More Praise for
Opening Our Hearts to Men

"What I longed to see was a book that would not only explain men to women but one that would help women to explore their anger toward men—one that would help them to stop viewing men as the enemy and look at them as human beings who have their own problems in seeking love, relationships and fulfilling lives. To my great joy, one has finally appeared. . . . Jeffers prescribes specific steps a woman can take to develop sufficient self-confidence, independence, self-love and love for other women so that they can open their eyes to who men are and choose men who are, in the deepest sense, good for them."

Howard Halpern
Miami Herald

"Finally a book that doesn't make men the enemy, but offers women practical tips for creating the loving relationships with men we deserve. *Opening Our Hearts to Men* is a much needed addition to every woman's self-help library."

Barbara DeAngelis, Ph.D.
Author of *How to Make Love All the Time*

"Challenging, honest, affirming, upbeat."

Warren Farrell, Ph.D.
Author of *Why Men Are the Way They Are*

"At last! A book that gives women permission to genuinely love themselves, and, in the process, allows them to open their hearts to men."

Tessa Albert Warshaw
Author of *Rich Is Better*

OPENING
OUR HEARTS
TO MEN

Susan Jeffers, Ph.D.

Fawcett Columbine · *New York*

A Fawcett Columbine Book
Published by Ballantine Books
Copyright © 1989 by Susan Jeffers, Ph.D.

Grateful acknowledgment is made to Hal Leonard Publishing Corporation and International Music Publications for permission to reprint excerpts from "No Wonder" by Alan and Marilyn Bergman and Michel Legrand. Copyright © 1983 by Emanuel Music, Threesome Music Co., Ennes Productions, Ltd. All rights in the U.S. and Canada Controlled and Administered by EMI April Music Inc. Rights in other territories Administered by International Music Publications. All Rights Reserved. International Copyright Secured. Used by permission.

Library of Congress Catalog Card Number: 89-91507

ISBN: 0-449-90513-6

Cover design by James R. Harris

Cover photo by Pamela Shandel

Manufactured in the United States of America

First Trade Paperback Edition: May 1990

10 9 8 7 6 5

To my beloved husband,

MARK SHELMERDINE

*When I finally learned
the secret to opening my heart,
in walked the most wonderful man
I have ever known.*

P.21 Plu mirror instead] magnifying gloss
P.94 purpose of Relationship
P.101 ATTRIBUTES Accolades

Contents

CONTENTS

Acknowledgments

Imagine having the blessed task of writing a book about LOVE! And included in this blessing are the following people who have contributed so much to this book and to my life . . .

Joëlle Delbourgo, my editor, who saw beauty in what I was doing and constantly reflected it back to me; *Dominick Abel,* my agent, who continues to be caring, optimistic, encouraging, and always available to me; *Suzanne Wickham,* my friend, who has guided my career in so many loving ways; *Mandi Robbins,* my assistant, who supports me above and beyond the call of duty; *the men's support group,* whose members invited me into their hearts; *the men who responded to my questionnaire,* thus contributing many insights about men's feelings; *the late Dan Casriel,* who taught me to stand tall; *my many other teachers,* who have kept me on the Path; *my many students,* who make it all worthwhile; *Larry Gershman,* my ex-husband/now-friend, who supported me in taking those first few steps such a long time ago; *Leslie Gershman,* my daughter, who provided me with valuable feedback and encouragement; *Gerry Gershman,* my son, who enriches my life; *Guy and Alice Shelmerdine,* my stepchildren, who continue to open their hearts to me; *Marcia Fleshel,* who is my real sister as well as my "soul-sister"; *Jeanne*

Gildenberg, my Mom, who continues to be my biggest fan; and *Mark Shelmerdine,* my wonderful husband, who brings mountains of love into my life and has taught me that I really can have it all!

*Opening Our
Hearts to Men*

INTRODUCTION: THE TELL-TALE SIGNS

Everywhere I go in my role as a public speaker, workshop and seminar leader, and in my personal life, I am constantly heartened by the wonderful women I meet. They fill me with joy. Their personal lives, however, often do not reflect the beauty I see within them.

Many are alone, although they don't really want to be. Some are divorced; some have never married; some want desperately to start a family and the biological clock is ticking. Yet, no matter how much they want a relationship, these women can't seem to find anyone with whom to share their lives. Love eludes them.

Many are married or living with a man, yet even within the relationship, they feel alone. The beautiful connection that was there in the beginning is long gone. They hang in there, hoping things will change, but it never does and when they get the courage, they leave—that is, if their men haven't been the first to reach the door.

There are some, far too few, who have found the secret to love. Along the way, they have learned the insights and tools that a healthy relationship requires. They know that the answer to the question "Where Is Love?" is quite obvious. And they wonder why the rest of us never tire of choosing the path that always brings us failure.

I have heard it said that the difference between rats and human beings is that when a rat finds there is no cheese at the end of a tunnel he eventually stops looking. Not so for human beings. We seem to keep going down that same tunnel despite the fact that there's nothing there! Certainly some of our experiences with love seem to bear that out. To see if this analogy might apply to you, answer the following questions. If any of your answers are yes, the likelihood is that you, too, are traveling down the losing tunnel in your search for a loving relationship.

Are you fearful of being hurt by a man?

Do you find yourself lonely even
when you are in a relationship?

Is there something wrong with every man
who comes into your life?

Do you always pick men who turn out to be
unavailable in some way or another?

Are you convinced that women are a superior breed?

Do you believe the commonly heard statement
"There aren't any good men out there"?

Are you always putting men down?

Do you feel that you are not lovable?

Do you feel your relationship would be great
if only *he* would change?

Do your conversations with friends always
revolve around problems with men?

At one point in my life, I would have had to answer yes to most of the above. There is no doubt that I was always looking down the wrong tunnel. In fact, it wasn't until I was in my forties that it occurred to me to try another path. And when I did, the fog finally began to clear and the love was able to shine through.

I thought I had it all figured out at the age of seventeen, when I found my proverbial prince. We both had expectations of living happily ever after; but sixteen years later, we had both turned into frogs—or, more accurately, he thought I had and I thought he had. A divorce was inevitable. I was then single for ten years. And while I truly enjoyed the single life, I still looked forward to the day I would find my "soul-mate" (the modern version of the prince).

After my divorce, it became habit to commiserate with my female friends about the lack of any good men out there. We lamented that we terrific women were simply not appreciated by the male of the species, and, in fact, believed that the more we improved ourselves, the fewer men there would be who would want us: we would be too much of a threat.

We all had our stories of the men who put us down, or withheld their love, or did all manner of things to give us grief . . . to punish us for our wonderfulness. We couldn't find men who could compare to our female friends—in their love, their openness, their sharing, their honesty, their humanness. We convinced ourselves that we were, indeed, the superior gender. We found men to be boring, closed, weak, and insensitive.

Today, my perspective has changed dramatically. Yes, I feel that women are as beautiful as before; in fact, much more so. But the big turnaround has come in my feelings about men. I have learned to love them as much as I love women. I can now see their courage, their vulnerability, their hurt, their desire to please. I can now see their longing to connect, to be loved and to love. I can now see their humanness . . . and I love who they are.

Why do I see this now when I didn't see it before? Have men changed? No, not really. I've changed. After I walked out on forty-two men (but who counted?), I took a good look at myself.

When I allowed the honesty in, I saw a woman who seemingly wanted a relationship, yet who pushed aside any possibility of having one. I saw a woman filled with anger and the self-righteousness that goes along with anger. Part of me loved the power of that feeling. It felt far better than the dependency I once knew. The price was very high, however. There is no peace of mind when one is angry all the time. I knew it all, and I'd fight to the death (of the relationship) to prove it. My sense of worth had to do with having the last word.

When I looked a little deeper, I also saw a woman filled with fear: fear of being hurt, fear of not being good enough, fear of being needy, fear of being helpless. Strangely, I had never really seen this before. My blinders allowed me only to see a woman who was independent, strong, confident, loving, and lots of fun. It was too painful to look beneath the surface. But, as I explain later in this book, there came the day when my fear and anger became glaringly obvious.

Recognition brings about transformation. If you don't see a problem, you can't change it. My honest look at myself was the first step on the road to finding love. It was painful at the beginning, because until that time, I had never seen myself as an angry person who really hurt inside. When I finally did see the truth, there was no going back into the lie. I had to move forward. And as I moved along the path of change, I eventually discovered the sublime joy of allowing my heart to open—of letting go of the anger, the self-righteousness, the fear, and the hurt—so that love could flow freely in and out. I learned what makes a successful relationship possible.

Along the way, I found a wonderful man to love, although in the beginning, when I was still filled with negative feelings about men, I was sure he wasn't my type. But he was patient, and ultimately I saw that he was perfect for me. We are now married and each day I am amazed at how wonderful he is. I know it is my new eyes that have created this miracle.

I am writing this book to pass on what I and other women who enjoy a loving relationship have learned along the way and to offer you some insights and tools that can open your heart to the enormous amount of love that resides within and around you.

Some of you will resist what I have to say. I know that if I had been presented with the contents of this book when I was in the heyday of my upset with men, I, too, would have put up a lot of resistance. I would have been far more receptive to the large number of books out there teaching me how to handle difficult men, hostile men, closed men, infantile men, and so on. I realize now that the answer to finding love does not lie in "handling" men. There is another, far more effective way to find love, and that is what this book is about. So keep an open mind. To love requires that you let go of many preconceived notions and begin to see men, and yourself, with new eyes.

Others of you will be more receptive to my message. You want to love men, but for some reason, it never works out. Men keep disappointing you and, as a result, you find your heart closed. You feel too vulnerable and too weak to withstand the pain that you feel men can create. If you fit into this category, you will learn how to have more trust in your ability to handle whatever a relationship brings you.

Still others of you have found some answers. You've worked long and hard at trying to understand your relationships, and you've come up with some profound insights that have transformed your ability to give and receive love. Your heart is opening more every day. If you belong in this category, you will truly identify and grow from the concepts presented here.

In whatever category you belong, the fact remains that we are all on the same path. Despite differences in outward appearances, we are all looking for the same thing: a way to love and be loved. As you read through this book, you will learn many things about loving yourself and others. You will learn:

- how to become more trusting
- how to create greater intimacy
- how to become more powerful and loving within your relationships
- how to deal with your anger
- how to feel more lovable
- how to understand that there's no such thing as a "bad" relationship
- how to see men in a more loving light
- how to be at greater peace with yourself
- how to feel more abundance in your life
- how to believe that things are not really as bad as they seem

... and much more.

And to You Men Out There ...

While the book speaks specifically to women, *I encourage men to read it as well*. Since all of our issues mirror yours, you, too, will find many insights about your own inability to find love and what you can do to create a love that works. This book will also help you to understand what women are struggling with in this very exciting, yet confusing, time of transition that affects us all.

To All of Us

The whole of the human species is crying out for love. If we all take the time to look into our hearts, we will ultimately feel complete and connected—within ourselves and as part of the human family.

1

MIRROR, MIRROR ON THE WALL

This is not a book about the women's movement; it is a book about love. Yet it seems clear to me that the two are inextricably entwined. To understand love, we must understand our ongoing struggle for identity. Whether or not we as individuals support the women's movement, we cannot escape the fact that it has greatly affected our relationships.

In these confusing times, we seem to be floundering in a sea of conflicting expectations. We don't really know what we want from men, and we certainly don't know what we want from ourselves. In 1963, Betty Friedan said in her book, *The Feminine Mystique,* which many believe signaled the beginning of the modern women's movement:

> I came to realize that something is very wrong with the way American women are trying to live their lives today.[1]

Surely, from all surface appearances, we can make that very same statement today. But let's take a closer look. Are things really as bad as they seem? Should we be thoroughly discouraged and consider all our efforts over recent years an exercise in futility? Not at all! It is important that we keep in mind the very significant advances we have made. It is easy to forget how helpless, trapped, and dissatisfied women were not so many years ago. Just to put some mind-blowing perspective on it, understand that our right to vote came only one year before Betty Friedan was born!

There is no question in my mind that we are on the right path. We just haven't quite reached our destination yet—that place of inner peace, fulfillment, and love that we all are seeking. Where we are reminds me of a lovely English verse that has often given me peace in moments of great confusion, and I pass it on to you:

> *Not to worry,*
> *Not to fret,*
> *All is well,*
> *But not just yet!*

It's true. All *is* well. We *are* on the right path. It's just that at this moment in time we are at a crossroads and don't know which way to go. There are some people who are even trying to convince us to turn around and go back to the way it was, who blame the women's movement for all that is wrong in women's lives today. And some of us may be tempted to agree. [Fear drives us to hide from uncomfortable places. Getting out into the world can bring silent screams of terror. But we won't find what we want by retreating. In going back, we will only find the silent screams of helplessness.]

No, we can't go back . . . we must go forward. But which path to take? Do we take the path that leads to the total breakdown of relationships between the sexes, which seems to be the way we are heading? Or do we take the path that leads to love? I seriously doubt that anyone reading this book would choose the former. (If so, this book is not for you!) I believe that deep within our hearts, we all have the human need to love and to be loved. Therefore, we need to figure out the next step that will take us in that direction, lest we travel too far off course.

The clue as to what that next step might be came to me as

I was teaching workshops on different aspects of love. I noticed that the women sitting in front of me were, for the most part, career-oriented and independent—or so it seemed. But when it came to their feelings about themselves and the men in their lives, it was as if they were in a time warp. Their lives were being run by the same insecurities, fears, and expectations that ran women's lives years ago.

I thought about all of the other women that I knew personally and professionally and realized this was true for most of them as well. Our exterior growth masks what is going on inside. In terms of politics, education, careers, creativity, and the like, we women have made great strides and are moving forward every day. But in terms of altering our sense of self, we've barely scratched the surface.

Seen in this context, the fog surrounding our next step begins to clear. The women's movement in its highest form has been concerned with uncovering the best of who we are. In order for this to happen, we must access that place within that is joyful, creative, action-oriented, strong, caring, abundant, warm, compassionate, truthful, confident . . . loving. It sounds great, doesn't it? Why would anyone resist! But resist we do. Our internal negativity continues to blind us to the great wealth within and, in terms of love, makes us "beggars" in disguise. In this regard, nothing has changed much over the years.

It is illuminating to look at "before" and "after" pictures of the situation. What were our feelings about ourselves relative to men prior to the women's movement, and what are they today? The "before" picture reveals that we were in the habit of pleasing men, or at least trying to. While we had female friends, the male of the species always took precedence. Many of you will remember the unwritten contract we had in high school: "If any one of us has a date and a boy calls, our date is off!" We were never angry with each other when this occurred, as we might be today. What came up instead was envy: "Boy, is she lucky!"

I knew few girls who did not prefer to be in the company of boys, even though, most of the time, we actually had more fun with our girlfriends. The more unpopular among us often appeared to be uninterested in boys, but I know they spent just as many nights crying alone in their rooms over some rejection as did the rest of us. They simply were playing the ever-popular game, "If you can't win, pretend you aren't trying!"

A lot of us married very young, and it was the joke of the time that we were all going to college to get our MRS degrees. But it wasn't a joke; it was the truth. Our hope of fulfillment was in finding the man of our dreams. My own story is illustrative. I met my first husband on the very first day of college. I stood in front of my dorm that day watching my father drive away, leaving me alone for the first time in my life. I then turned around and literally bumped into the man who would be my husband one year later. From that very first day, we were inseparable.

In effect, I earned my MRS degree that first day on campus. The relief I felt was enormous. I didn't consciously realize it then, but I had just "substituted heads": my husband-to-be took over where my father had left off. It is significant that the song I picked for my wedding was "Someone to Watch Over Me." It was my plan to be happy forever in my new role as wife, and later as mother to two wonderful children. Such was not the case.

This plan for happiness went awry for an incredible number of us who fulfilled the dream we were taught to dream. Adulthood was supposed to bring independence. Instead our dependency needs grew. We were raising children, yet we hadn't gone beyond the level of the playpen ourselves. Our self-respect diminished with time. We soon found ourselves feeling empty, insecure, lost, bored, and angry. "Is this all there is?" was the question uppermost in our minds.

In retrospect, the more fortunate among us in terms of self-growth and self-respect were those who were initially "unlucky in love" or those rare exceptions who really were not interested in marriage at such an early age. Both were "forced" to go out and take care of themselves before marrying and raising a family. The majority of these women stretched, grew, and gained confidence in themselves. The rest of us stood by with envy and watched as our husbands and children stretched, grew, and gained confidence in themselves.

We felt very guilty about our unhappiness. To make matters worse, we were told by our psychologists, if we had one, to go home, accept our role, and be more appreciative of our blessings, thus confirming our feeling that, indeed, something was terribly wrong with us. We looked at our wonderful husbands and our beautiful children and tried harder to be happy . . . with no success.

I was one of the lucky ones. I found a sympathetic medical doctor who diagnosed my extreme fatigue as boredom and a lack of self-fulfillment. He said, "Some women are meant to be full-time wives and mothers, and some are not. You are not. If you don't find something outside the home to fulfill yourself, you're going to find yourself in very bad shape." He warned me that I would be heavily criticized if I pursued anything outside the home, but that my emotional survival depended upon it. I didn't realize how ahead of his time he was.

It was then that I decided to resume my college education and get something other than my MRS degree. Immediately, I began to feel alive once again. My doctor was right. He was also right about the criticism I was to receive. It might surprise you to learn that the bulk of the criticism came from other women. To be a woman fulfilling herself outside the home was to betray all of womankind. What might surprise you more is that my then-husband was my biggest support. He was thrilled to see me come alive again. Yet my guilt about needing my own interests remained. I couldn't understand why remaining in the home as housewife and mother was so destructive to my sense of well-being.

And then, with great relief, I read *The Feminine Mystique* and found out that I was not alone, that there were many women who were dissatisfied with their assigned role. Friedan even gave a name to the "problem that had no name"—*the housewife syndrome*—and told us that we were in the middle of an identity crisis. We were being only half of what we could be. She pointed to the growing amount of psychological data that showed that women who were filling their full potential— self-actualized women—were happier, more secure, more loving, and even more effective as wives and mothers than those who subjugated their needs for their husbands and children. What a discovery . . . and what a relief!

If I were to summarize the feelings we had about ourselves and our men prior to our attempts at self-actualization, the list would look like this:

A Look at Ourselves, Pre–Women's Lib

We didn't like women very much . . .
particularly ourselves.

We felt we were second-class,
less important and inferior to men.

As "little" women,
we looked up to and depended on men
to take care of us . . .

Yet we were, consciously or unconsciously,
extremely angry at them.

Time moved on, and as the women's movement took hold, we banded together and began the search for our lost identity. Where we once felt isolated in our dissatisfaction, we now had millions of other voices to validate our feelings. We were buoyed by the righteousness of our cause. And . . .

What gave us the greatest impetus of all was our creation of a common enemy, a target for us all to attack: men.

Clearly, it was *their* fault that we had lost our identity, our confidence, our sense of self-esteem. They kept us from becoming all that we could be, but they couldn't hold us back any longer!

Our anger was unleashed en masse. For the first time in many of our lives, we felt a sense of power. Where we once competed with other women, we now began a fierce competition with men. Some of us, turned off by the extremists, began to change the fabric of our lives in a quieter way as we began to venture forth, slowly and surely, outside the home. And some of us, who didn't have the courage to act, simply smiled and watched and waited, hopeful that someday we would have our chance. Of course, there were those of us who resisted any change, who cared only that things remained the same. But for most of us, one thing was certain: blatantly or subtly, we were united in seeing men as the enemy.

Many years have now passed. On the whole, we as women have won many battles and have made many gains in changing perceptions and feelings, especially in the area of realizing our career goals. In fact, the pendulum has swung so far to the other side that it is now considered the norm for a woman to have a career. "Occupation: housewife" has lost its status and "self-actualization" is in. A multitude of new opportunities exists for women today, and these opportunities are increasing in number daily as both women and supportive men continue to fight the inequalities that remain.

Yet a huge problem still exists. The Housewife Syndrome has ceased to be an epidemic. We have set off on our path toward self-realization, but we are still haunted by dissatisfaction and confusion. A new "problem with no name" seems to have emerged with no solution in sight. While healthy relationships were difficult prior to the women's movement, for too many of us, they seem to be impossible today. Why can so few of us find love? Even within existing relationships, our battle with men goes on. Given the many gains we have made, why hasn't our anger abated? Why, for many of us, has it actually increased?*

I was forced to deal with these questions about five years ago. Prior to that time, I thought I was doing pretty well. I had been happily divorced for ten years and had accomplished much relative to my career. In terms of men, I dated a lot and had a number of meaningful relationships. Unfortunately, there was always something "wrong" with the men I picked (does this sound familiar?) and I usually ended up walking out in a rage. Yes, I was angry, but so what. They deserved it, and who needed them anyway! I delighted in my newly found female camaraderie. "If only I could find a man who was just like my girlfriends" was a common lament. We were united in our anger toward men who were almost obsessively our main topic of conversation.

And then came something that was to dramatically change my life. I was three years into a typically—for me—turbulent relationship with Mark, who was later to become my husband, when I found out that I had breast cancer. For years I had been teaching people in my workshops to let go of the "victim" mentality and start taking responsibility for what happens to them in life. So, after the initial shock wore off, it was natural to ask myself, "What am I doing or not doing in life that could be creating disease in my body?" At that time, I was rather unconscious of matters of health, so I began to investigate. I found out that there were a number of things that were associated with breast cancer. Some were controllable, some were not.

I went to work on the controllable ones, two in particular. The

---

*Some of you may not feel you have made men the enemy; nor do you feel anger toward men. As you will see, anger is only one problem in relationships. Remember to take what applies to you and let the rest go.

first was *diet.* Changing my eating habits was a relatively easy thing to do. The second was not so easy to change; in fact, I can't remember anything being quite as challenging. That, of course, was *letting go of my anger.* What made the challenge so great was that the basic requirement of getting rid of my anger was to take a brutally honest look at myself instead of pointing my finger at men.

I really didn't want to do that. I was comfortable with my negative feelings about men. My female friends and I delighted in sitting around putting down men. It was as though we belonged to an exclusive club, and I certainly didn't want to give up my membership. I even liked my anger and the power I felt when I unleashed it. It motivated me and gave me an impetus to grow. But one thing was certain: I did not want my cancer to recur, so if letting go of my anger and resentment would give me even the slightest edge in terms of survival, I was prepared to bite the bullet and proceed.

The only time I remember working so hard on my inner self was after my divorce. Then it was to find my identity and to become an independent person. Now it was something else. As I look back upon that time, I realize that I was about to discover inadvertently what I believe to be the next step in the women's movement. While the process was difficult for me at times, the rewards were monumental.

So what was this "next step" that I took? It is best described by a wonderful line I recently heard:

"Pick up a mirror instead of a magnifying glass."

On reflection, this is exactly what I did. With the help of various teachers, books, and workshops, I was able to "look in the mirror" and ask on behalf of all us confused women out there, *"Mirror, mirror on the wall, what is the problem with us all?"* The mirror reflected back loud and clear:

You have worked hard for your rights. That is good. The "problem" is that, in the process, you have closed your hearts to men. You've substituted the "Housewife Syndrome" with the "Closed Heart Syndrome." Your task now is to continue moving forward in your quest for wholeness, *but with an open heart.* In doing so, you will come much closer to finding the fulfillment you seek.

I know. At this very moment, there are many of you out there revolted by the very sound of it!

"What! Open our hearts to *them!* It's their hearts that need opening, not ours! And anyway, why should we open our hearts to them? They are the ones who are causing all the problems in the first place!"

Believe me, five years ago I had the same reaction. But I've learned a lot since then. And it is my purpose in writing this book to share with you the liberating (and sometimes painful) truths revealed with the help of that magic mirror. It might help you to relax a bit when I tell you that the cure for the "Closed Heart Syndrome" does not require that we give up anything that we have gained in our struggle for identity; on the contrary, I have found that it only adds to our sense of self, our completeness, our capacity to love and be loved. It also makes us far more effective as we venture out into the world.

So trust me and let me begin by showing you an interesting "loss" that we as women have suffered over the years that helps to explain in part some of the problems we are having today. In our society, it is common to label such qualities as soft, warm, passive, and nurturing as "feminine" and such qualities as strong, assertive, and goal-oriented as "masculine." I believe these labels were originally meant to describe polarities in the wide spectrum of human qualities that exist in all of us. They were not meant to differentiate men from women.

22

Yet, somewhere along the line, society confused the issue and interpreted these labels literally to mean that the female's role is to display only the feminine and the male's role is to display only the masculine. There are some people who go so far as to insist that these polarities are inherent, thus discouraging either sex from exploring the dormant potential that lies within. This societal pressure results in half-men and half-women and those of us who attempt to cross these trait barriers are accused, even today, of being unmanly or unwomanly. Traditional relationships reflect these lines of demarcation, as the following model illustrates:

TRADITIONAL COUPLE

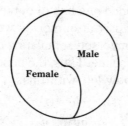

Here, the man provides the "masculine" half of the whole and the female provides the "female" half. One without the other is only half a person:

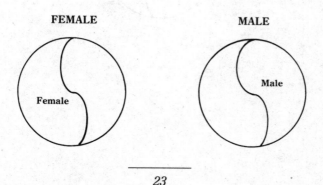

FEMALE   MALE

You can see what lopsided individuals we become when we lose our other half! In this framework, with which many of us still identify today, our expectations of each other are enormous. We require that our mate provide the other half of who we are, which, as most of us have discovered, leads only to bitter disappointment.

Instinctively, I believe we have always known that there was something terribly wrong with this model—that it created two half-people instead of two whole-people. This was, in fact, the model that instigated the beginning of the women's movement. In the heat of our dissatisfaction with the roles that we had been assigned, we began our search for wholeness.

But in our eagerness to find the other half of who we were, many of us simply traded one half of ourselves for the other by dissociating with that part of ourselves we considered weak—the feminine—and, conversely, emulating that which we considered strong—the masculine. Thus, the pendulum made its swing and many of us are now left with this:

FEMALE

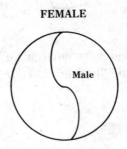

Male

instead of our old pattern, which, as you recall, looked like this:

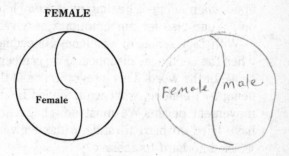

Interesting, isn't it? We're still lopsided! We simply seem to have replaced one half of ourselves with the other half! In order to find the part of us that is strong, assertive, independent, and action-oriented, we have moved away from that part that is nurturing, warm, and receptive. Naturally, the true picture is not as exaggerated as the model makes it out to be. It is meant only to describe the process of what seems to be happening to many women today.

What I think all of us would agree to be the ideal relationship is one which comprises two whole people:

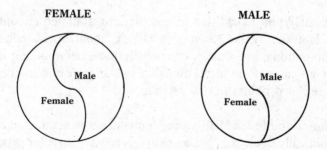

In this model, both sexes are in balance, equipped with more tools for finding joy and satisfaction in life. For example, women are not only nurturing, warm, and receptive, but they are also strong, assertive, and protective. These qualities can be called upon when needed. Feeling more complete, we do not depend on anyone else for our emotional survival.

With this sense of wholeness, neediness disappears. And when the neediness disappears, we can begin to love in the true sense of the word. This integration of all that we are capable of being is, I believe, what we intended to attain as the women's movement began. We must now begin to reclaim all that we have tried so hard to stifle without giving up what we have worked so hard to achieve.

In trying to understand the problems we are having today, it helps to take a look at the underlying—or, more accurately, hidden—reason for our banding together and making men the enemy. On the surface, we simply assumed they deserved it; they *are* the enemy! In picking up the mirror instead of the magnifying glass, we see another picture. Philosopher Sam Keen gives us a clue. He describes the way in which tribes and nations have typically maintained their strength:

> Normally, social cohesion is maintained by projection and paranoia. We deny our own aggressive, destructive, hostile impulses and attribute them to an enemy.[3]

Ouch! When I read this line, something sounded uncomfortably familiar. While Keen was talking about social cohesion within nations, he could just as easily have been talking about what we have done in relationship to the men in our lives.

Keen also points out to us that:

> One of the few ways that we human beings seem to have politically of saying "we're okay" is to have another group who we say is not okay. Certain processes exist— The first is the process of psychological numbing. We don't kill *human* beings, psychologically speaking: We have to

dehumanize them before we can do it. We have to have some way to make them seem unlike ourselves.[4]

Reread this statement. It is very important in understanding what so many of us are doing with the men in our lives. We can better understand the concept of psychological numbing by looking at the military. Bombardiers in the air force, for example, have to numb themselves (close their hearts) when they drop a bomb on enemy territory; otherwise, it would be too painful for them to think of the humanity that lies in the target range. Soldiers are trained to kill only the enemy, not human beings. Even at weapons plants, psychological numbing occurs. Nuclear bombs there are called "reentry vehicles"—the word "bomb" would make it all too real, too horrifying.

In a less obvious sense, when we made men the enemy, we numbed ourselves to the fact that they are *human,* and in that, their struggle for survival is just as hard for them as it is for us. To keep them the enemy, we have blocked our vision to the pain, fear, and emptiness they so often feel. Even more significantly, our anger has served to mask the truth of what is really going on within ourselves. It has delayed our having to deal with our own pain, fear, and emptiness, which, even in our well-defended personalities, pop up painfully at times. Ironically, it is from this place of pain that our capacity to empathize and to love emerges. I have noticed that those (men or women) most numbed to their own deepest pain can be the cruelest of all.

A closed heart helps us deny our own "shadow," our dark side, as Carl Jung called it. While we attribute greed, ugliness, and aggression to the enemy, we cannot see it within ourselves. And just as importantly, when we blind ourselves to the beauty in others, we can't see the beauty within ourselves. While we might feel superior, we certainly don't feel good about who we are and how we are behaving. Thus, totally cut off from our essence, it is no wonder that we are confused about who we are and what we should be doing for the rest of our lives.

A closed heart also keeps us from having to take responsibility for what is going on in our lives. When we have an enemy who is responsible, we're let off the hook as to what part of the problem we have created—and continue to create—all by ourselves. While taking responsibility is a very difficult thing, it is our only hope of making any significant changes. When we abdicate responsibility, we are victims, and victims are powerless. As long as "they did it to us" remains part of our thinking, we won't find the identity and joy and satisfaction in life that we all are seeking. When each of us can say, "I am responsible for changing what I don't like in my life," then, and only then, is true growth really possible. When we pick up the mirror instead of the magnifying glass, we can begin to create life the way we want it to be.

In its healthiest sense, the women's movement is about freedom with responsibility. It is about becoming the best that we can be. We must take responsibility for who we are and what we are doing. Looked at in this way, *the women's movement has nothing to do with men!* We must stop focusing on men and concentrate on changing ourselves. We must also stop seeing them as our enemies.

The truth is that there are no enemies. There are only human beings, all doing the very best they can. I don't care what the surface looks like; *everyone* wants to love and be loved. We can now allow our hearts to feel and recognize the pain that we all—men and women alike—share as human beings. We need to help each other . . . we need to help (not change) our men . . . we need to help the world.

When I first presented these ideas in my workshops, I expected to encounter a lot of resistance. While there was some, I was surprised to find that the majority of women acknowledged with words and nods, and sometimes tears, that this is indeed what they have done to themselves and the men in their lives. I then asked them to take an even more uncomfortable look at what was really going on with them. I asked, "Although we have made great strides in many areas, what has really changed when it comes to the men in our lives?" I asked them to be really honest with themselves about this question. And, with great reluctance, they answered, "Not much." They concluded the following:

A Look at Ourselves Today

Despite the bravado,
we still don't like our ourselves very much . . .

We still feel second-class, less important,
and inferior . . .

We still want to "look up to" men
and be taken care of,
especially financially . . .

And we are even angrier than before.

The women in my workshops acknowledged that they still had very low self-esteem. They acknowledged that their fear still kept them locked in many of the beliefs, expectations, and actions that existed prior to the women's movement, and we discussed these at length. I thanked them for their honesty and pointed out that there was nothing inherently bad about the way they were feeling, and that it was only with this kind of honesty that we could begin to find answers to the many conflicting emotions we still have today about men and about ourselves. It is only with this kind of honesty that we can begin the next step.

Once again, let me suggest that you see the positive instead of the negative in terms of our progress. Our banding together for strength and making men the enemy was perhaps a necessary step as we left the security of hearth and home and ventured forth into new territories. Perhaps without this strength we would not have made the strides that we have made. Perhaps it was also necessary to cut off parts of ourselves that we associated with weakness, thus forcing us to access the "stronger" parts that we had previously denied. Perhaps the anger was necessary for us to have made the impact on society that we have made. Perhaps we had to first pay attention to the externals—our political, educational, economic, and "social" rights—to prepare us for the really tough job of looking within. And with all this behind us, perhaps it is time to allow ourselves to reclaim those parts of ourselves that we have long denied.

As a group, it is safe now to move on. We have proved much to ourselves and to the rest of the world that we needed to prove and we don't have to hold on so tightly anymore. We don't need enemies any longer to unite us and make us strong. Although we may differ on many issues, we are united in spirit and we are strong. We are ready to go forward. We are ready to let go of the anger and the blame. They have outlived their usefulness.

En masse, we unleashed our anger.

En masse, let us unleash our love.

Wow! What a great world we have the power to create!

And so, if we were to look at what our next step will bring, it is this:

As We Open Our Hearts

Women loving women

Women loving men

Moving to this next step is not an easy task. The problem lies, not with the men out there, but with the need to move from the security we feel as part of the "tribe." To move ahead requires that we not only let go of our own anger, but that we distance ourselves from others who are angry and accusatory and who have made themselves victims of their own beliefs. Because of this, beginning can be a lonely place. We have to move away from the consensus of opinion in order to find new answers. This takes a lot of courage. But to create a love that works requires that we destroy those perceptions and ideas that have thus far only created painful relationships—with ourselves and our men.

My plan is to show you how you can take responsibility for many aspects of a relationship in a way that will heal the hurts and build your self-esteem. Until both men and women feel good about themselves, we will continue to hurt each other. So the task at hand is to really look at what we are doing with the purpose of feeling better about ourselves and perhaps in the process, helping our men to feel better about themselves as well. *— they do themselves!*

Some of what you read might not be comfortable, but if we can all lighten up and not take ourselves so seriously, the task will be much easier—in fact, it will be fun. Probably our biggest sign of growth is to be able to laugh (in acceptance and in love) at our human "flaws."

With that in mind, let's move on and begin to find some cures for the "problem" that now has a name: *the closed heart syndrome.*

2

ANGER: HOW SWEET IT IS!

One of the biggest enemies to an open heart is anger. I know! You are reading the words of a person who really used to love the feeling of anger. As Merle Shain said in her lovely book, *Hearts That We Broke Long Ago,* "Anger is a passion, so it makes people feel alive and makes them feel they matter and are in charge of their lives."[1] So true!

I remember times when my anger felt nothing short of sublime. It gave me a heady sense of power. It made leaving easier. It motivated me to make healthy changes in my life. It drove me to prove to everyone (especially myself) that I was competent and that I could do anything I wanted to do in life. Anger insidiously, but mercifully, masked the fear and pain and poison within. Actually, if I hadn't been concerned about a recurrence of my cancer, and if I hadn't wanted a man in my life, I might have remained angry forever!

For a very long time, I didn't know I was an angry person. I repressed it beautifully. Even if I had known, I probably wouldn't have let it out anyway. I was too much of a people-pleaser and wanted everyone to like me. I was too "sweet" and concerned with being pretty and feminine, and society had taught me that anger and femininity simply did not go hand in hand.

I'll never forget the first time I really got in touch with my anger. In an effort to save our marriage, my first husband invited me to go with him to a new form of group therapy he had discovered called scream therapy. My first reaction was, "Scream therapy! You've got to be kidding!" He wasn't kidding. Partly out of curiosity, partly because of my fear of the marriage ending, and mostly to prove him wrong, I agreed to go with him. I remember feeling self-righteous and above it all as I entered the room where the group session was being held. I was hardly prepared for the "show" that was about to begin.

Having just received my doctorate in psychology from a very traditional university, you can imagine my shock as, one by one, all the weirdos in the group began to scream out their pain, anger, joy, and so on. One by one, with tears running down their faces, they shared the deepest and most intimate parts of their lives. Had they no shame? Certainly this was not something I would do! Air my dirty laundry in public? No way! You have to understand that, not only was I self-righteous, but I was also a person very concerned about my image and my makeup.

To make matters worse, I was a person totally out of touch with my feelings, most of all my anger. I was numbed as to what was going on within me as well as what was going on within others. Needless to say, there was no way I was going to stoop to such an unladylike performance in front of all these strangers!

And then it was my turn. Dan, the leader of the group, was obviously used to dealing with numbed, self-righteous people. He asked me what I was feeling. And I told him, "Nothing." He then chided, "Well, have you had *any* feelings today?" I told him I had been a little angry at my husband that morning. He then instructed me to go around the room and to each person simply say, "I'm angry!" That sounded harmless enough, and, convinced he would get nothing out of me, I began the go-around.

To the person on my left, I very demurely said, "I'm angry." It was barely a whisper. As I moved on to the next person, the eighteen members of the group yelled, "louder!" So I increased the volume a wee bit, still making sure my dignity was intact. "I'm angry." Each time I said it, the members of the group yelled, "Louder." And the level of my voice continued to rise as I went from person to person.

"I'm angry!"

"Louder!"

"I'm angry!!"

"Louder!"

"I'm angry!!!"

"Louder!"

"I'm angry!!!!"

"Louder!"

This went on until I came to the eleventh person in the group. Then something happened.

The mild-mannered "lady" in me was replaced by a raving maniac. Somehow the self-conscious, rational and covertly scared, insecure, and helpless part of my mind was sidestepped and what came through was a strong, angry, self-confident, assertive, and determined human being. Years and years of rage were suddenly unleashed, and what sprang forth was seemingly another person—a part of me I had been hiding from myself for all these years.

What a sight! I outperformed everyone in the room with the crying and screaming. I even embellished my performance with a whole string of four-letter words. Everyone else had dealt with their feelings sitting down. I loomed up from my chair as if this power within demanded to be expressed by a person standing upright and tall. Someone much bigger than I had ever been willing to be was screaming to come forth. I don't know how long I continued this incredible release of anger and power, but it was clear that my self-image was transformed forevermore.

When I finally stopped and came back to my "rational" mind, I stood there amazed at what had come out of me. I felt a bit shaken and embarrassed until Dan told me to look around at the faces of everyone in the room. I began looking around at what earlier I had perceived to be a bunch of hostile strangers. I now was able to see what I was incapable of seeing before—warmth and smiles and, most of all, connection. I had become a real honest-to-God human being for the first time in my life, as opposed to an insecure, people-pleasing, passively hostile fashion plate totally out of touch with my feelings. Just as importantly, I felt as if someone had taken ten tons of weight off of my shoulders. I felt light and free. And I felt powerful.

During my marriage, there had been many screaming matches to be sure, but there was no power attached to my yelling—only the helpless flailing of a child having a temper tantrum. This scream was different. It was the scream of a person totally capable of writing her own script, the scream of someone who was going to have to make drastic changes in the way she lived her life, both inwardly and outwardly.

As you might have guessed, I became one of those "weirdos" and attended the group for another six months, at which point I mustered up the courage to leave a marriage that should have been left years before, not because my husband was a bad person, because he wasn't. We had just gotten married too young and had bought into the fairy tale prince and princess myth. We were both trying to live a lie and it didn't work. When you try to live a lie, everything becomes twisted.

In any case, I finally discovered the powerful feeling of "entitled" anger, and for the next twelve years I used it to its fullest. Man after man felt the brunt of it as I bolted out the door of many relationships feeling self-righteous, judgmental, and incredibly determined to handle my own life. In that, the anger

was a beautiful feeling. No one was going to tell me what to do!
It was, as the song says, "My Turn" now.

I discovered over the years that I was not alone in my loving
the feeling of anger. Most women (and men) who allow themselves to get in touch with this very powerful emotion report
really loving the feeling and can't imagine why it should be given
up. Understandably, when we move from passivity and frustration and helplessness to a wonderful sense of power, we really
want to hold on to it.

One of the reasons anger feels so great is that it distances.
Just as being perpetually ladylike and sweet numbs, so does
being perpetually angry. It keeps us safe from really feeling our
underlying pain . . . or anyone else's. Anger is also a great
unifier. As I discussed earlier, it was anger that gave the
women's movement its great impetus. It creates camaraderie,
a common cause, a common enemy to hate and to fight. It lifts
depression and gives us a feeling of well-being. It makes us feel
superior, righteous. In short, anger has a lot to be said for it.

But eventually the emptiness in our heart, or in my case, the
cancer in my breast, makes us take a second look. When we do,
we are pained to see that our unresolved anger has created
dis-ease in our bodies, minds, and souls, dis-ease in our relationships, and ultimately dis-ease in the fabric of our entire society.
And until we get in touch with our anger and effectively deal
with it once it is uncovered, we will continue to be run by it. It
will have its way.

I believe that our unresolved anger, whether overtly or covertly expressed, explains why so many of us are alone or unhappy in our relationships. You may be asking:

"But aren't we entitled to our anger? After all, society has
dealt us a dirty blow. It isn't easy being put in the role of
second-class citizens. It isn't easy trying to be Superwomen. It isn't easy getting ahead in a world that is run

by men. It isn't easy taking a backseat. It isn't easy that
all the good men are taken. It isn't easy when they won't
help with the house and kids! It isn't easy that we are torn
between career and family and they aren't!"

And so on . . .

Yes, it's true! Life isn't easy. And, yes, we are entitled to
our anger. And, anyway, whether we are entitled to it or not,
we cannot escape it. It lives within all of us. It is part of what
makes us complete as human beings. I love the story of the
monk who lived in a cave for five years, meditating and cleans-
ing himself of all negativity. When he decided to enter humanity once again, he felt assured that he had transcended his
humanness and had become one with the gods. He came down
from the mountain with peace in his heart, blissfully strolled
into the marketplace, and was accidentally jostled by a pass-
erby. At which point, he turned around in a rage, ready to
attack his assailant.

His lesson was that to be human we have to include our
anger; we cannot meditate it away. Just as we will feel fear, pain,
loneliness, love, excitement, and so on, so we will feel anger. We
are born with it, as you will notice watching your newborn child
screaming out the rage of his or her unmet demands. And we
will die with it. We might learn how to stifle it at a very young
age, but you can bet that it never goes away.

I've often been asked if anger is an appropriate emotion.
My answer is that anger is always appropriate; it is our response to it that often is not. The reason that anger is appropriate is that it indicates an underlying problem. It is a wonderful guide:

anger

It tells us when our needs are not being met.
It tells us when we have work to do on ourselves.
It tells us how unclear we are about who we are
and who we want to be.

It tells us that all is not right with the world
and changes need to be made.

But once we get these valuable messages, we need to take
action to correct the problem and then work on releasing the
anger. It is clear to me that unresolved anger causes a multitude
of sins—against ourselves, our relationships, and our planet.
But how do we begin to deal with it all? It seems so overwhelm-
ing! As always, the answer is:

"Pick up the mirror instead of the magnifying glass!"

I know, many of you are convinced it is *they* who should be
picking up the mirror, not us! The truth is that we all need to
pick up our mirrors. However, since we can only be in control
of who *we* are and what *we* do, as always, our most powerful
plan of action is to take action ourselves. That being the case,
let me move on and show you how you can begin to deal with
the anger that holds you back and keeps you from living the kind
of loving, caring life that all of us are entitled to have.

As I see it, dealing with anger is a five-step process:

1. Get in touch with the anger.
2. Vent it in an appropriate way.
3. Pick up the proverbial mirror and stare into it until you
   determine where the upset is coming from and why it is
   there to begin with.
4. Make a plan of action to correct the situation that created
   the anger in the first place.
5. Then let it go so that you can get on with your life in a
   loving way.

In order to get in touch with your anger and vent it in an
appropriate way, you need to acknowledge that it is there. Be-

cause we have been trained that anger is unattractive in women, many of us have been careful to hide it, especially from ourselves. You may insist that you really don't have any anger or that you used to be angry but have already dealt with it. Don't believe it! We all have anger, even those who have been working on it for thirty years, or who are saints-in-training, or whose lives are gloriously abundant. Many of my students who think they've already worked through their anger are surprised at what comes up for them when we do anger exercises in class. The anger may be well hidden, but it is there!

There are many ways of dredging up anger carefully kept. Naturally, one of my favorites is screaming, not to your mate, but in private or with a good friend.* Since screaming in one's home may bring in the neighbors and the police, or both, it helps to be a little resourceful. I used to drive to a secluded area and sit in my car and scream and scream and scream. If that isn't convenient for you, it helps to scream into a pillow, or to turn up the stereo, which masks the screams. You begin, as I did, by simply repeating "I'm angry" over and over again, increasing the volume with each repetition.

Pounding a pillow is also effective in bringing up anger. Kneel by the side of your bed, and with both arms stretched straight above you and with your hands clasped, come down hard on a pillow on the bed over and over and over again. Sometimes it takes five minutes of pounding to begin to bring up the anger. It helps to think of some person in the past or present that you would like to punch in the face. And we all have someone like that.

You could also buy a rubber bat, called a bataca, which is often used in therapy to release the stress of anger. With the bataca, you can pound away at the anger you've had for your parents,

*While "scream therapy" involves much more than just screaming, the simple physiological release that the scream allows is beneficial to body, mind, and spirit. Unreleased anger is like a poison eating away at our insides, causing all sorts of physical, mental, and spiritual decay, leaving us dissatisfied and joyless. Yuck!

children, bosses, and particularly the men in your life. You might even want to pound away at all those seemingly wasted years when you hadn't done what you really wanted to do in life. Just get it out. You can be sure that anger unexpressed will be taking its internal toll in the form of depression, illness, addictions, fatigue, guilt, and so on.

NOTE: Remember to take responsibility for your health. If, for example, you have back problems or any other disorder that this kind of exercise might aggravate, try something less physically taxing. After all, you don't want to add to your list of things to be angry about!

Physical exercise releases some of the tension that the anger creates. Use the swing of your tennis racket as a means of whacking out your anger. Or use each step that you jog to reinforce your commitment to make changes in your life.

I know there are many people who will tell you that when you feel anger toward someone, you should get it out directly at them. Sometimes we can't seem to stop ourselves, and sometimes "direct screaming" is quite effective, depending on your goal. This approach certainly does vent the anger, but it doesn't do much for the relationship! Hurling epithets at someone is not exactly a loving act (even though it might feel great, as well as justified, at the time). This doesn't mean that, in certain situations, the person with whom you are having a problem doesn't need to be confronted. It simply means that it is better to confront him or her after some of the steam in your pressure cooker has been released. And, as you will soon find out, your reaction to what someone is doing is not their fault!

Interestingly, many of us have expressed, and seemingly resolved, our anger on many levels. We are wonderful friends, and loving daughters and mothers; we are generally interested in working for the good of the world by involving ourselves with humanitarian efforts. We are the picture of gentle, caring human beings. But we haven't cleared the biggest hurdle: releasing our anger toward the men in our lives.

Generally speaking, we can find ourselves in one of three categories:

passive / aggressive

1. The *passively hostile* describes those of us who have not as yet gotten in touch with the rage that lies within. Not that we have hidden it from those near and dear. Those around us can't help but notice the way our anger oozes out in subtle and not so subtle ways, such as our being late all the time, or spending too much money, or being constantly ill, or "sweetly" putting them down, and so on. We fear our anger because of our even deeper fear of losing our feminine identity, or worse, someone we love . . . fear of being out of control . . . or fear of having to make changes in our lives. For us, it is better not to rock the boat than to face the unknown.

2. The *openly* hostile describes those of us who certainly have gotten in touch with our anger in a big way. Some of us uselessly flail around with it, simply blowing off steam. And some of us use it to make really significant changes in our lives, if only out of spite! Some of us feel great about our anger, convinced that the male of the species is a legitimate enemy to fight! Some of us are not so happy with our anger but haven't a clue as to what to do to resolve it.

While it might not seem so to those who are being attacked, I believe that open hostility is at least a step in the right direction. Again, while it doesn't do much for relationships, it does symbolize our willingness to take a risk and move away from an unhealthy, albeit safe, image of what it means to be a woman, and to explore more of the person that lies within.

But we can't stop there. As I discussed earlier, unresolved anger, either open or passive, numbs us to what is going on within ourselves and what is going on with others. Until we allow ourselves to feel, we cannot be friends and lovers to the men in our lives—and this leads us to the next category.

3. The *inner sleuth* describes those among us who have learned to use our anger to uncover more of who we are. While our tempers still flare on occasion, we have learned to release our anger in a "safe" way, so as not to hurt unfairly the people we care about. We then pick up our mirror and ask the all-important question:

> "What are we hiding from ourselves that is causing us to lash out?" *pain*

When we begin to look inward with questions such as this, we begin to feel the feelings, no matter how painful, that have been locked up inside. We begin to open our hearts to the breadth of possibility of what it means to be a human being. We become conscious seekers of parts to the human jigsaw puzzle. And as we connect the pieces, we are amazed at the richness of the picture that emerges.

For the first time in our lives, we begin to understand what it means to really take responsibility for our lives. We see that our anger is simply a clue that something has gone awry within ourselves, not without, and in that it is very valuable. We continue to ask ourselves empowering questions:

> "What is the *real* reason for our anger that lies beneath all the lies we have told ourselves?"

After much soul-searching, our mirror has told many of us that the underlying cause of our anger lies in the fact that we still are not feeling good enough . . . strong enough . . . entitled enough. We find out that:

> Our anger is about the actions we are *not* taking to correct the matter at hand!

Our mirror tells us, for example, that if we are living with a man who is unloving and hurtful, our anger is really not at him (although his behavior is not to be condoned), but at the fact that we are choosing to stay . . . that we don't have the courage to leave . . . that we don't trust that whatever happens, come what may, we can make it on our own. This lack of trust fills us with unwarranted self-loathing. Ultimately, no one can be harder on ourselves than we are.

Why are we so fearful of taking appropriate action in so many hurtful situations in our lives? I believe that basically our sense of self in relationship to men has changed little over the years, despite the fact that we have made many significant advances in the outside world. There is a part of us that still feels second-class, a part of us that still wants to "look up to" our men, a part of us that still hopes to find someone who will take care of us from now to evermore, a part of us that does not trust that we have within us what it really takes to survive on our own.

Even when we are actually "making it" financially in a big way, there is still a part of us waiting for someone to come along so we don't have to work so hard or worry so much. There is still a part of us that is scared and tired and wishes that we could turn it all over to someone else so that we didn't have to deal with really taking responsibility for our lives. There is a part of us that still feels inadequate, helpless, and alone. That is the part of us that is angry. And that is the part that has kept us from being all that we can be.

It is not only in the world of work that we have deep anxiety; we also fear making simple changes within the home. For example, even if we don't want to, we continue to wash the dishes, prepare the meals, subjugate our careers, focus our attention on others, not act on what we really want to do in life, insist on being Superwomen, all because there is a part of us that is afraid to say "NO!" . . . a part of us that is afraid of the loss of our men or loss of the image of ourselves as women if we don't.* *We do what we don't want to do because, first and foremost, we crave approval.* Our sense of survival is tied up with it. And we will sacrifice our sense of self in order to get it. We don't have enough confidence to understand that we can be who we want to be in life and still be loved, not necessarily by the men we are with, but certainly by others out there who are more secure.

It is not because of men that we are trapped in unwanted roles. It is because of our anxiety about separating ourselves from the known, which, no matter how distasteful, is safe and accepted by the society around us . . . and the child within us.

It is interesting that alone, many of us do fine. As soon as we get into a relationship, however, all our insecurities are triggered, and we revert to familiar and unsatisfactory patterns. So many men report being attracted to women who are independent and strong. As the relationship progresses, these very same women turn into weak, helpless, and needy "little girls."† What is going on? Where has the mature woman gone? Why, when she is so often capable of functioning as an adult in the world of work or parenting, is she incapable of functioning in a parallel way in her relationships?

The story of Joan is illustrative: After a brief marriage, she was left alone to take care of herself and her young daughter. For thirteen years she had supported both of them by teaching in the local high school. Recently, she remarried, and that is when the "trouble" began. She came to me distraught, con-

*I am not talking about those women who choose homemaking as a career and find deep fulfillment and satisfaction in that. Obviously, these women will not harbor the anger of those who are unwillingly playing that role.

†Men, too, often revert to old patterns because of the same kinds of insecurities that are triggered by relationships.

vinced that she had made a terrible mistake in marrying Ted, and then proceeded to tell me how he was letting her down.

One of Joan's complaints, for example, was that the repairs in their new house were going too slowly and it was making her furious. I asked her, if it was bothering her so much, why she didn't tell her husband that, since he was so busy, she was going to take some of the burden off his shoulders and work with the contractors on her own. She looked startled, as if that thought had never entered her mind (it hadn't) and went on to insist that it was _his_ job to handle the house repairs. I asked her why it was his job. All she could come up with was "Because it is."

I asked Joan who had handled all the house repairs in the years prior to her meeting Ted. She said she had. I asked her what had changed. She couldn't answer that and impatiently went on to a new complaint. "And his children don't call before they visit. They just drop in whenever they feel like it. I like my privacy!" This was something to be cleared up, indeed, but hardly the reason for all her upset. She even objected to the fact that Ted loved to cook—she felt that that was her job. (I pointed out that there were probably 100 million women who would trade places with her at a moment's notice!) Her complaints went on for an hour with her "yeah, buts" popping up each time I showed her how she could alter the situation.

Usually, when we (male or female) fight about little things, the underlying issue is often some form of dependency. I finally asked, "Joan, what is _really_ going on?" It was then that she broke down and began to cry, stating that for some reason she felt small and unimportant. She was even thinking of leaving her teaching career because "what did it all mean, anyway?" She was threatened by all the beautiful young girls at her husband's office and was really feeling old: "Why would he want me, anyway?" In truth, she had abdicated her identity, her sense of self, and, indeed, had begun feeling (and acting) very inferior and insecure in terms of the relationship. She had let herself become a dependent child. She went into the relationship as a whole person and then "attached" herself to Ted, expecting him to be her tower of strength. (No wonder men die young!) And to mask all her self-loathing, her unsuspecting husband became the scapegoat.

In reality, Ted was trying desperately to make her happy, as Joan later began to see when she took off the blinders. If he had been a more secure person, he might have been able to say: "Joan, grow up. Start working on why you feel so put upon. I am doing everything I can to make you happy, and I realize now that something is going on within you that is keeping you depressed. I'll help you work on it if you wish, but I refuse to be your dumping ground."

On the contrary, the more Joan dumped, the more Ted tried to please her. Certainly, if this pattern had continued, she would have created a self-fulfilling prophecy: Why *would* he want her, anyway? (Unless he was a glutton for punishment!)

I gave Joan a program of exercises to help her pull up her own power instead of expecting Ted to be powerful for her. I also told her to make a list of all the loving things he did for her each day and thank him. (It is interesting to note that at the beginning of her session with me, Joan could think of nothing that her husband did for her. By the time the session ended, she had listed thirty items.)

After doing her exercises for a short time, Joan began feeling like a "person" once again. She learned to pick up on the cue that whenever she was in a complaint mode, she was not taking responsibility for her own life. She could then pick up the bag of tools that I had given her and begin to work on herself (instead of finding fault with her husband). In so doing, she began to see what a loving man she had attracted into her life. And just as importantly, she was able to keep in the foreground the loving person that she really wanted to be, instead of the whimpering child that she loathed.

I am not saying that all men are as loving as Joan's husband, but no matter what the situation, the same principle applies:

> As we begin to feel better about ourselves, we react in appropriate ways to change situations that do not support our growth.

But the question remains: What happened to Joan in the beginning of her marriage? What triggered her insecurities? Where did the beautiful, strong, competent, loving woman go and where did the insecure, frightened, spoiled brat come from?

A useful framework for helping to explain Joan's behavior is found in Eric Berne's theory of transactional analysis.[2] Berne states that within every one of us, male and female, are three ego states. At any given moment in time, one of these three ego states is in charge and thus determines what we are thinking, feeling, or doing, and how we are doing it. Let me introduce you to these three ego states:

The Child-Within—This is the part of us that has not yet grown up. It is who we were when we were young and who is still present within us. On the positive side, it is the part that is curious, playful, and filled with joy. On the negative side, it is the part that is filled with fear, helplessness, and rebellion—all the emotions of the defiant child, who, on the one hand wants to show its independence, and, on the other hand, is petrified when Mommy or Daddy is out of sight. In most cases, this is the part of us that is responsible for our anger.

The Parent-Within—This is our built-in judge or nurturer, as the case may be. Most often it is our judge. This is the part of us that has picked up the dos and don'ts of our society and our parents. It can be cruel in its demands and far more punitive than our real parents ever were. All our "shoulds" and "shouldn'ts," as well as the "I told you so's", come from the Parent-Within.

On the positive side, the Parent-Within can be taught to be our security blanket that comforts us when we are feeling needy.

The Adult-Within—This is the logical, reasoning part of the mind that isn't attached to childish or parental demands. It has the ability to objectively appraise any situation without interference from the Child-Within and the Parent-Within or any other subpersonalities that lie within. The Adult-Within can interpret reality in a most constructive way. When used effectively, it can serve to bring out the best of who we are.

Applying this to Joan's situation, we can see that when she was on her own, her inner Adult and inner Parent had been the dominating characters in her life. With all her responsibilities as mother and teacher, there was not much chance for the inner Child to emerge. As soon as she found herself under the "protection" of a man, however, the insecurity of the Child was automatically triggered and emerged with a vengeance, masking the strengths of the woman she had become and exposing the anxieties and fury of childhood and adolescence that had never been resolved.

I use the word "triggered" because:

It is believed that certain events remind us of times long past and replay the feelings that were attached to those earlier times.

This would explain why so many of us revert to the Child when we are in a relationship. When we are functioning in the world on our own, dependent feelings are not as easily triggered. But as soon as we are involved with a man (a father figure, indeed!), the Child automatically emerges and we can't figure out on a conscious level what is going on.

After my divorce, I decided I was going to become a very independent woman, and, to be sure, I managed very nicely on my own. Every time a new man came into my life, however, I would revert back to old dependencies, demands, and patterns in my life, and, of course, old anger. I would blame all my unhappiness on whoever the "he" happened to be at the time. Ultimately, I would leave the relationship hoping I would find someone better the next time around. And each time I would get into a new relationship, the same thing would occur.

I finally came to realize that each time I fell for a man, I literally "fell" into a childlike state in terms of my emotions. My inner Child emerged with a full vengeance. The men in my life were like an automatic release of all the feelings of insecurity, fear, and helplessness that I actually had as a child. This awareness ultimately enabled me to switch into present time and call forth the stronger and healthier part of me which was able to soothe my frightened inner Child with positive self-talk:

"Not to worry. All is well. We can survive, with or without a man. I am powerful. I can take care of you. Let go. I am always with you. We'll handle whatever happens. You have a relationship, but you are more than your relationship. Stop worrying about what you are going to get from this man; instead, focus on what you have to give to this world."

This kind of positive self-talk was able to pull me from an unloving state toward the man in my life into one that was more loving.* It was possible for me to see that, in fact, my upset was because of something internal and had nothing to do with him. Again, I am not suggesting that all the men in my life were gems. Hardly! Some of them were horrors! But the real issue is not that they were horrors, but that I chose to be with them in the

---

*An *affirmation* is another form of positive self-talk. I've included a list of affirmations at the end of many of the chapters. Consult Appendix A to learn how to use them most effectively.

first place. And that's the "something internal" that I had to look at.

Over time I have learned that the scared Child-Within will always be there. So will the punitive Parent-Within. What we need to do is to recognize when they are there and replace their voices with messages from a higher part of our being. The power of this kind of "inside look" is tremendous.

Let me illustrate how our three inner states work by using a common complaint of women: "I'm tired of being chief cook around here!"

Parent (within): You should cook dinner for your husband. It is the *right* thing to do.

Child (within): I don't want to cook dinner. I want someone to cook dinner for me.

Parent: That's a bad way to think. You're being very selfish.

Child: But I don't want to cook dinner! And I'm fed up with having to do everything around the house!

Parent: But you won't be loved if you don't cook and clean. That's your job and that's what men expect. Remember that there are plenty of good women out there just dying to meet a man. You'd better cook that dinner!

Child: All right, I'll do it! (because I can't face the consequences of what will happen if I don't do what I'm supposed to do!) But I really don't want to! And I hate *you* for making me do it.

While the *"you"* we hate is really our critical inner Parent and more significantly our gutless, inner Child, we turn all our hatred outward to the innocent (and hungry) man who has just walked in the door and who has no idea that he has become a monster in your mind. Granted, he might expect you to have his meal on the table every day of his life, because that is what he has been taught that women should do, but he certainly does not have the power to *make* you cook his meals if you really don't want to. You can choose to say no! Every day you take on the role of chief cook is one more day you confirm your man's expectations and entrench them as part of the "contract" of the marriage, thus making change more and more difficult.

So why don't you say no? Because the inner Child feels that it couldn't cope if it was abandoned and left behind. Unless we can somehow assure it that it will always be cared for by the inner Adult and the supportive (as opposed to judgmental) inner Parent, it can never make any healthy changes. We can do this by strengthening the voice of the Adult and nurturing Parent who can promise protection from the most reliable source of all: the power within. I will talk more about getting in touch with the power within in later chapters.

So far, I have talked about recognizing and venting our anger (Steps 1 and 2 in our five-step process of dealing with anger). I have also talked about the underlying cause of our anger (Step 3). It's time to move on to Step 4: taking appropriate steps to correct the situation that is troubling us. Going back to the cooking example, what might our inner Adult have to say about the situation?

"Obviously, this cooking arrangement is not making me happy. I don't know how my husband will react to my wanting to change it. Who knows? He could leave. I know it frightens the hell out of me (the inner Child) to think of losing him; on the other hand, if I don't take care of my own needs, I will be incapable of being a loving person. I'm beginning to resent him already.

"What are my alternatives? First, I'll talk it over with him. He doesn't even know how unhappy I am in the role of chief cook. And if he doesn't like it, he'll just have to learn to deal with it. I really want to do other things with my time. Second, I'll come up with some alternatives: We can have food sent in or we can go out three times a week or he can be responsible for the food three days a week. The important thing is that I am clear I don't want to cook every day of the week . . . *and I am willing to act on it."*

While all this is taking place, your Parent, of course, is resisting with, "You're a bad person." "You won't be needed any more and he'll leave." And so on. The Child is yelling, "Oh, my God, what'll I do if he leaves?" The key is to feel the fear and do it anyway, knowing that somehow, come what may, you will survive. It requires that you choose the voice of your inner Adult to keep affirming:

> "Whatever happens, I'll handle it!"
> "Whatever happens, I'll handle it!"
> "Whatever happens, I'll handle it!"

You finally get up the courage to confront your husband with what is making you unhappy and present him with your alternative plans. What you don't realize is that the real test is yet to come!

After you've rationally presented your proposal, he starts to resist. You have to remember that his inner Child is also frightened of changing the status quo ("I'm not as important to her anymore and she might leave") and his inner Parent is filled with directives ("You'll be a wimp if you let her get away with this. Be a man and stand your ground!"). So he might retort with something like:

> "I can't believe I'm hearing this from you. You know how much I enjoy your cooking. Why would you want to deprive me of one of my great pleasures?"

Guilt! Guilt! Fear! Fear! "If I don't cook, I'm a bad person and he won't love me anymore!" For the health of the relationship, it would be wonderful to be able to keep your Adult at the forefront:

"I know you might feel upset with this change, but you must understand that I am only thinking of the relationship when I insist that some changes have to be made. I find myself feeling trapped and resenting you instead of feeling warm and close. Let's see how we can change the situation so that we will both be happy. Do you have any ideas?"

The resistance will most likely persist and even heat up a bit:

"You're really selfish, you know. I don't hear other women complaining. They're appreciative of what their men do for them. What's your problem?"

Guilt! Guilt! Anger! Anger! If we are saints-in-training and can still keep the Adult and its clarity at the forefront, it would say:

"I know it feels as if I am selfish, but I need to do this for myself. And I hope you will understand that, but if not, so be it! This is my plan and I intend to put it into action. I hope that you will support me. I love you very much, but I have to take responsibility for my own happiness and cooking every night does not make me happy. It has nothing to do with my love for you. I am appreciative of all you do for me. You are a wonderful husband. And that has nothing to do with the fact that I am no longer cooking dinner every single night of the week. That is final."

It is then important to put your plan into *action*—and stick to it—despite the hostility of your mate, which will probably increase for a while. Ultimately, when he realizes that you truly mean business, he will in all likelihood go along with the plan.

You might have observed that the script doesn't usually go like that, however. Instead, our scared Child, who desperately needs approval, comes forward to "prove" itself, and the battle begins:

"What do you mean, selfish? I've been picking up after you for ages and I don't want to do it anymore!"

Your husband shouts back:

"Well, who's been paying most of the bills around here!"

And so it goes. Two inner Children with closed hearts, each unable to see the fear and pain in the other. The battle will continue, but in the end we women usually back down to the wishes of our men. I believe it was Betty Friedan who said, "If it were a real war, we'd lose. We need men too much!" I'm not so sure we need men any more or less than they need us. *But I do know that it is our giving in when it goes against the very grain of who we are*—not their demands—*that incites our rage.*

When our Child is at the forefront, we are too frightened to "leave home" and make any real changes in our lives. And, in the earlier example, we remain stuck in our old unwanted position of chief cook. Whenever we show the slightest bit of guilt, ambivalence, or fear about what we want, our man will persist until we finally give in. The pattern of self-loathing continues, and, of course, so does our anger.

Keep in mind that our men (and children, parents, and friends) will almost always resist changes in our behavior (as we resist changes in theirs) and we have to be prepared for it. One thing is clear, though:

We can't blame men for walking all over us. We can only notice that we are not moving out of the way.

I will never forget what Dan, the leader of our group sessions, said to me as I was hurling out all the real and imagined "injustices" my ex-husband had perpetrated against me over the years: "Susan, you talk as if you were a butterfly on the asshole of an elephant. All you had to do was move out of the way!" I must say that nobody had ever explained it to me that clearly before!

So it is up to us to take action, to sculpt our lives as creatively as we can. There are many of us who are already doing just that, despite the fear provoked by our inner Child. We have learned to call forward that strong and steady inner Adult and we have reeducated our inner Parent to be more nurturing so that we always have internal support to help us when the going gets tough. It is clear that in order to have the strength to make the changes that will rid us of our anger, we first must learn how to love and nurture ourselves. Our anger signifies the fact that we have not reckoned with our inner Child as yet, i.e. we have not grown up. You can bet that the angrier we are, the more dependent we are, despite what the outer circumstances look like.

There are those of us who marry young and never really try our wings in the outside world. Not that you can blame us; the blanket of hearth and home can be very warm indeed. Some of us have found happiness, meaning, and purpose there . . . and that is good. That is what we are all seeking. But others of us find that the shoe doesn't fit and we come to hate the sense of helplessness we feel. We then decide to get out of our self-imposed trap and become strong, independent women. We know we have the right to get out there and make something of ourselves, just like the men do. And it is here that we get stuck, afraid to make the big hurdle. Subconsciously, our inner Child becomes terrorized:

"Oh, my God, you mean I really have to go out there and face rejection, face fourteen-hour days, face failure? Am I really equipped? Am I really good enough? Can I make the mark? Do I really want to work that hard? I can't even balance my own checkbook. How am I going to make it out there?"

At some point we subconsciously decide that we are not ready, and in order to hide our insecurity from ourselves and anybody else that might be watching, we save face. We make it *their* fault, thus putting off taking those fearful steps into the unknown.

"If there were more equality in the workplace,
    then I'd really be making it."
"If I didn't have to stay home with the children,
    then I'd really be making it."
"If women had the same opportunities that men have,
    then I'd really be making it."

If we are still blaming, it means that we still haven't come to terms with the fact that equal opportunity in many ways *does* now exist—but equal opportunity doesn't mean equal achievement. You've got to get out there and work for that on your own, which requires incredibly hard work. This isn't to say that there are no inequities in the home and in the workplace where women are concerned. There certainly are! And we have to take the responsibility to see that these inequities are changed. But, as those who have actually pushed through the fear and have actually turned their lives around can attest, where there's a will, there's a way. When we don't handle the fear our *will* becomes a *won't* and we find it necessary to create a scapegoat to mask our inability to take action. The truth is that dependence and anger go together. When we get rid of our dependency needs and our feeling of helplessness (by handling the inner Child), magically, our anger abates, and our hearts begin to open.

Given all this, how can we begin to take control of our inner Child and begin to make appropriate changes in our lives? Since fear is the underlying cause of our paralysis, I suggest you read my book *Feel the Fear and Do It Anyway,*[3] which has many tools for pushing through fear and addresses in depth much of what I have been discussing. When all is said and done, we see that it is our fear that creates our anger. I know that there are many things that seem to justify our legitimate anger, such as infidelity, wife beating, nonpayment of child support, and so on. And it helps to keep "pounding the pillow" to discharge the hurt. But then we must move on with our lives and make the necessary changes to assure that we are taking care of ourselves, physically, mentally, emotionally, and spiritually. When we do, we come to realize that there are effective recourses to infidelity, wife beating, nonpayment of child support, and so on, that allow our integrity and sense of self to remain intact.

We are in pain when people hurt us. It helps ease our pain to keep in mind that those who hurt, hurt others. As most vividly stated by Zig Ziglar, "Every obnoxious act is a cry for help!"[4] When we take responsibility for moving out of the way of those who try to hurt us, we can begin to open our hearts and see the pain that lies within their souls. We can begin to understand that no matter how heinous the "crime" that was perpetrated, it is the act of a very frightened Child who is fighting for its survival in the only way it knows how.

Again, this is not to condone such people's behavior but to ease our own gnawing pain and confusion. It helps us to recognize that people's pain drives them to do destructive things, not their malice. But given that, we don't have to remain in a situation where hurtful behavior continues. I once heard the expression, "First time, shame on you. Second time, shame on me." It is up to us to take the steps necessary to remove ourselves from an unloving person. However, unless there is physical violence involved, it pays to take a good look inward before we make any changes. Often it is our vision that is unloving, not our man. As Joan discovered after working on her self-esteem, her husband was really pretty terrific, after all.

If we find ourselves in a very hurtful relationship, it is important not to be angry with ourselves. That is only compounding the hurt. Instead, we can use the experience to notice what we are doing, with the ultimate goal of taking appropriate action. But the first step is always the noticing:

I notice that I'm having a very difficult time letting go of this unhealthy relationship . . . *instead of* . . . That creep is making me so unhappy.

I notice that I constantly draw critical people into my life . . . *instead of* . . . I can't believe the way he puts me down in front of his friends.

I notice that when a man really treats me well, I turn off. I'm drawn to inconsiderate men . . . *instead of* . . . Would you believe he kept me waiting for three hours!?!

And so on . . .

When we see everything as a learning experience, no matter how awful the situation may appear, there is no reason to be angry with ourselves. As long as we use all our experiences, even our bad relationships, as a mirror and begin to make changes as a result of what we see, it follows that we can do no "wrong." It's all part of the process of learning and growing.

It also follows that once we begin to alter our perceptions about the offending parties, forgiving and letting go (Step 5) become easier. If we can see their insecurity and pain, their inexcusable behavior becomes excusable—although not necessarily acceptable. If we see our experiences with them as an opportunity to learn more about ourselves, we can look back and thank them instead of hating them. If we see the part we've played in our own drama, our feeling of "victim" dissipates and we don't feel so put upon.

We have to work on forgiveness. It doesn't come naturally. One of my favorite forgiveness exercises is as follows:

Find an empty room and turn off the telephone. Put on some quiet music. Sit down in a comfortable chair and close your eyes. Focus on relaxing all parts of your body from the top of your head to the tips of your toes. Think of a man (or woman) who brings up a lot of anger, pain, or guilt in you. If there is no one in the present, think of someone in the past. Picture him in front of you. First surround him with rays of loving white light and tell him that you wish him only joy and happiness in life. Thank him for whatever he has given you, no matter how little you think that may be. Repeat this process over and over again, once a day, until you can actually look at the individual in your mind's eye and wish him only love.

Sounds easy? Wrong. You will be surprised at the amount of rage and withholding and sadness this exercise can pull up in you. It can really get you in touch with the huge amounts of resentment you are harboring—resentment that can only cause self-destruction to you and everyone around you. Allow yourself to scream at the person in your mind's eye, call him names, or whatever, then keep coming back to the task at hand—sending love and all good wishes. It may take weeks for you to really forgive and embrace this person with your love. Remember that the one with whom you find this exercise the most difficult is the one you most need to forgive.

You might need to forgive someone who is no longer alive. Just because someone is no longer here doesn't mean that you have resolved your anger toward him. I know many people who have never forgiven their loved ones for dying and leaving them. I know it doesn't sound "reasonable" to be angry at someone for dying, but our Child isn't a reasonable character.

As we begin to melt our anger, we also begin to see the part we played in creating the course of events. As I stated earlier, we then become angry at ourselves. Continue this exercise until you forgive yourself as well. See yourself having all the wonderful things you are entitled to. See yourself as the beautiful human being you really are.

This is truly a healing exercise and one that, in some form or other, is used by many in the health professions to help people heal their bodies. It gets dramatic results.

In a similar vein, Gestalt therapy uses the "empty chair" technique. Here, you imagine the person who is the object of your anger in an empty chair you have placed in front of you. The person could be someone who is alive or dead. You begin a dialogue by telling him or her what you are feeling. (It is very effective to play the role of the other person and actually switch chairs to do this.) You, in effect, become the other person and answer for him or her. Keep going back and forth with this process. You will be amazed at the insights you will have and the empathy that you will begin to feel as you literally put yourself in another's shoes.

As a variation, you can even put different parts of your personality in the empty chair (such as your Parent, Adult, or Child). Or create a dialogue in a journal with the person who is the object of your anger. I am always amazed at the creativity of our subconscious mind. Everything we need to know is there for the asking!

Another useful angerbusting tool is the game I created for my students called Switch. Let me use myself as an example of how the game is played: I am married to a very loving man who has my best interests at heart. Therefore, when I am feeling angry at him, I have learned to suspect there is something going on within me that is causing the problem. I then ask myself this question:

"What am I not doing for myself that I am expecting him to do for me?"

Interpreted another way, *how am I not taking responsibility for what I want?* I usually come up with an answer. For example,

Mark always makes our airline arrangements. On one occasion, I was unhappy about where we were seated. My first reaction was to get angry at him. "Why didn't he check? He knows I like the window seat! Now my trip is ruined and it's all his fault!" Obviously, these are the thoughts of my Child, certainly not the intelligent loving part of myself! I have taught myself to listen for that nasty voice of my Child within, and when I hear it, to quickly switch to my inner Adult (even though I am still feeling like the Child!). In this particular case, my Adult quickly was able to surmise that if I have specific needs in an airplane, it is up to *me* to make sure that my needs are met. It is up to *me* to call the airline and check on the seat arrangements. As soon as I got in touch with that, my good ol' inner Parent started to do a number. "You idiot, if it means so much to you, why didn't you call the airline and confirm that you had a window seat!" Once again I had to switch into the Adult mode and reason:

"This is a good lesson. Next time I will know what to do. Let's see if I can 'get off my position' that this is a bad seat and really enjoy the trip anyway. Isn't it wonderful that the two of us are together? Isn't it wonderful that I am going on a trip? Isn't life wonderful?"

Using the game of Switch, I melted all my anger . . . I learned something for future trips . . . I focused on the positive instead of the negative and, in the brief few minutes that it took me to process all of the above, everything switched from upset to ecstasy. This game of Switch (or a better name for it might be Grow Up!) is magical if you can remember to include all the components.

1. Decide what the Child within is angry about. (Remember it is always the Child who is angry.)
2. Switch into the Adult mode and change your perspective.

3. List the ways you can take responsibility for the situation.
4. Focus on the positive instead of the negative.
5. Allow your heart to open to the person to whom you are projecting anger and see that the person is really doing the best he can.

In my airplane drama, the only action I had to take was to change my perception. Often solutions are more painful and not that easy. Sometimes it requires that you leave the situation you are in. But playing the game of Switch allows you to leave with compassion instead of anger, forgiveness instead of resentment. For example:

Complaint: I will never forgive that man for the pain he has caused me. After twenty years, how can he leave me and go off with another woman? How can anyone be that cruel? I'll never forgive him! I'll make him pay for this!

Switch: I know that I will be feeling a lot of pain and loss for a while, but that too shall pass. I'm so sorry that the marriage has ended, but I am grateful for the many years we had together. They weren't twenty wasted years. Even though he was really difficult at times, he did support me in many ways and I am grateful for that as well. We had many good times together. We gave each other a lot, especially our two great kids. I don't know how I am going to make it on my own, but I trust I will find a way. I will see it as the end of one era and the beginning of another. Who knows what possibilities lie ahead? Maybe I'll go back to school and pick up where I left off so many years ago. There are so many things I have wanted to do over the years and never got around to doing. Workshops to take, friends to make, community projects with which to get involved. I guess now is the time to begin. I (the Child-Within) am scared to death . . . but I'll find my way.

I know that the switch can bring on an enormous amount of sadness. I believe that is why anger dominates so many divorces. It is easier leaving with anger than with sadness. But sadness is part of life, and healthy sadness has a bittersweet feel to it. Things change. Life moves on. We must learn to go along with it; go with the flow, as they say. I'm sure you have heard it said time and time again, that you can't have any control over anyone else, you can only have control over yourself. And when you take that control, the world begins to open up for you.

I suggest you take out a pad and pen and begin to write down the many things that make you angry in life, whether they have to do with your job, your friends, your family, or the man or men in your life. Put only one complaint to a page, leaving room for the game of Switch. Begin to see how you can turn around your complaint into action on your part that will assure that your needs are met. I know in certain areas this is easier said than done. But if you keep in mind that the purpose of your anger is for you to gain insight about yourself, this can be a very valuable exercise.

The ultimate goal of the process is for you to end up with a plan of action that will improve your sense of self-esteem. Be creative. The more difficult the situation, the greater the reward when the answer is found. You might even want to do this with a friend so that you can contribute feedback to one another when one of you is blocked on a solution. You will be surprised at how clever you can be if you set your mind to it. The following is one more example of how to play the game.

Complaint: I'm angry he is such a workaholic.

Switch: I have all this free time. I'll bet there are some wonderful things I could be doing for myself. I'll exchange babysitting with my girlfriends so I won't have to spend money on that. I understand that my husband is working so hard because he is pressured to bring home the bacon. Maybe I can get a part-time job while the kids are at school, or even start a business from my home. That will take some of the pressure off him. That would really be exciting, creating my own business from home. Maybe one of my friends and I could do something together . . . and so on.

This happens to be an actual story from one of my students. She soon began to really enjoy her "free" time when her workaholic husband was doing his own thing. As she began to gain enthusiasm for what she was doing, and got off his back, guess what happened! He began to get more interested in her and less interested in his work. Prior to her switch, she really was a drag to come home to. She was always mildly depressed, with no energy, and was always putting him down as having more interest in his work than in her. When she began to "rescue" herself, everything in the relationship changed. The irony is that she got so involved in her new business that she is the one who has become the workaholic and he is the one freeing up his schedule so he can spend more time with her!

There are some women, of course, who realize that they do not want an absentee husband. They play the game of Switch for real—by getting out of the relationship and finding someone else who is more interested in truly sharing a life. That is another creative solution. We have to decide what we will tolerate in a relationship and act to change what we won't—to tolerate the intolerable is to kill a piece of who we are.

I think you get the picture. The key is to take action in life, instead of complaining that the world is not making you happy. Once we get off the "victim" routine, it is amazing how creative we can become. We begin to pull up our power and fill ourselves with enthusiasm and a sense of wonder at the possibilities. A victim mentality brings only upset and is an incredible waste of valuable energy. If I seem to be belaboring this point (and I am), it is because it is so important for us all to understand.

> We have to stop playing the role of "poor us" and instead create a new model for ourselves—that of loving, creative, powerful, and abundant adults. With this new model, life becomes easier and more joyous . . . and we have far less to be angry about.

I think that if we continue on the warpath, bashing our men, instead of loving them, the time will come in the not too distant future when a counterattack will be mounted. I see glimmers of it already. Of course, men harbor their own anger as well: they too are only human. But as a group, they have remained on the defensive, not the offensive. As a group, they have not as yet created *us* as the enemy. Given the direction that we seem to be headed, a full-scale war between the sexes is a distinct possibility. I don't believe any of us really want that. I don't think we understand fully the losses both sides would incur. The answer lies in becoming lovers instead. And it would take so little on our part to turn it all around.

What we don't fully understand is that most rational men are in favor of the women's movement; what they are not in favor of is our anger. In my workshops, many men reported that what really turned them off about certain women was their anger, not their newly found strength and independence. That, they liked. It took some of the responsibility off of them. They also found strong women more interesting to be with. It became clear to me, as I taught class after class about relationship and connection, that *most men like us much more than we like ourselves.* They have their own insecurities to be sure, but in truth, they want the same thing we want—to love and be loved.

The time to deal with our anger is now, before we get hardened in our positions. Anger wastefully expends energy that could be used for helping the world instead of hurting it. We need to send positive vibes into the world instead of negative ones. We can't decry war when we are in combat ourselves. We need to learn how to love again. And why shouldn't we be the ones to make it happen? Certainly, without a doubt, we have the power to make it happen . . . beginning right now.

Affirmations for Releasing Anger

I am taking action.

I am now taking control of my life.

I am reclaiming my power.

I am powerful and I am loving.

I have nothing to fear.

I have choice in my life.

I am sculpting my life as I want it to be.

I see the pain in those who hurt me.

I am moving out of the way of those who hurt me.

I am moving out of my own way.

I am drawing beautiful people into my life.

I am melting my anger and letting go of the pain.

I am creating a life filled with love.

Everything I need to know is within me.

Whatever happens, I'll handle it.

I am sending positive energy into the world.

I have the power to control my life.

I relax and I let go of my anger.

3

DAMNED IF THEY DO AND DAMNED IF THEY DON'T

"How many women here think they would like to trade places with men?" . . .

"That many, huh?"

"How many women here would willingly and without resentment take on the financial responsibility of the relationship? . . .

"No hands, huh?"

"How many women here expect a man willingly and without resentment to take on the financial responsibility of the relationship? . . .

"That many, huh?"

"Once again, how many women here think they would like to trade places with men?" . . .

"No hands, huh?"

And so it goes. I am struck when I teach my classes on relationship to see that so many traditional expectations still hold at a time when we are seeking equal rights. This isn't good or bad; it just confuses the heck out of us (as well as our men)! And since this is a book about opening our hearts, I think that it is critical for us to look at those conflicting expectations that get in the way of love.

As you read this chapter, you might find your "yeah, buts" screaming out in protest. I ask you to hang in there, hating me if you must, until you get some rhyme out of my reason. Keep remembering that our purpose in this book is to take a good look in our mirrors, not our magnifying glasses. In no area do we need to look at ourselves more than in the area of our expectations. Unreasonable expectations are the basis of so much of our disappointment in our relationships with men and our relationships with ourselves. It is also the basis of so much of our anger.

We women have been fighting for equality for many years. Yet let's take a look at what many consider ideal protocol for a first date:

He is the one who calls. *He* is the one who picks the restaurant (the more expensive, the better!). *He* is the one who picks us up. *He* is the one who opens the door. *He* is the one who drives. *He* is the one who tells the waiter our order. *He* is the one who gets the waiter's attention if something is wrong with our food. *He* is the one who pays. *He* is the one drives us home and takes us to our door.

One of my students suggested that not only does she expect the man to do all of the above, but she also expects him to call the next day and tell her he had a wonderful time. A similar variation exists if we are married and going out with our husband for the evening. Tell me, if you can, how this is any different from that of a parent taking a child out to dinner! And, if you are anything like me, you *love* this entire arrangement! I love it so much, that I can't understand why men don't want the same "equality"!

Some do, but some don't, as some of you may have already discovered. Men are sometimes very threatened as we try to take some of the responsibility off of their shoulders. The reason they are threatened is because, just as our femininity has been defined by being taken care of, so their masculinity has been defined by being the caretakers. Old self-images die hard! Again, neither is right or wrong—our feelings and behavior simply reflect our training.

I watch a young woman's face light up as she talks about the date who picked her up in a limo, bought her flowers, and fed her champagne and caviar. (Every woman's fantasy at some point in her life!) The fact that her date was extremely self-centered and more interested in impressing her with all his accomplishments than finding out anything about her doesn't seem to stop her from waiting by the phone for him to call.

I don't see the same sparkle in her eyes when she talks about the date who met her at the restaurant, split the bill, and, because they had separate cars, didn't see her home. Even though he was a great guy, had many things to share, was warm and open and obviously interested in her, her interest in seeing him again was nil. Yet this woman considers herself a feminist.

It is clear to me that:

> What many of us find attractive in our men is inconsistent with what we say we want our men to be, and, as a result, inconsistent with what we say we want ourselves to be.

This inner conflict translates into the anger we feel for the men in our lives. It seems to me that if we want to become more complete as human beings, and if we want to be considered partners with our men, then we have to change who we are and how we see ourselves in relation to men.

A great many of us have already begun to alter our expectations of ourselves—and of our men. Our tastes *are* changing. What used to look good to us in men, no longer does. The Bill Cosby image is beginning to look better than macho man. In fact, I believe it is only a matter of time, when we will all look back at our Child's version of the ideal man and cringe. Our eyes are slowly becoming accustomed to a more realistic version of the "prince."

But the process is slow. Some of us get very impatient with ourselves. We seem to know what is best for us, but our "eye" hasn't yet received the message. Over and over again, we are attracted to the wrong type. And our relationships end up in a shambles. We still don't see as attractive men who would support the best of who we are. What we can learn from this is very simple: *our type is not really our type*. Yet many of us continue to be our own worst enemy when it comes to the selection of our men.

There are many explanations for our irrational behavior. My favorite is the following: it seems that before we make our perception of what is attractive consistent with what we say we want, we need to go through a "re-visioning" process. We need to transform our mindset, to create what educator Robert Fuller calls a "psychotectonic" shift, a big word that means:

A change in the deepest assumptions we hold about ourselves, a shift in what we take for granted, in what we think we are capable of.[1]

Fuller illustrates by asking us to imagine living in a country where slavery seemed perfectly normal and natural. This, of course, describes the America of not so long ago. Yet today the idea of slavery is repugnant to Americans, and it is hard to believe it actually existed in the "land of the free and the home of the brave." Fuller points to this as an example of the kind of profound transformation in thinking that entire societies are capable of making. In the same way, I believe that we women are capable of making profound transformations in our thinking about men and about ourselves.

I would embellish on Fuller's words by noting that there must have been a lag time after the shackles were cut until slaves actually felt free and were seen as free. It must have been terrifying for slaves to leave the security of their master, and, at the same time, it must have seemed odd for employers to hire ex-slaves and treat them as employees. But there came a point in time when the re-visioning occurred, and ex-slaves felt and were considered to be free from bondage.

Now, what does all this mean to women and our quest for healthy relationships in the context of equality? Plenty. It helps to explain many of the inconsistencies in our thinking and our behavior that even we can't understand, let alone the men who are trying to please us. While we have declared ourselves worthy of equal rights (our own version of the abolition of slavery), we are experiencing a normal lag time between our declaration of equality and the new behavior and beliefs that would support that declaration. I believe this lag time, hence our confusion, is simply part of the process of transformation. I also believe that we won't act as equals, nor will we be treated as equals, until this shift in our inner vision occurs. When this happens, we will stop our wavering and really take our "equality" seriously, at which point the rest of the world will take us seriously as well.

Some of us have made this shift on an individual level and it has transformed the way we see the world . . . and the way the world sees us. But for the rest of us, confusion and unhappiness reign. I hope that what I am telling you will eliminate some of the mental anguish you may be going through. Transition, by definition, brings with it confusion: we are not quite out of one stage and not quite into another. But in time, the big inner leap occurs, and our ambivalence and confusion are laid aside. The new becomes the norm and the old is outdated.

A good analogy can be found in the world of fashion. When we are accustomed to wearing short skirts, we don't immediately like the newer fashions that feature long skirts. At some point in time, however, our eye adjusts; short skirts no longer look so good and the long skirts look great! When we look at the styles in old magazines, we laugh and wonder how we ever thought they were beautiful.

It is really important for us to understand the broader implications of what I have just said:

Just as we are in a transition period and have not yet made the requisite mental leap for equality to occur, *the same can be said for men.*

This explains the fact that while most rational men (and that's a heck of a lot more than you think!) support equality for women, their "eye" hasn't become accustomed to the new look. They, too, are confused and ambivalent. Their minds and hearts know what is fairer for women and for themselves, yet they "see" as attractive many aspects of the old model. As many of us are still attracted to the idea of men being the primary breadwinner, so many of them are still attracted to the idea of women taking care of hearth and home. In time, they, too, will make the inner leap necessary for them to enjoy women in other contexts. It is already happening in the corporate world. Many men report that they enjoy working for women, for example, whereas at one time this arrangement was unthinkable. I believe it is only a matter of time when equality in the household will be the accepted norm as well.

A further implication of all this is that:

The sooner *we* make the inner shift, the sooner the men will. Once our tastes change, their behavior will shift to accommodate those tastes.

Most men really want to be loved and appreciated by women. When we are clear that the "new" man looks better than the "old" man, you will find a lot more "new" men around. The question men ask women most often in my workshops is, "What do women want?" We can only assure them that someday we will be clear about that ourselves! But keep in mind that:

We can't be angry at men for not having accepted equality between the sexes, because we haven't accepted it ourselves!

The big question we have to address is "Can we make this inner shift happen faster than it appears to be happening?" Men and women are becoming more and more polarized and entrenched in their positions. We must stop the war which only weakens all of us and, instead, begin to give each other strength. I believe we can start by creating our own re-visioning campaign. I remember, years ago, there was a "Black is Beautiful" campaign. It didn't take long for everyone I knew, including myself, to sport an Afro hairdo, whereas prior to the campaign, we didn't consider this hairdo attractive. We can create the same kind of campaign for changing our expectations and perceptions of men. By making the new look ever present in our eye and by affirming the beauty of the new, the inner shift can be speeded along and we can let go of our inappropriate expectations.

Please don't be impatient with yourself as you go through this process. I suspect that letting go of our expectations is one of the most difficult things we can do in our lifetime. It is letting go of the myth, the fantasy, the imagined safety. It is letting go of the anger, which, as we already know, provides us with a sense of power, camaraderie, exhilaration, leadership, and so on. *But what we get in return is self-esteem, caring, a new kind of safety that derives from our own inner power, an open heart, the ability to love, and a feeling of bliss so great that one can't help but look up and give thanks.*

So let's begin the re-visioning process by looking at our old visions and the preferable re-visions. Of course, not everything will apply to your particular situation. Simply take what you can use and discard the rest. One thing is sure: What doesn't apply to you will definitely apply to someone you know. Remember to keep an open mind and a smile on your face!

Re-visioning Our Expectations

Without a doubt, the three most difficult areas in terms of our expectations about men, in order of importance, are money, money, and money! I have seen so many wonderful women turn into wicked witches when it comes to money. This is not really very surprising since this is an area in which we feel most insecure.

It is quite clear from my professional and personal experiences that the majority of women still expect men to be the primary breadwinners and, as a result, often look at the trappings of the men rather than the men themselves—the cars they drive, the restaurants to which they take us, the gifts they buy us, and so on. The following are a few statements made by some of my students:

"I really know I won't end up with him. He'll never make enough money so that I could really feel secure and have the things I want to have in my life. I mean, I'll always make my own money, but I still want to feel secure in his being able to take care of me."

"If a man does not make as much as I do, I figure there is something wrong with him—he's having problems getting along with people on the job, or problems making up his mind as to what he wants to do in life, or he isn't very ambitious."

"If a man expects me to split the check on our first date, I wouldn't go out with him again."

"Any man that asks for alimony is a leech."

These are not atypical statements. The women who uttered them were young. Some of them argue that since women don't make as much as men, this is the way it should be. Some women don't . . . and some women do! I know women who make annual salaries of over $100,000, and I know men who make $20,000. It is true that a significant gap exists between women's and men's salary in certain segments of the economy, and we must continue working to close the gap. But the issue here is that whatever our salary, most of us women look down on a man who does not make as much money as we do or who does not bear the brunt of the financial responsibility of the relationship.

This isn't to say that there aren't a huge number of us who are supporting men who are out of work or going through school. However, after a "respectable" amount of time, most of us get annoyed and resent their inability to bring in an income and often break off the relationship. Thank goodness men generally don't feel the same annoyance! It is very true that some men are threatened when we earn more than they do, and you now know one of the reasons why: they feel they will lose our respect . . . *and they're right!*

But the fact that we so generously hand over the financial responsibility to men has little to do with the fact that they are often threatened by our earning capacity. It has more to do with our failing to "see" ourselves as competent enough to provide all the finer things in life for ourselves and our families. We still feel that we need a man to give us all that.

Also, we have not made the inner shift that allows us to look at a woman who supports a man and see it as perfectly normal. We assume he isn't capable enough, or that he is looking for a mother, or that he's lazy, or all of the above. Yet most of us still see it as perfectly natural if a man is supporting a woman.

This combination of our insecurity and the lag time in the re-visioning process creates such jokes as, "What's yours is mine and what's mine is mine!" And we laugh and think this is cute. When the inner shift finally takes place and our heart begins to open, we will look back and see that it isn't so cute. We will wonder how we justified it. We will see it as selfish, unfeeling, and self-defeating. (Our men will look back and wonder why they went along with it!) But until that inner shift actually takes place, the idea of being in a genuine partnership with our mate is still too new to feel normal, but it will happen.

Making this transition isn't easy, and some of us don't even want to make it. We want equal rights without having to uphold our part of the bargain. Handing over our hard-earned money for such things as the mortgage, utilities, and so on, can be agony for many of us in the beginning. Certainly it was for me. I met my present husband just as I made a change in career. My income was negligible in the beginning and he became my chief financial support, a role which he took on willingly and lovingly. When I finally began earning money in my new career, I noticed that I had this incredible urge to bank it and let him continue to pay all the bills. (Do you recognize the inner Child here?) Another part of me (the inner Adult) recognized that this arrangement is not exactly a modern definition of a partnership, and I forced myself to share until it felt good. What staggers me about what I just told you is that *for the twelve years I was single, I totally took care of myself with no help from my ex-husband . . . and it felt great!* I felt confident, strong, healthy, and happy. As soon as I remarried, the inner Adult disappeared into the background and the inner Child stepped in, bringing all my old expectations about money to the fore.

So what are some steps we can take to speed the re-visioning process when it comes to money? The first thing we can do is to focus our awareness on our old vision and invent the re-vision. For example:

Old Vision

Men should be the primary breadwinners.

Re-vision: Why? It is terrific to see a woman out there making enough money to support her family. It doesn't mean that her man is a failure. It doesn't mean that she is a fool. She is just a capable woman who happens to be making more money than her mate! He is not a parasite! He may be supporting her in a multitude of other ways.

Old Vision

Women who ask for alimony are entitled.

Men who ask for alimony are gold diggers.

Re-vision: Why? If we believe alimony is appropriate for women, then it is just as appropriate for men, given the same circumstances. A man is not a leech if he asks for alimony, he is an equal human being. Men *and* women who withhold money that is legally or morally due their mates are selfish and uncaring!

Old Vision

On a date, men are the only ones who need their wallets.*

Re-vision: Why? It is demeaning to a woman for a man to pay for everything. Even if a woman can't afford expensive restaurants, reciprocation is important for self-esteem. "New" women don't expect everything to be handed to them but show appreciation for the gifts of their dates. They send flowers and thank-you notes, and do all the things they expect their men to do for them. A man who can't handle this is an "old" man and someone we definitely want to pass over!

---

*For those old enough to remember, our mothers or fathers always gave us "mad" money when we went out on a date; that is, just enough money to get us home if we got mad at our boyfriends. Some of us have never given up this practice!

Old Vision

Women can't earn as much money as men.

Re-vision: Why not? Look around. Women are capable of earning very big wages. Some have even accumulated great wealth on their own. While the percentage is small, the percentage of men who earn very big wages is small as well! We are not victims in this world. While it is true that it may be more difficult in many cases for women to excel, it is not impossible. Today's world offers us exciting challenges, and we women are up to the challenge!

You get the idea. While I can hear some of your "yeah buts" from here, given enough exposure, the re-vision will look more appropriate than the old vision. Just keep looking at your expectations about money and see how you can envision another way of being. You might want to make a list of all your own personal expectations and write your own re-vision. By questioning your old expectations with a "Why?" or a "Why not?," you begin the process of changing the underlying belief systems that keep you stuck in confusion. It also helps to look at each re-visioning statement and create a little meditation for yourself. Shut your eyes and spend a few minutes picturing yourself comfortable and happy in the new scenario.

In addition to becoming aware of those areas that need re-visioning, there is something else we need to do:

Women must learn more about how to handle money effectively and, in the process, change our "relationship" to it. Improving our relationship with money will definitely improve our relationship with men.

Even some of the most successful women I know resist feeling at home in the world of finances. To get you moving in the right direction, I suggest you read Tessa Albert Warschaw's book, *Rich Is Better*. Warschaw feels that women put up stumbling blocks against the full use of their power, particularly in the area of money where we are run by fear. Now is the time, she contends, for women to enter a period of "expansive abundance." (Just saying those two words makes me feel good!) She describes it as "the art of living a life that never loses spiritual and ethical meaning for all its material conquests; the art of adding richness to others, indeed to the very planet, while at the same time acquiring and achieving."[2] And she gives a lot of tools with which we can do that.

What you could also do is to go to workshops about money or talk to others who are experts in the field. Or perhaps you could start a self-help group with a few friends, making your fears and expectations about money your primary focus. It's not that women and finance don't go together (that's an old vision). The number of female experts in the world of finance is growing every day. Actually, it's a wonderful field for women. Make learning about and playing with money one of your hobbies, if you don't make it your profession.[3]

A third action you could take to help the re-visioning process is to familiarize yourself with the inequities that still exist for women in the workforce today. You can actually get involved in the process of political and legal change, whether that means writing to politicians, or getting out there and marching. There are many dedicated women and men working for our rights, and they have made enormous progress. It is up to us to make sure this progress continues.

A fourth way you can speed up the process is to use money in a way that you've never used it before. Is there something you've always wanted but have been conditioned to think that a man is "supposed" to buy for you? Hence, you wait? Stop waiting! Save up your money and buy it yourself—a piece of jewelry, or a trip to the Orient, or that expensive camera, or whatever.

Also, use money in a new way when it comes to the men in your life. One of my friends offers us a great example. A workshop leader, she had just returned from a ten-city tour during which she had collected a large sum of money from the sale of her tapes and books. She looked at her hard-earned cash and was struck with a loving "Aha!" She decided to gift-wrap the take, which was mostly in cash, and present it to her husband as a gift to be spent any way he wanted. How did he feel? He was moved to tears. No one had ever given him money in that way. The gift was made more precious knowing how hard she had worked for the money. He certainly didn't need it, as he was a large earner, but he said that he never felt so honored. She said that for her it was a transformational experience. She felt strong and capable and loving.

So begin using money in ways that are atypical for women. Be creative. You will be surprised how much your generosity will be appreciated. As a start in the right direction, send some flowers to a man in your life. Many men tell me that they have never received a bouquet of flowers, yet they all report how much it would mean to them. One man said, "I'd love it, but it has never happened."

Aside from money, what other expectations need re-visioning? Let's have some fun here.

Old Vision

Men are supposed to give us their
jackets if we are cold.

Re-vision: Why? Is it really OK for us to be warm at their expense? Are we that frail that we will catch cold if they don't warm us up? Hardly! According to the mortality tables, I suspect we are the healthier sex and should offer them *our* jackets!

Re-visioning exercise: Would you take the coat of a female friend if she were also cold? No way! So be a friend to your man as well. If he is cold, do not take his jacket. Sit there and be cold, and you'll definitely remember to bring along a heavier sweater the next time!

Old Vision

Men are supposed to do all the driving.

Re-vision: Why? Don't fall for the commonly held belief that women are lousy drivers. We're great drivers! So why don't we offer to share the load? Could it be the old "Prince on His White Charger" fantasy coming into play? Could it be that we are l-a-z-y? It could be that he feels demeaned having a woman drive him around. Build him up and tell him a real man is not threatened to have a woman do the driving . . . and you see him as a real man!

Re-visioning exercise: Tell your mate or your date that as a gift to him, you are doing all the driving for the next month so that he can just relax and enjoy the scenery. This will get you off the automatic assumption that driving is a man's job. After the month is over, you can share the driving.

Old Vision

I want a man I can look up to!

Re-vision: Why? This only results in a stiff neck! By definition, a man to "look up to" means a man who will "look down upon"! Again, a conditioned response, one that needs re-visioning. While "looking up to" may simply be an unfortunate metaphor for respecting our man, in truth, there are many of us who don't see it as a metaphor. We really want men who are "more" than we are—who have more success, more money, more status, more strength, and so on. A physically bigger man perpetuates the conscious or unconscious hope that we will be protected. What is it going to be for you? A looking-up-to-and-being-looked-down-upon relationship or one that is eyeball-to-eyeball?

Re-visioning exercise: Every time you see a man that we would consider short in our society, say to yourself, Short men are beautiful! Short men are sexy! I love short men! Just think of Dudley Moore and Michael J. Fox and consider them your modern-day sex symbols.

Old Vision

Men are supposed to do all the pursuing.

Re-vision: Why? I've asked hundreds of men if they would be upset if a woman called them or made the initial approach. Without exception, they said they would love it! If a man objects, he is definitely an "old" man and one to be avoided. "New" men love to have women show an interest in them.

But let's tell the truth about all this. The real reason we don't pursue men is, not because they object, but because *We are chicken! We can't stand rejection!* Yes, it's difficult to face rejection, but keep in mind that *men are expected to face rejection all the time . . . and it hurts them just as much as it hurts us!* Many men report that it sometimes takes seven approaches before one woman accepts. Think of the pain! One of my female students said she tried approaching one man and it didn't work. So she quit trying. Can you imagine what would happen if the men felt the same way? We'd never get together!

Re-visioning exercise: In safe environments, go up and tell three men to whom you are attracted that you would like to invite them to have lunch with you one day the following week. You might be rejected, but so what! You'll handle it! I'm not saying it won't hurt a little, but make it hurt a two instead of a ten. Most importantly, you'll get to see what men go through all the time. What a heart-opener that is!

If you are married, there are many opportunities to "make the approach" to your husband—sexually, sending flowers, creating candle-lit dinners, etc. Be a lover in the true sense of the word, in the same manner that you want to be loved.

Old Vision

It's inappropriate for a man to stay home and take care of the children while his wife works.

Re-vision: Why? Some fathers are more nurturing than some mothers. Wouldn't it be more appropriate that the best nurturer be the one to spend more time with the child? While some professionals profess that women are inherently the nurturers and men are incapable of nurturing, I *strongly* disagree. Recent evidence suggests that when men are put in the role of single parents, their nurturing skills are just as good as women's. Certainly my ex-husband was a far better nurturer than I was! I believe the day is not far in the future when Mr. Mom will be as much the norm as Ms. Mom!

Re-visioning exercise: Rent videos of *Kramer Versus Kramer, Three Men and a Baby,* and *Mr. Mom.* All three movies are about men who "learned" how to mother (just as in the beginning, we "learned" how to mother). You also might want to rent *Baby Boom,* which is about a career woman who has to learn how to mother. I don't believe mothering comes as naturally to women as we are led to believe. Don't forget that we had a lot of "training" as girls while playing with our dolls, which men never had. And "training" it definitely was!

Old Vision

Men prefer women who are not so successful.

Re-vision: That's a cop-out if I ever heard one! It's true that some men are very threatened by successful women, but is this the kind of man with whom you want to share your life? The answer is yes if you are still too frightened to get out there and be successful. The answer is no if you are ready to accept the challenge of testing yourself in new waters.

The truth is that, as time goes on, men are becoming less interested in marrying dependent women and taking care of them for the rest of their lives. The men in my workshops almost unanimously reported that they wanted interesting and independent women who could take some of the financial responsibility off their backs. They also felt that successful women add to their self-esteem. *What turned men off was not that a woman was successful, but that she was angry, judgmental, and self-righteous, and had a chip on her shoulder!*

Re-visioning exercise: Ask fifty single men if they are turned off by successful women. I can almost guarantee that the majority will say that they truly enjoy successful women.

Those are just a few examples to get you started. You can make a game of this with your friends and begin to really look at how your expectations are stuck in the dark ages. This awareness will set the stage for the ultimate mental leap when we will truly understand and enjoy what equality really means.

To help us further with the re-visioning process, we must begin to notice how our expectations are subliminally programmed through radio, television, song lyrics, women's magazines, and so on. Ask yourself if the messages you are receiving support your growth or are keeping you a narcissistic child. If you suspect the latter, write to the source and let them know you object.

Subliminal programming also takes place through many long-held traditions, some of which are very hard to give up. For example, I just came from a wedding at which the father gave the bride away. While this part of the ceremony is sure to bring tears to many an eye, it reinforces the image of woman as child. Symbolically, the bride went from the support of one man to another. A little thing, perhaps, but maybe not.

Although my dearest uncle wanted to "give me away" when I married for the second time, I explained that this no longer fit the person I had become. Not to hurt his feelings, I gave him an honored place in the wedding party and told him how much he meant to me. What my husband and I chose to do was to walk down the aisle together, not with my arm in his, but holding hands, symbolically walking through life side by side. I can't tell you the psychological difference that this simple alteration of the wedding ceremony made for me. I don't know how many of us out there are ready to make this switch in the wedding ceremony, but it is something to consider.

We can further speed the re-visioning process by noticing where our expectations are conflicting. These expectations are impossible for our men to fulfill, yet they create much anger and upset within us when they are not fulfilled. For example, we want a man who is successful in business but who also spends a great deal of time with us. In many ways, these are mutually exclusive and our expectation is unrealistic as well as unfair.

I went out to dinner recently with a couple who have a traditional relationship. She feels it is important to be at home with the children rather than to earn money to support the requirements of the household. As a result, he is under great pressure to "perform" financially. Yet she is very resentful of the long hours he has to work and never ceases to let him (and everyone else) know that she is annoyed by his absence from the house. He wants desperately to please her and is always in there trying. He hasn't as yet figured out that she is, in fact, unpleasable, but it will hit him one day and he will leave. And her friends will hear no end to the story of how she was "wronged" by this man for whom she gave up so much of her life.

A very wise teacher once told me, "Susan, you can have anything you want in life, but you can't have everything." One choice precludes another. The sooner we learn that, the faster we will be at peace with ourselves . . . and at peace in our relationships.

To be attracted to a man because of his status, his power, and his wealth blinds us to the characteristics that create beautiful relationships. Warschaw points out that many powerhouse women, in particular, unconsciously create unhappy personal lives because they only want men who are "gladiators." Gladiators, she points out, leave women exhausted, unfulfilled, and hurt. These women don't even look at men who are sensitive, supportive, and ready to fill intimacy needs.

Women are often told that if we want to find a man, we must lower our standards. I don't think we need to lower our standards; rather, we need to expand our hearts to see the beauty in another person. *Perhaps we should call it raising our standards!*

I'm talking about growing up . . . and growing up is never

easy. Because of all the struggle that we encounter in the process, many of us are tempted to go back to the way it was. And there are many men and women in the media suggesting that, because of our present-day dissatisfaction, the way to go is, not forward to the next step, but back to the way it was. I don't agree with this analysis.

Yes, there is a lot of dissatisfaction, not because we are headed in the wrong direction, but simply because change brings disruption and resistance. In this sense, disruption is not necessarily a negative sign. It's like moving to another town. Before, and even for a short time after the move, there is fear, upheaval, fatigue, confusion, irritability. We question whether we have made the right choice. But after a time, when all the settling in is done, we begin to feel comfortable once again, perhaps even more comfortable than we felt before.

We are in the middle of a much more formidable "move"— from one state of consciousness to another—and it involves the entire fabric of our being and society. Social change is a long process, and we have a long way to go. But we mustn't lose sight of how far we have come.

One of my students said, "I'm grateful to be growing, but I really don't want to grow." I understand. There is a part of us that really doesn't want to give up the many privileges and imagined safety that childhood allows. I understand why we want to hang on to much of the old but enjoy the privileges of the new. Yet there is another part of us that will love the strength we derive from feeling whole and standing side by side with our partner in life, and not hanging onto him for survival. As Harold Kushner wrote, "No matter how cute and charming a child might be, there is something incomplete about him."[4]

This, of course, applies equally to women. It is this incompleteness that creates our insecurity and lack of self-esteem. It is time for us to grow up; this includes us out there in our forties, fifties, and up. It is obvious that childhood has nothing to do with age!

So what can we expect from our men in a healthy relationship? What in an ideal world—in a fair world—would we ask them to give us? In a fair world we would ask only that they treat us with respect; that they support our being the best that we can be; that they love who we are, including all our flaws; that they be on our team, not on the opposing one; and that they want what is best for us, given that it doesn't conflict with their becoming the best that they can be.

But even these "fair" expectations carry with them some measure of risk. Perhaps our man, for whatever reason, is not able to fulfill them. Not to worry! There is a way to create a relationship based on a guaranteed, no-risk, no-disappointment expectation! Simply decide the following:

The *only* purpose of the relationship is for me to learn how to become a more loving person—to myself and to my partner.

Each day you affirm:

"Today I am encountering new situations that teach me more about who I am and what I yet have to learn about loving myself and others."

Seen in this way, each person that we choose to have in our lives becomes a "practice person." We can assume that we chose them in order to work out something that we haven't quite resolved within ourselves. This beautifully fits in with the original mandate of this book, which is to pick up a mirror instead of a magnifying glass.

As you can see, this approach removes so much of the anguish that traditional expectations create. Even if the person we choose is one we later decide to leave, or vice versa, we will not have lost a thing. If we keep our focus on the learning and

94

growing that each relationship provides, we will *always* come out a winner . . . and so will he.

You might notice that there are lessons that some of us need to learn over and over again. So be it! Eventually we get the message and begin making better choices in life, thus making all the interim relationships valuable learning experiences. *In this way every relationship—good or bad—is a no-risk relationship.* It would be wonderful if we could enter all our relationships with the following contract with ourselves:

I understand we are both beautiful human beings doing the very best we can. My only expectation of this relationship—whether it lasts one week, twenty-five years, or until death-do-us-part—is that I will learn more about opening my heart and becoming a more loving person. I accept this as one of my highest purposes in life.

Inner Shift Affirmations

Warm men are beautiful!

Sweet men are beautiful!

Open men are beautiful!

Equal men are beautiful!

Men are beautiful!

Strong women are beautiful!

Assertive women are beautiful!

Successful women are beautiful!

Equal women are beautiful!

Women are beautiful!

Women breadwinners are beautiful!

Men who stay home and take care of the children are beautiful!

Men who get alimony are beautiful!

Women who pay the expenses on a date are beautiful!

Men who accept women paying the expenses on a date are beautiful!

4

How Do I Judge Thee? Let Me Count The Ways

In the beginning, everything is wonderful. He is so perfect and our hearts are filled with undying love. We have found him at last—the man of our dreams. Time passes and the glow dims a bit. He isn't making us as happy as he was before. The initial high is falling lower and lower. Our rose-colored glasses become severely scratched until all we can see are blemishes—imaginary, perhaps, but real to our distorted vision. The judgment begins. If enough time passes, we even come to hate the way he eats.

A familiar scenario! And then we ask ourselves and each other, "What happened to Mr. Wonderful?" Some of us go through man after man, finding that the emergent flaws are too much to handle and we leave, or we become so critical that the men's self-respect makes them leave first. Ultimately, we come to the conclusion that what we had hoped was fiction is actually fact: *There really are no good men out there!*

Are men really all that bad? When I do workshops with women, I ask them to yell out to me *what is bad about men.* Here are some of the answers I've gotten:

They're manipulative, selfish, controlling, afraid of commitment, unemotional, egotistical, childish, lazy, dependent,
closed, cheap, insensitive, lying, possessive, immature, un-
interesting, know-it-all, angry, hostile, inflexible, unaware,
unfaithful, nonsupportive, judgmental, crude, arrogant . . .

That bad, huh? As the words keep tumbling out, one can
almost feel the air become saturated with hostility and disdain;
similar, no doubt, to the air that permeates many relationships.
This is not the kind of energy in which love can blossom, to say
the least. In fact, it is the kind of energy that signals the ultimate
death of a relationship.

I then ask these very same women to yell out *what is bad
about women,* and they respond:

We're dependent, demanding, manipulative, selfish, living
in a fantasy world, afraid of commitment, looking for a
perfect man, self-righteous, moody, unappreciative, needy,
untruthful, fearful, angry, hostile, lazy, only interested in
men's money, stingy, judgmental, crazy-making, bitchy,
complicated, possessive, unfaithful . . .

That bad, huh? Now the air fills with laughter as we realize
how many things we women have in common with our men! At
this point, I ask them to make a deal with me:

No more criticizing men until we handle what is wrong
with us!

That's right! I remind them that the only way that women will
move forward is to stop trying to fix men and begin working on
ourselves. I don't say this out of altruism, but out of healthy
selfishness. The lesson of the day is, once again, to pick up the
mirror instead of the magnifying glass. *We all want to have loving*

relationships, and I know of no quicker or more satisfying way to get this result than to eliminate our negative judgments about men.

To give my students a preview demonstration of how this works, I next ask them to yell out *what is wonderful about men.* There is initial hesitation, to be sure, but once they get going the accolades come tumbling out:

> They're strong, generous, fun, sexy, loyal, cuddly, depend-
> able, loving, caressing, huggable, encouraging, faithful,
> considerate, kind, enthusiastic, giving, passionate, coura-
> geous, delicious, warm, good-humored, protective, sensi-
> tive, easygoing, easy to please, sweet . . .

I wish you could be present to experience the change of energy in the room as the women shift their focus from negative to positive. If you didn't know any better, you would think that someone switched the people in the room! They even look different—warmer, softer, more loving, and certainly more lovable. It's hard to believe that these glowing words come from the same women who had such negative things to say just a few minutes earlier. This is an amazingly simple demonstration of how a change of energy can be achieved with a simple switch of mindset.

And then, adding to the positive energy in the room, I ask the women to yell out *what is wonderful about women:*

> They're giving, open, loving, loyal, humorous, soft, cuddly,
> sexy, curious, sensitive, faithful, smart, considerate, kind,
> interested in others, warm, always trying to learn more
> about themselves, tender, soothing, encouraging, sweet,
> nurturing, compassionate, healing . . .

As they acknowledge the beauty within, the women take on an air of confidence, self-esteem, and pride in who they are as human beings.

Clearly, when we are judgmental of either ourselves or our men, we lose our joy and lightness—qualities that come only from seeing with loving eyes, not hostile ones.

Can you imagine what the world would look like if we kept this sense of appreciation of ourselves and each other within our hearts all the time? Well, we can! Or at least we can improve the percentages! Throughout the rest of the chapter, you will find exercises that will show you how to create a shift in the context of your relationship from complaint to appreciation. You also will notice yourself happier than you've been in a very long time. If you are not in a relationship, use others in your life as "practice people"—parents, children, the boss. You will love how your relationship with *everyone* improves when you become a "lover."

Appreciation Exercises

1. *Stop complaining about men.* It sounds easy, but wait until you try it! When I give this assignment to my students, most of them report that they have an incredibly difficult time doing it. Many couldn't do it at all. One student said that the only way she could do it was to tape her mouth shut! This exercise made them aware of how much male-bashing they actually did. One woman said that if she and her friends were not complaining about men, they had very little to talk about. Silent lunches! From the demonstration at the beginning of the chapter, you now know that men really do have good qualities; it's just that so many of us seem to focus on the negative ones. If this description fits you, it is now time to learn how to shift your focus.

The first place to begin monitoring your complaints is at lunch with a friend. It's a good idea to come early so that you can eavesdrop on the conversations taking place between women at other tables. Whether these women are surgeons, secretaries, business managers, housewives, psychologists, or whatever, if they are at lunch with a friend, you will notice that they spend a lot of time talking about the Universal Equalizer—problems with the men in their lives or men in general. You will hear very little, if anything, about what's great about men. This isn't to say that women talk only about men. It is to say that for those of us who are not in a relationship or who are in an unsatisfactory relationship, men dominate our thoughts, hence our conversations.

Back to your table. Your friend arrives, and after a few words of greeting and small talk, you will notice that the complaints begin.

Would you believe that Joe put off our vacation?
I wonder why he can't get it together to make a commitment.
He expects me to work all day and then come home and cook and clean. I'm really fed up.
I wish he'd call when he says he'll call. I sat around waiting all night and I could have gone to the movies with friends.
He really puts me down in front of other people and I don't like it.
I really hate men. They really can make life miserable.
I wish he'd open up more. Half the time I feel like I'm talking to a wall.

All of the above may be true. There definitely are issues between men and women that need to be worked out. Given that, how do you move yourself from the "moan and groan society" to the "live, love, and be happy society?" As was just demonstrated by the women in my workshop, it is very easy to create beauty where ugliness once existed by simply shifting your focus. You can begin slowly, by adding an "and" after each negative phrase, followed by a positive statement. For example:

Would you believe that Joe put off our vacation?

AND

I'm really appreciative that he works so hard making it possible for our kids to go to private school.

I wonder why he can't get it together to make a commitment.

AND

I appreciate that he's never lied to me about the fact that he's not ready for marriage.

He expects me to work all day and then come home and cook and clean. I'm really fed up.

AND

I have more fun with him than any person I know. He really makes me laugh.

I wish he'd call when he says he'll call. I sat around waiting all night and I could have gone to the movies with friends.

AND

He is very attuned to me when we go out together. He really listens when I talk. I get the feeling he really cares.

He really puts me down in front of other people and I don't like it.

AND

He can be so tender at times, it makes me cry.

I really hate men. They can make life miserable.

AND

I really love the way men can bring pleasure into my life.

I wish he'd open up more. Half the time I feel like I'm talking to a wall.

AND

He tries so hard to please me.

Practice doing this until it really feels comfortable. Keep in mind that this is not an exercise in denial; certain things in relationships need to be handled. As for the above complaints: We need vacation time. We need to structure our lives so that we don't have to be Superwomen. We need to let our men know that when they say they are going to call, we expect that they do (or, we go out and have a good time with our friends instead of waiting around for the call). We need to let men know that it is not OK for them to put us down in front of other people. We need to open up communication. But everything that we need to confront in a relationship will have a much better chance of being resolved when we come from a *loving* stance instead of a judgmental one.

When this first phase of the exercise becomes really comfortable, move on to Phase 2, which is to drop the negative statement altogether and simply go with the one that is positive. Just as the complaint is about to come from your lips, switch to the positive:

I really appreciate that he works so hard making it possible
    for our kids to go to private school.
I appreciate that he's never lied to me about the fact that
    he's not ready for marriage.
I have more fun with him than any person I know.
He is very attuned to me when we go out together. He
    really listens when I talk. I get the feeling he really
    cares.
He can be so tender at times, it makes me cry.
I really love the way men can bring pleasure into my life.
He really tries very hard to please me.

What happens when you do this is that the conversation flows from positive statements instead of negative ones and a whole new mindset is created. This is very important. In this way, we begin to see the beauty in our men instead of the flaws. I am always amazed at how we women talk with disdain about a man at lunch and then expect to create a loving relationship with him over dinner. What do we think is going to happen in the interim that makes all the bad feelings go away? Do we really think that he isn't going to sense, at some level, that we've made him the enemy? What we are doing, in fact, is creating a self-fulfilling prophecy. Remember the Universal Law: Like attracts like. If we come to dinner with hostility (covert or overt), we are more likely to attract hostility. If we come to dinner with love and acceptance (I am not talking about neediness), we are more likely to attract love and acceptance. Keep in mind, it's impossible to have a loving relationship with a man in the context of "men are to blame for everything that is wrong with women." It is only possible to have a loving relationship when we create a context of "I love men!"

To make matters worse, when we are negative, we add "mass" to our position that men are to blame, making it much more difficult to get out of this self-destructive mindset. It requires great strength to say "I was wrong." The more heavily we are invested in our negativity, the harder it is to see another viewpoint. We ignore the positive and work harder to "prove" how terrible men are!

I must tell you that when I first began to talk positively about men, I felt very uncomfortable, as if I were being disloyal to my own sex, a traitor to the cause. I had invested so much in my position that men were to blame for all the evils of the world. My discomfort was reinforced by the disdain I felt from some of my friends when I changed my tune and began to look at what was good about men. They didn't want to hear it. Also, since complaining about men was habitual for me, it was difficult to create a new frame of reference. My initial discomfort soon wore off, however, when I began to draw more positive men (and women) into my life. And life became more and more satisfying.

Thankfully, some of my old friends were actually pleased with the new way we began playing the game of "lunch." We became partners in learning a new way. We realized that the basis of our friendship had been at the expense of our men. (A pretty unattractive picture, indeed!) We decided that beauty, not negativity, should come from our friendship.

What was most satisfying, however, was the new feeling we began to have about ourselves. *I don't believe that any of us respect ourselves when we are constantly putting others down.* At the time I began opening my heart to men, I was very involved in anti-war activities, which was totally inconsistent with the hostility I had been perpetuating by my critical attitudes. As I turned my thinking around, I felt myself come into harmony with the more beautiful part of my being—my soul, if you will—and I began to feel much more at peace with myself.

A woman I know once commented that she found it much easier to get over a relationship by focusing on what was terrible about a man rather than what was great about him. Yes, it does make it easier to break the tie with criticism rather than with love. As I said earlier, I believe this is the reason for the extreme hostility that transpires between divorcing couples. It's much easier to say, "I hate you. Get out of my life!" than "I love you and I'm so saddened by the pain we have caused each other." And if hostility is what is needed to get us out of a bad time, so be it. Perhaps it is just part of the process.

But there comes a time when we must deal with the pain of our loss so that we can move on with our lives. The faster we do this, the better. We have to keep acknowledging what was positive about the relationship and see it as a great learning experience instead of a waste of our time. That is to say, we must focus on what we got out of the relationship, not on what we gave up. This makes the healing take place at a much faster rate.

If you want to become responsible for your life, become responsible for your mouth! It can make the difference between loving relationships and hostile ones. It's up to you. Which leads me to Step 2 . . .

2. Don't buy into the complaints of your friends. You sit down to lunch with your girlfriend and she starts complaining about the man in her life. How do you respond? It's simple. Since she is playing devil's advocate, you can play angel's advocate! As she complains that her boyfriend is not ambitious enough, you say, "Yes, *and* he is so sweet in so many other ways. I thought it was great he cooked dinner for you the other night." That is to say, you are to point out what is positive about her man.

You first might want to explain what you are doing, or you risk losing your friend! You may lose her anyway, since she may not be ready to get off her negative position about men. Don't feel guilty. She will find many out there with whom she can commiserate. It's more important that you begin to surround yourself with positive friends. It always helps to have a *growth buddy,* a friend to whom you can look for support and feedback as you do your self-growth exercises, and vice versa. We need to help each other out. We need to become each other's teachers as we learn. It is true that we teach best what we want to learn most!

3. Use your judgments as tools for self-discovery. Try as we may to eliminate judgment from our minds and our mouth, we will not always be successful. The truth is that there always will be a judgmental part of ourselves with which we will have to contend. It's just a part of being human. But not to worry! Negative judgments can be transformed into a valuable tool for self-discovery. They can serve as a signal that something within needs fixing, and when we pick up our mirror to see what that "something" is, we see that:

> Our disapproval of someone else often signifies that we are out of touch with our own inherent beauty and, as a result, are not feeling good enough about ourselves.

When we do not feel good about ourselves, we often live with the childlike insistence that the world makes us happy. By looking into our mirror, we can instead pick up our bag of self-esteem tools and begin to work on bringing up our level of strength and confidence. This is the key to handling our reactions to whatever is going on around us, no matter how painful the situation may be. Without this awareness, we remain in the helpless position of blaming others for what is wrong with our lives.

One woman I know obviously doesn't feel good about herself. She hasn't spoken to her husband since he left ten years ago, which makes communication about the kids somewhat difficult, to say the least. He's as happy as a lark in his new life and she is still stewing in her own juices, not realizing that the only person she is hurting is herself . . . and perhaps the children. Her ex-husband gave her the big house in which she lives and, because of the divorce settlement, she doesn't have to work a day in her life. There is so much that she could be doing . . . so much that she could be offering the community . . . so much that she could be offering another man . . . so much joy she could be giving and getting. But her hate keeps her from seeing the incredible abundance in her life. Instead of thanking her ex-husband for the nine years they had together and appreciating the easy life his fourteen-hour workdays provide her, she bad-mouths him whenever anyone will listen. One soon understands why he left her!

Hence we need to transform our reactions. A very important part of that process is to:

Stop asking why other people act the way they do. The important question is why we react the way we do.

Whenever anyone asks me "Why do men need to do this or that?" I tell them that it's an irrelevant question. The relevant

question is "How do I explain my reaction to their behavior?"
We need to switch our inquiry about men into an inquiry about
ourselves. For example:

Inappropriate	*Appropriate*
Why did he leave?	Why can't I let go?
Why won't he commit?	Why don't I find someone who is ready for a commitment?
Why doesn't he pick up his clothes?	Why do I pick up his clothes for him?
Why doesn't he give me more money?	Why don't I find a way of making extra money?
Why won't he stop drinking?	Why don't I attend Al-Anon meetings?
Why does he need to fool around with other women?	Why do I stay with a man who constantly needs other women?

It helps to write down your complaints and then do some
soul-searching to get to the root of the problem. Put one complaint at the top of the page and take yourself through the paces
with as much honesty as you can. Remember that honesty is not
about self-blame, but about self-discovery. Your self-analysis
might look like this:

Complaint:

It really makes me angry that Peter is always late!

Self-inquiry: I wonder why it upsets me when Peter is late.
He's always been late ever since I've known him. I know
I'm not going to change him, so why does it upset me so?
Why don't I prepare for his lateness, such as by telling him

to be there earlier than I intend him to be, or by bringing a book to read, or by enjoying the quiet time when I could just people-watch? Is it that I need something to hold over him? Is it that it gives me an opportunity to look superior? Is it that something else is really bothering me?

If you continue this process for at least a half hour, you might get some very important insights into why you react the way you do. Again, this isn't to say that Peter is acting appropriately when he shows up late. But we are powerless if we try to change Peter. We can only change our reactions to what Peter does. After we look at the whys of our reactions, the next step is to devise a plan of action, such as the following:

1. I will tell Peter that from now on I will wait twenty minutes, and if he has not arrived, I will leave.
2. I will always have an alternative plan, so that I don't sit around for the evening and brood.
3. If we are going to a party and he has not arrived in time to pick me up, I will simply go off on my own and leave him a note to meet me there.
4. I resolve not to be defensive or angry, but just to tell him that I am taking care of my needs so I don't have to be angry at him when he is late.
5. If we are meeting at a restaurant for dinner, I resolve to enjoy the passing show. If I am hungry, I will order my appetizer. I will be responsible for making myself happy no matter what time Peter appears.
6. I also resolve to get off his back about time. He knows my feelings; what he does is up to him. What I do is up to me.
7. I resolve to keep in mind that his lateness is nothing personal. He is late wherever he goes. I will stop taking it personally.
8. I resolve to keep in mind that if I want to be with Peter, lateness is part of the package. If I can't live with his

lateness, it is up to me to find someone who loves to be on time.

Whatever plan you come up with, the key is to *stand by it!* Using the above example, if Peter has not arrived in the allotted twenty minutes, then leave. When you are ready to leave for a party and he has not yet arrived to pick you up, go on your own. Again, when you do this with love, eventually he might get the message and begin showing up on time. Maybe not. In any case, this exercise is not about manipulation; it is about taking care of one's needs.

If your man starts to put you down for taking action, and it's a given that he will, it is important that you are clear in your own mind that it is his behavior that is inappropriate, not yours, and that there is no need to be defensive. You simply say:

"I understand why you might be upset, but I am taking care of my own needs in the event you are late. Then I have no reason to be upset with you. I care about you and I don't want to constantly be angry at you."

Do not accept the guilt trip he might try to lay on you. It might not all go smoothly at first, but keep practicing. It gets easier as you go along.

Borrowing an Al-Anon idea, when we don't handle our reactions and instead spend our time trying to change the other person, we become "co-partners" in their negative behavior. But when our judgment is used as a mirror, we are able to break our need to control the other person. It's a much more powerful way of being. When you can see everyone in your life as "practice people," reflections of what you have to work on within yourself, the judgments, that were once self-defeating, now take on a whole new healthy glow. They become tools for self-enlightenment instead of weapons to use against the people in your life. Going back to our lunches with our friends, when our judgments are used as tools for self-discovery, they most definitely do become appropriate lunch-time conversation once again.

Remember that this is never to be used as a self-bashing procedure. Exchanging male-bashing for self-bashing is not the order of the day. The trick is to stand back and be the observer. "Aha, here I am doing it again. Isn't that interesting?" I always see myself as Sherlock Holmes, trying to fill in the pieces of the jigsaw puzzle called life. Every once in a while, part of the picture becomes clear and there is that moment of "Aha!" that moment of enlightenment. I realize that I probably will never get to see the totality of the picture, but as my self-sleuthing continues, I see things with more clarity and as a result am able to take more control of my life.

4. Learn how to take. When we are constantly judging other people, it's safe to say that we are feeling scarcity at some level: something is "not enough" in our lives. We scramble to build up the stockpile of whatever we feel we are missing, but somehow it is never enough. We can never get enough praise, enough money, enough love, enough anything. The "not enough" syndrome signifies that we have not learned to take in the abundance that surrounds us. Whether there is a loving man in our lives or not, we need to see that the abundance is always there in some form or another.

The sun shines *and* our car starts *and* we have a roof over our heads *and* too much food in our bellies *and* friends and family that we love and enjoy *and* flowers that make us smile *and* sunsets that take our breath away *and* a heart that is still beating *and* books to read *and* walks to go on *and* service to provide to the community *and* animals to love *and* movies to see *and* on *and* on *and* on.

One of the exercises I give my students is to create a Book of Abundance. Each night before they go to sleep, they are to make a list of *at least* fifty things they have to be grateful for that day. Focusing on our blessings is a wonderful way to nod off to sleep. They balk in the beginning. "Fifty things!" As they commit to doing the exercise, however, they find themselves going through each day looking for what's great about their lives instead of continuing their habit of only noticing the gloom and doom. Needless to say, this tool is a great life-enhancer.

I ask you to create your own Book of Abundance and include in your list at least five items that acknowledge the gifts that men bring to your life. If you are not in a relationship, acknowledge the gifts of your male friends, your father, your boss (if male), the bus driver who got you safely home, the man who pumped your gas. *Begin making men part of the blessing of what it means to be a woman in this world.*

Start recognizing when you are being given something, no matter how small. I know that when we are in relationships for a long period of time we start to take things for granted. One way of rekindling the flame is to become more appreciative of the blessings. Even if you think you are in a "bad" relationship, appreciate the gifts. They are really there. If your man is lazy or silent or always putting you down, realize you are still getting something from the relationship or you wouldn't be there. Notice what that something is. It might simply be, "I'm not ready to be on my own right now. I'm thankful that I'm not alone." And know that when you are ready to leave an unhealthy relationship, you will leave with a sense of appreciation for what the relationship allowed you. There are always positive things to find in the man in your life. Things are given us, but our eyes are often blind to the gifts. As you begin to go through life with a sense of appreciation, the feeling of scarcity disappears and a feeling of abundance comes in. If you notice and appreciate long enough, you begin to feel nourished and lose the sense of neediness that signals the destruction of most relationships.

This same sense of neediness also prevents relationships from even getting started. I have known many women to strike out with men on the first date because their neediness is coming through. *Needy people can't love,* and men are wise to run away from needy women (and vice versa). When we feel that our cup runneth over, we can be much more loving in our relationships. We stop collecting injustices and begin collecting blessings instead.

5. Begin saying thank you to men. This exercise is an extension of the previous one. After you have brought to consciousness the blessings that men bring to your life, the next step is to thank them.

Do you know how good you make a man feel when you let him know he makes a difference in your life? And do you know how good you will feel when you see his face come alive with joy in being reminded that he does, indeed, make a difference?

For some of us, the experience is very foreign. We don't say thank you very often. I've noticed that there are a number of reasons why we don't thank people in our lives:

1. Our self-esteem is so low that it never occurs to us that our opinion really matters to someone else. Believe me, it does! Human beings need validation from the people around them. And, strangely, *it enhances our self-esteem to enhance someone else's!*
2. We withhold thanks when we are angry at the other person. We choose to judge instead. We don't want to do anything that would make him feel good! If we can get past the hostility and thank him, our heart begins to melt.
3. We feel so powerless in our own lives that we don't want anyone to know that we need him. We feel it gives that

person power over us. Yet when we see a positive response, we begin to understand that the pathway from
pain to power lies in giving to other people.

4. We are subconsciously so afraid of becoming dependent
on anyone else that we don't even admit to ourselves that
what that person gives is important to our lives. When we
acknowledge someone's gift and learn to thank people in
our lives, we can feel the heavy burden that we've created
for ourselves lifting off of our shoulders.

For many reasons, saying thank you to significant others in
our lives can be extremely difficult for many of us, particularly
when we say it to our men. One woman reported that she would
rather have her teeth pulled!

As an experiment, right now, put down the book and thank
the man in your life for all he has contributed to you. If he
isn't there, pick up the phone and call him or write him a letter. If you are not in a relationship, call up some man from
the past and thank him. It could even be your father. This is
another one of those easy-sounding exercises that is virtually
impossible for some of us to do. The amount of withhold we
feel is enormous. If you find yourself unable to utter those
words of thanks, you'd be wise to master the anger exercises
in Chapter 2. When you handle your anger, it is much easier
to give thanks.

To make it a little easier to get going, begin by thanking
people in more neutral circumstances—clerks in department
stores, police officers, colleagues at work, and so on. "Thank
you! Thank you! Thank you!" Get these two words so firmly
entrenched in your consciousness that they flow easily from
your lips. Giving away thanks is a big step in opening your heart.

I've created the letter on the following page to get you
started. While you may not agree—or identify—with all the
items I've included, it is the spirit of thanks that is important.
If you experience very mixed or negative feelings as you read

it, just pick up the mirror and notice these feelings. When we withhold our appreciation of others, it is usually an indication of our anger, insecurity, and pain.

On the other side of the coin, there will be men who also are experiencing anger, insecurity, and pain, and, as a result, may not be ready for our thanks. If you are with such a man, you may ultimately decide you don't want to be with a person who can't appreciate your loving him. But it is more likely that the man in your life or men in general will love this new way of relating and respond with loving compliments. Remember, the more we bolster another's sense of personal power, the less they will have to seek it at our expense.

Interestingly, as the men in our lives respond more lovingly, we may find that we are the ones who are resisting. Change is difficult, and if we aren't proficient at being lovers, then our hostile behavior will feel safer. But keep at it! New behavior requires a lengthy training program—usually one that lasts a lifetime.

A Thank-You Letter to Men

This is a letter of "thanks," a word that you don't often hear from women. Consider this the dawning of a new day. We are at last beginning to catch glimmers of the warm light of the Soul that shines within us . . . and within you. At such times our Hearts sing with appreciation for the gifts that you bring into our lives. Just as a beginning:

THANK YOU . . . for taking the enormous risk of rejection and asking us for that first date . . . most of us refuse to be put in that position.

THANK YOU . . . for going to battle for us, where you have often paid a big price. And thank you for not demanding that we join you.

THANK YOU ... for working so hard and worrying about whether your family will have enough.

THANK YOU ... for your delicious bodies that warm and pleasure us ... thank you for loving our bodies as well.

THANK YOU ... for the pleasure of your company ... we delight in being with you.

THANK YOU ... for paying our way ... especially at those times when we could well afford to pay our own way.

THANK YOU ... for being strong and protecting us when we feel frightened. How well you hide your own fear to make us feel secure.

THANK YOU ... for defending us when other men don't have our best interests at heart.

THANK YOU ... for trying so hard to please us ... even when we are unappreciative of your gifts.

THANK YOU ... for seeing the beauty within us long before we saw it in ourselves.

THANK YOU ... for listening and loving and caressing and cajoling and laughing and trying and hoping and caring and being and doing and buying and taking and supporting and sharing and helping and nurturing and protecting and walking the walk and talking the talk.

From our hearts to yours ...

The many women who love you

———

6. *Sidestep your negativity.* When we are feeling inwardly critical of someone, it often helps to go to another part of ourselves (our Higher Self) and say something loving to them instead. The times when this approach is appropriate are when we know our criticisms are "off the wall"; that is, when we are not taking responsibility for something in our lives and are blaming our man for it.

An example would be, "I'm really upset he waited too long to get theater tickets. Now we can't see the show." The truth is, "If I really wanted to see the show, I should have been the one to get the tickets. I was just too lazy to do anything about it!" Or maybe we are upset about something at work and subconsciously blame our husband for not being a millionaire so we didn't have to work to begin with! (Yes, our minds do work that way sometimes.) We express this hidden agenda by wanting to lash out because he left the top off the toothpaste. Other times we are feeling particularly critical and moody and we don't have a clue as to the reason why. These are all appropriate times for acting from a more loving part of ourselves. Let me give a few examples from my own experiences of how this technique works.

One summer day, Mark and I were driving merrily through the beautiful countryside, but I was secretly stewing about something stupid. Just as I was ready to pounce on him, which was my old pattern, I bit my lip and, *while still experiencing the emotion of hostility,* sidestepped my negativity and said, "I'm so glad we have this afternoon together. I love you." I wasn't feeling glad. I wasn't feeling loving. But I said it anyway. When I did, he reached out and touched my hand and said, "Yes, it's really great, isn't it? I love you, too." What could be more heavenly! The hardness in my heart melted immediately and so did my upset. *What happened was that I created the atmosphere for love to occur instead of a fight.* I had to learn how to keep opening up the space for love, instead of blocking it by putting judgment in the way. In this way, I helped create a wonderful afternoon filled with appreciation instead of a tense afternoon filled with fighting.

Another time, Mark expressed concern about a meeting he was going to that morning, the success of which meant a great deal to his company. At the time, I was in a career transition and wasn't bringing in any money. When I am not earning my own income, I become very fearful when it comes to my husband's income. (Does that sound familiar?) Hence, when he expressed his concern, my fear loomed up and my mind went right into judgment. "Why doesn't he have control over the situation? Why isn't he better prepared?" Such thoughts were going around and around in my head. My inner Child really wanted to know that he had it all handled.

Since my upset at him was totally inappropriate, this was the perfect time for loving words to transform the negative thoughts. With this awareness, I was able to call forth the inner Adult and nurturing Parent and express encouragement to him when he really needed it. Even though I was feeling filled with inner worry, I was able to say, "Don't worry about it, honey. It will turn out all right. Even if the meeting doesn't go the way you want it, we'll handle it. We always do and we always will. We can handle anything! Not to worry!"

What happened inside me as I was saying these words was nothing short of a miracle. I began to feel immediate relief. As I was soothing his distress, my distress disappeared. I felt comfort and safety, and a wave of calm came over me. The positive affirmation to Mark acted as a tranquilizer to myself. I began to feel that what I was saying was absolutely true (and, of course, it was!). My hostile and judgmental feelings about him turned immediately to empathy, compassion, and appreciation of the support he was giving me as I moved from one career into the other. (This is a perfect example of the denumbing process I discussed earlier in the book.) The transformation within myself from fear to love truly was nothing short of a miracle!

As a postscript, Mark called me later in the day to tell me that everything went well and to thank me for the encouragement. He said he went into the meeting keeping my words in mind and thus felt no desperation about the outcome. My positive words were helpful, not only in getting rid of my fear and hostility, but also in creating the outcome that I wanted.

The implications of this phenomenon are enormous: *We don't have to change our negative thoughts before we can be a support to someone else . . . or ourselves. We just have to change our words which automatically make the shift for us.*

Sidestepping our negativity is best used when we know that our upset with our partner is the result of something within us and has little or nothing to do with him. It takes a certain amount of awareness to know when that is the case. Practice being your own observer and ask yourself, "Is my upset with him reasonable or is there something I am not taking care of in my own life?"

Sidestepping our negativity is telling the truth when our mind is telling us lies about the man in our life.

Read that statement again. It's confusing, but true! It is important to learn that so many of our judgments come from false perceptions. We can actually learn to change our perceptions by the words we speak; hence, my firm belief in the power of affirmations.

7. Try some nonverbal loving. We can sidestep our negativity in a non-verbal way. To illustrate, one of my students was having great difficulty communicating with her father. Each day when she came home from work, she faced a tyrant who verbally took out all his frustrations in life on her. Her response was to shout back in kind. My assignment for the week was for her to let him know she loved him, which she dearly did underneath all her hurt.

One day as he was screaming at her, she was about to yell back when she remembered the assignment. Instead of yelling back, she just sat there and silently repeated over and over again: "I love you, I love you, I love you." As she kept repeating the words, she noticed a melting in her heart. Instead of feeling the old anger she normally experienced, she began to feel compassion for the man she called her father who never dared to live his dreams.

And then it happened. Her father suddenly stopped, looked at her, and apologized profusely for making her the brunt of his anger. She didn't even have to say it aloud. Her message was heard. Remember, as she began to say the "I love you"s in her mind, she wasn't feeling it. But the constant repetition shifted the energy in her body as well as the energy in the room.

8. Make friends with all of who you are. When I talk about being in touch with all of who we are, I do mean *all* of who we are—the wonderful and the horrible. I have already talked about many aspects of the self—our male aspects, our female aspects, our Higher Self, our Child-Within, our Adult-Within, our Parent-Within. These are only some of the multitude of subpersonalities that lie within, many of which are unconscious to our conscious mind. Psychologists have referred to the hidden parts of ourselves as the "disowned" self. Usually what we choose to "disown" represents the dark side or the "shadow within," as psychiatrist Carl Jung called it.

What the various models suggest is that human beings are comprised of many polarities—good and evil, greed and generosity, peacefulness and aggression, kindness and hurtfulness, and so on. This explains why at one moment we may feel loving and an hour later we may feel hostile. It just depends on which inner subpersonality is in charge. Jung suggested that there could be no peace in this world unless each nation recognized its own "shadow," that is to say, its own dark side. In the same way, there can be no peace in relationships unless we each recognize our own personal dark side. I will discuss this in more detail in the next chapter. Just remember that it is a given that whatever "evil" we see in someone else can be found within ourselves as well.

Knowing this, we can once again begin to use our judgments as our mirror. We can ask ourselves, "What am I hiding from myself?"

HE IS SELFISH!
Isn't there also a part of me that is selfish?

HE IS INCONSIDERATE!
Isn't there also a part of me that is inconsiderate?

HE IS MANIPULATIVE!
Isn't there also a part of me that is manipulative?

When we can finally acknowledge, accept, and ultimately embrace the totality of who we are, then, and only then, can we do the same for someone else.

I remember an old "Twilight Zone" episode about a Scrooge-type of character who always complained that people were a scourge and that the world would be better off without them. With a bit of magic, he was able to create a world without people. But that proved to be too lonely. Then he decided he would simply create a world where all the inhabitants were exactly like him—the ultimate reflection in a mirror. When he got over the shock of seeing his dark side in other people he accepted the fact that people, with all their faults, are beautiful, and, that this is indeed the best of all possible worlds.

Ultimately, love comes when we can embrace the "flaws," along with the beauty, in others. This is only possible when we have embraced the flaws, as well as the beauty, within ourselves. Interestingly, we may find that it is just as difficult for some of us to accept our beauty as it is to accept our flaws. Can you imagine what that does to our relationships?

9. Discover your negative belief systems and change them. We all have our own personal sets of belief systems. If our belief system is *men are bad,* we will notice what is bad about men. If our belief system is *men are good,* we will notice what is good about men. It's that simple. When we believe that something is a certain way, we choose experiences that validate our belief patterns. If we believe that men are selfish, inconsiderate slobs, we will collect evidence to absolutely justify that belief.

Our belief systems have been formed over many years and it takes a great deal of reprogramming to change them, but it can be done. What I suggest you first do is make a list of your negative beliefs about men. Some beliefs that my students came up with are:

Men give you pain.

Men fear commitment.

Men lie.

Men fool around.

Men are inconsiderate.

I next asked my students to turn their negatives into positives:

Men give you joy.

Men want to commit.

Men are truthful.

Men are faithful.

Men are considerate.

The truth is that some men give you pain and some men give you joy and some men give you both. Some men fear commitment, while others want it. Some men are liars, others are truthful. Some men fool around, while others are faithful. Some men are inconsiderate, while others are very caring. We can take our choice as to which belief systems we want to carry into a relationship with a man. The belief system we choose can make all the difference as to whether that relationship will succeed or not.

Begin the transformation process by listing all your negative belief systems and changing them into positives. Repeat your new belief systems over and over again daily until they become firmly entrenched in your mind. If you need some help, look at the *appreciation affirmations* at the end of this chapter. As much of a male-basher as I was in days gone by, I have become a male-lover through this process of changing my belief systems and re-visioning the way I look at men. And what a beautiful sight I am seeing. Come and take a look!

Appreciation Affirmations*

Men are
Terrific!

I love men!

I love men!

Men are
Wonderful!

Men are
Loving!

I love men!

Men are
Caring!

I love men!

Men are
Generous!

I love men!

Men are
Delicious!

I love men!

I love men!

Men are *Loyal!*

I love men!

Men are *Kind!*

I love men!

Men are
Dependable!

I love men!

Men are
Protective!

I love men!

Men are
Considerate!

I love men!

Men are
Faithful!

Men are
Strong!

I love men!

Men are *Sexy!*

I love men!

Men are
Cuddly!

I love men!

Men are *Sweet!*

I love men!

Men are *Fun!*

I love men!

Men are
Warm!

I love men!

*To be repeated at least once a day with gusto!

5

ALWAYS RIGHT...BUT NEVER HAPPY

Do you always need to be right? Do you always need to have the last word? And when someone points out to you that you are self-righteous, do you self-righteously try to prove that you are not self-righteous . . . simply always right?!?

Take it from one who knows, if the answer is yes to any of the above, you have much to learn about loving yourself and loving others.

It wasn't too long ago that I discovered I had a serious case of self-righteous-itis. Although my children were regularly pointing it out to me, I just assumed "kids will be kids"—always critical of their mother! And then came the day when sixty adults in a workshop I attended confronted me with the fact that, indeed, I was a queen of self-righteousness. If there had only been fifty-nine people in the room, I might have been tempted to prove them wrong, but sixty was an awesome number! I began to monitor my behavior and, discovered, alas, they were right.

It was clearly time to learn some new lessons in life. As an ancient sage once said, "When the student is ready, the teacher will appear." I was standing at the top of Mount Palitana in India when my first teacher appeared. He was a Jain monk who was giving a talk to twenty-five of his disciples. (My Path has led me to many interesting places, indeed!) There was something very spiritual about the setting. I was receptive to his words:

"You will find throughout life that people have the need to be right. And you can let them be. When you find yourself with someone who needs to have the last word, let them have it. You don't need it. Just look at them and remind yourself that they've never been to the top of Mount Palitana. They don't understand."

The next party I attended offered me the opportunity to test his suggested strategy. One know-it-all (it's so easy to see our flaws in someone else!) was self-righteously putting down an opinion I had just expressed. I felt my blood begin to boil and was just about to counterattack when I remembered the words of the Jain monk. I bit my lip and just repeated to myself over and over again:

"He's never been to the top of Mount Palitana."
"He's never been to the top of Mount Palitana."
"He's never been to the top of Mount Palitana."

And it worked. I was able to keep my mouth shut. To say this was easy would be to tell a lie. There was a part of my being that was screaming "Kill! Kill!" but I kept quiet. I went home that night feeling very proud of my remarkable self-control.

I kept practicing until I weaned myself of the need to have the last word . . . no minor feat! But after a while I realized that there was something very incomplete about this strategy. While it kept futile arguments from escalating, it didn't take away my need to feel superior. I hadn't stopped looking down upon people who disagreed with me; I was just quieter about it. Obviously, there was more to the issue than having been to the top of Mount Palitana.

Confronted with my own self-righteous behavior, I became an observer of it in others. In time, I concluded that:

Those who constantly need to be right are, in truth, fighting a battle with a part of themselves that feels very inferior and unsure of itself. And it follows, the more self-righteous, the bigger the battle within.

In order to let go of the need to be right, it is necessary to soothe that place within that feels so threatened, which, as we all know, isn't so easy to do. What keeps us feeling inferior and unsure of ourselves is our inner Chatterbox—that negative voice within that fills us with messages of gloom and doom and, in some way or another, always tries to convince us that we really are not good enough. You will recognize it as the voice that sounds something like this:

I really blew this interview. God, I wish I had worn a different dress. It kept riding up on me as I was sitting in the chair. I hope he didn't get the wrong idea. He seemed very cold. I wonder if I said anything to make him clam up that way. Maybe I shouldn't have told him that I haven't worked for two years. He might think I couldn't find a job or that I was lazy. Maybe I should have acted more excited about the company. I wonder if I asked the right questions. Maybe I didn't come across enthusiastically enough about the company (and on and on and on . . .).

The Chatterbox, thankfully, has its counterpart in the form of the Higher Self—the spiritual part of ourselves that fills us with messages of abundance and tells us that, not only are we good enough, but we truly make a difference in this world. The Higher Self sounds like this:

I will get this job or I won't. I did the best I could and I trust that if the job is meant to be mine, it will be. If not, there is a better job out there waiting for me. I know I have much to offer this world, and I trust that I will be able to express my gift in an appropriate way. I have within me what it takes, and I will rest easy knowing that I will continue to learn and grow from whatever experiences come my way. I can rest easy knowing that it is all happening perfectly.

When we are able to call forward this spiritual expression of who we are (which few of us know how to do), we feel a sense of inner peace and abundance, an inner knowing that all is right with the world. Perhaps that is what the Jain monk really meant when he talked about having been to the top of Mount Palitana, having been to that place within that knows only peace, beauty, creativity, joy, abundance, love, and compassion.

I have observed that women in today's world seem to have a bigger problem with self-righteousness than do men. This isn't because we are less in touch with our Higher Self than men. (None of us score very well in that department.) It is because the women's movement has come at a time when society, in general, has lost its spiritual ground of being. Both men and women alike have been concerned with *body* and *mind,* but *spirit* has gotten lost in the shuffle. Many of us deny that the spiritual part of ourselves even exists!

In my experience, this lack of spirituality affects women more than it does men simply because we've been in the process of greater change. As a result of the women's movement, we are putting ourselves out in the world in new and frightening ways. We are transforming our self-image. We are going against the accepted path and putting ourselves in unfamiliar territory. Even those women who are not in favor of the women's movement are affected, as they are forced to question values long held inviolable. With all this, we need as much help as we can get—inside and out!

Yet at a time when we most need the inner guidance and comfort from our Higher Self, we are at a loss as to how to summon it. We have no way of reaching the top of Mount Palitana, so to speak. We are at the mercy of our Chatterbox. We have no way of giving ourselves that sense of inner peace and confidence that we so desperately need. Without this "centeredness," looking in our proverbial mirror has been too difficult. It makes sense that:

> Without backup from the "best" of who we are, it has been much too painful to take a look at the "worst" of who we are. As a way of avoiding ourselves, we focus on the "worst" in our men instead.

In my workshops, I do a very telling exercise. I arrange the room so that all the men are seated on one side of the room facing all the women seated on the other side. The instructions are simply for the men and women alternately to ask each other questions. Generally speaking, the men seem to have an attitude of sincere inquiry:

> "What do women look for in a man?"
> "How do women like men to make the first approach?"
> "How do women feel about splitting the check?"
> . . . and so on.

What comes through is a desire to please women, combined with a total confusion as to what women really want.

On the other hand, a large number of women (not all, of course) present a very different picture. They sit forward in their chairs with a hands-on-the-hips pose and a look of disdain upon their faces. Their voices are hostile and their questions reveal an unmistakable self-righteousness. The blame comes pouring forth:

"Why don't you men ever want to make a commitment!?!"
"Why are you men only interested in sex!?!"
"Why don't you men call when you say you'll call!?!"

(I love the answer one man gave to the last question: "I guess for the same reason you women give us fake phone numbers!") The general stance of these women immediately puts the men on the defensive. And when the men begin to respond, they can't get a word in edgewise. The women jump in to disagree, to confront, and to negate anything the men have to say.

We can see this same kind of behavior on talk shows that capitalize on the popularity of angry and bitter women attacking men on a variety of feminist issues. The shrillness and venom that come from the mouths of these women are painful to watch. It occurs to me at moments such as these that while we accuse men of not relating to us, we don't get such high marks for relating to them either.

We can begin to see that because we are so out of touch with our Higher Self, our self-righteousness steps in to serve a number of protective functions:

It gives us a sense of superiority (albeit false) at a time when our self-esteem is very low.

It keeps us from having to look in the mirror and ask ourselves, "How might I have contributed to the circumstances in my life that don't work?" at a time when we can't face the answer to that question.

It allows us to blame others, thus keeping us "victims," so we don't have to take action at a time when we are too frightened to act.

It serves as self-talk at a time when a part of us needs to be convinced.

This last point needs some explanation. As we put ourselves out into the world in a new way, we are not always sure of the "rightness" of many of our actions. We have not let go of the old and are uncomfortable with the new. To stop ourselves from falling back into the comfort of old patterns, we need to put all our energy into going forward. Defending our position is one way to do this. As we try to convince someone else of our wisdom, we are convincing ourselves as well. It follows that we become inappropriately strident when anyone tries to weaken our resolve by suggesting that we are making a mistake (God forbid!).

As an example, if we choose to leave the traditional role of mother-who-is-home-when-the-children-get-home-from-school and move out into the world, the way we handle our guilt and insecurity about our new role (if we are not in touch with our Higher Self) is to hang on desperately to the belief that we have made the right decision. We will look for—and find—evidence supporting our point of view from articles, books, talk shows, and mental health professionals. We become defensive if anyone suggests that it is better for our children that we go back to the way it was.

It works in reverse as well. If we buck the trend and go into a traditional mothering role, we invest all of our psychic energy into proving (mainly to ourselves) that we are doing what is absolutely best for the child, and if any other mother does not make the same choice, she is a bad mother. Once again, we will find evidence to prove our point of view and, once again, we will become defensive if anyone suggests that we will create a better role model for and a sense of independence in our children if we get out into the world and fulfill our own potential as human beings.

As we begin to develop inner confidence, we eventually reach the point when we are able to drop our self-righteousness. We know we have finally reached this point when someone can disagree with us and we can say, "Thank you for sharing," take in what they have said, and then go merrily on our way. But developing this inner confidence takes a great deal of time, as you have already found out! The one way we can speed up the process is by learning how to get in touch with the best of who we are—our Higher Self.[1]

In effect, we have to learn to be our own best friend and build ourselves up when we are down, pat ourselves on the back when we've done something right. We need to affirm and live into the idea that:

> "I am a beautiful being who has much to contribute to this world."

When this idea becomes an inner certainty, our self-righteousness "miraculously" disappears. There is no longer any need to prove anything to anyone else since most of our prior arguments were only meant to convince ourselves that "we are beautiful beings who have much to contribute to this world!"

When we can get to this place of beauty within, we can also begin to drop our destructive competitiveness with men. Again, our competitiveness is a natural progression in our search for wholeness. For so many years, we have considered ourselves to be second best. Instead of trying to become equal to men, many of us are striving to prove that we can become "best." This sets up a battle that makes loving relationships impossible, either at home or in the workplace. We are all familiar with the distance-producing sayings, such as "A woman is a better man for the job!" which can only serve to threaten men more than they have already been threatened. *It's time that we stop trying to be better than men, and instead try to be better as women.* In that, we can begin to develop more loving relationships. As psychologist Toni Grant points out:

> "Some highly accomplished and intellectually evolved women do indeed have satisfying personal relationships

with mature men. But these are special women who are in touch with their feminine aspects and therefore relate to men in a non-competitive manner."[2]

When we stop trying to compete with men, but instead focus on expanding our boundaries of what it means to be a woman, we will be able to relate in a way that is more powerful, more creative, more compassionate, and certainly more loving.

How do we expand our boundaries? In terms of self-right-eousness, an important direction to explore is the area of the disowned self that I touched upon earlier. It is important for our own mental health, our relationships, and probably the survival of the world, that we uncover our shadow. There are those who speculate that unless we do, the world will blow itself up, each side trying to prove that the other is the "bad guy" and not acknowledging the "bad guy" that lies within. Certainly most of us have "blown up" many relationships by trying to make our partner the "bad guy."

How do we find that elusive disowned self? From noticing what we loath in someone else. Hence, as we screamingly ac-cuse men of all manner of things, we can be sure that we are disowning parts of ourselves that are just as loathsome. For example, when we accuse men of greedily avoiding their ali-mony payments, we deny the part of ourselves that is greedy as well; when we accuse men of avoiding intimacy, we deny the part of ourselves that avoids intimacy as well; when we attack men for seeing women only as objects, we deny the part of ourselves that sees men as objects as well. In the same way, when we condemn another woman for allowing a man to take care of her, we deny the part of us that also wants to be taken care of; when we condemn another woman for being vain, we deny our own vanity . . . and so on.

It follows, then, that in order to gain peace with ourselves, we must not only get in touch with the best of who we are—our Higher Self—but we must also get in touch with what we consider the worst of who we are—our disowned self. The purpose of this is not to punish ourselves, but to understand that to be human is to be filled with polarities: one good trait does not exist without its opposite, nor does one bad trait exist without its opposite. We have to understand that to be human is to be both:

Dependent and Independent

Greedy and Giving

Cold and Warm

Weak and Strong

Insecure and Secure

Scared and Confident

Dishonest and Honest

Hateful and Loving

I don't know why the human species was made this way; perhaps to teach us humility! In any case, this is the way it is. And the sooner that we can accept it (no exceptions), the sooner we can get off our false position that we are "better than" and begin to relate in a more loving fashion, not only to others, but to ourselves as well.

We then become aware that when people manifest their negative side, it is because they have had painful life experiences. Somewhere along the line they have been hurt, put down, and humiliated. No matter how outwardly "successful" they may be, they have never been taught to feel good about themselves. They have never been taught that they make a difference. When we understand this, it makes it easier to have compassion for someone who is manifesting destructive behavior. And with this compassion we are able to thaw our frozen hearts and find ways to build others up, not tear them down.

Conversely, those who are able to express the more beautiful side of who they are are not "better than." They simply have had experiences in life that have made them feel good about themselves. This doesn't mean that they have had more money or status in life. Some of the most insecure, self-righteous people I know belong in the category of the "rich and famous." No, I'm talking about those of whatever background who have learned that they have purpose and that they make a difference. As a result, they act in ways that are loving and supportive of other human beings. This doesn't mean that the "bad stuff" doesn't exist within them; it just means that life has treated them a little better.

When we are able to reclaim our disowned selves, we no longer need to hold onto our self-righteousness. There's no longer anything to hide, from ourselves or others. Strangely, we may find it very hard to give up our self-righteous qualities for the simple reason that self-righteousness has its delicious side. It feels so good to be superior. Just as anger has its sense of power, so does self-righteousness. But give it up we must . . . that is, if we are interested in experiencing tranquility, love, joy, and abundance in our lives and in our relationships.

So, how do we begin? Psychologists Hal Stone and Sidra Winhelman suggest that a good starting point is to think of who it is in your life you can't stand.[3] Who "pushes your buttons"; that is, who enrages you? These people are direct reflections of your disowned self. You simply look at each person and ask yourself, "What part of my disowned self am I seeing in him (or her)?" This is another way of picking up the mirror instead of the magnifying glass. In this way, your enemies become your allies, your mentors, your teachers.

Another way to discover our disowned selves is simply to put in motion the intent to find it. You don't have to understand how the process works. What you should do is send signals to your subconscious that you are ready to find some answers and to let go of old belief systems. Remember that the purpose of finding our disowned self is not so that we can punish ourselves, but quite the opposite: so that we can accept ourselves as part of the human race and not work so hard to be perfect, or expect perfection from anyone else. Examples of statements that are useful in discovering your disowned self are as follows:

> I am sick and tired of my self-righteousness and I now commit to learning about what it is within me that I have denied from myself.
> I am sick and tired of my anger and I now commit to learning about what it is within me that I have denied from myself.
> I am sick and tired of my unrealistic expectations and I now commit to learning about what it is within me that I have denied from myself.
> I am sick and tired of my "judgmentalness" and I now commit to learning about what it is within me that I have denied from myself.

Another tool for ridding ourselves of self-righteousness is "Listen and Learn." I stumbled upon the true meaning of this familiar phrase a number of years ago. At the time, I was passionately involved in the anti-nuclear movement and was associate producer of an anti-MX missile documentary for the BBC in London.[4] As part of my research, I set up an interview with a public affairs person at one of the plants in California that was building the MX missile.

I had not told the public affairs person in advance of my vehement anti-nuclear stance. During the interview, he was proudly going on about the effectiveness of this amazing new piece of weaponry. I sat there with a phony smile on my face, nodding in feigned agreement as I was self-righteously thinking to myself:

"This man is an idiot. This man is dangerous. He is definitely an 'enemy' to peace. It is the likes of him that is going to blow us all up. He has zero regard for humanity! He couldn't care less about what happens to this world. All he cares about is his stupid missile."

As he rapturously went on about the advantages of the MX missile, I happened to look down at his desk and saw a proudly displayed picture of this "killer's" beautiful wife and children. My eye was then drawn to the wall behind him, on which was tacked a piece of "art" with the scrawled words, "I love you Daddy." And *truth* then struck me like a bolt out of the heavens:

"This man *isn't* an enemy! He *does* care about humanity! He feels! He loves! He gets scared! He prays! He hopes! He desperately wants to make a difference in this world! In no way does he want the world to blow up! He has a wife he loves! He has kids that he wants to see grow up healthy and happy! He wants to make a better world for them."

Then I looked into this man's eyes—I mean, *really* looked— and saw a Soul who, indeed, wanted a world in which it was safe to live . . . who was doing what he thought necessary to reach that end . . . who really was a caring human being. His ideology became unimportant. I saw only a man doing the best he could with what information was available to him at the time. The fact that his information was different from mine didn't make him any less beautiful. What a heart opener!

When I realized who I was really talking to—a loving Soul— my whole approach to the interview softened. The barriers created by my belief systems began to crumble, and I actually began to hear what he had to say and to learn something new in the process. I began to "walk in his shoes" and understand how, from his perspective, he could believe in nuclear weapons as a way of saving the world. And from this place of understanding, I was able to state my position in a more effective, non-threatening way. I opened the space for him to hear me as well. The miracle was that I came into the room going for the kill and came out finding another human being to love.

While I never did agree with his idea that the MX missile was one way of creating a better world, and I would continue to work toward a nuclear-free world, I was for the first time really able to hear the way he saw things and learn from his vision. From this expanded perspective, I was able to respect his position and discover the incredible sense of freedom and inner peace that not-needing-to-be-right allows. I could feel the stress dissolve from my body as I was able to go with the flow of what was happening in the room.

This experience brought home to me a realization that I was able to generalize to the rest of humanity (it was so obvious that I felt stupid for not having seen it before):

If *I* truly believed in the rightness of what I was saying, then *they* also believed in the rightness of what they were saying!

Imagine that! Any person with whom I was arguing was feeling just as right as I was. This "profound" kind of thinking led to the further realization that maybe, just maybe, there was some merit to his or her way of thinking and I should listen to new ideas instead of shutting off my ears. What a good idea! Why hadn't I thought of it before? And, indeed, it was a good idea. As a result of this simple but transformational decision, I began to expand my limited vision to include the viewpoints of others.

This experience brought a new question to my mind:

What if there really were no "right" positions? What if there were only "different" positions?

How relaxed the world would look from that perspective! I'm reminded of the words of Ram Dass,[5] another one of my teachers, who was reprimanded by an activist friend for not being more "passionate" about the anti-nuclear movement. He explained to his friend, that while he believed nuclear weapons were wrong, who was to say what the "Grand Design" really was meant to be. He said he would stand up for his belief in the inappropriateness of nuclear weapons, but he wouldn't invest emotionally in the outcome. After all, who was to say who was right and who was wrong? None of us, in our awesomely limited perspective, can really be all-knowing as to how life is "supposed to be."

What a powerful way of being in the world—standing up for what you believe in with the realization that you may be wrong! What a loving space from which to present your messages to the world, to manifest your purpose. And what a relief to know that you don't constantly have to defend your positions!

"Maybe I'm right and maybe I'm wrong!" I'm always looking for an opening to tell the following story which my daughter lovingly passed on to me. (She's another one of my teachers!) I think it fits in beautifully here:

A long time ago there was a Russian farmer who had an enlightened view about life. And so when the other farmers told him how lucky it was that he had a horse, his answer to them was, "Maybe it is . . . maybe it isn't."
Time went on, and one day his horse disappeared. The other farmers came to him and told him how unlucky it was

that he lost his horse. His answer to them was, "Maybe it is . . . maybe it isn't."

One day the horse returned home, bringing with him another horse he had met along the way. Now the farmer had two horses. The other farmers came to him and told him how lucky it was that he had two horses. Once again his answer was, "Maybe it is . . . maybe it isn't."

One day his son was taming the new horse, which was rather wild. In the process, the son ended up with a broken leg. The other farmers came and told him how unlucky it was that his son had broken his leg. And you guessed the farmer's response: "Maybe it is . . . maybe it isn't!"

The following day the soldiers came to the farm in order to recruit the farmer's son into the military, but because of the broken leg, the son was spared military service. The other farmers (who never seemed to learn) came once again to tell our hero how lucky it was that his son was not taken away from the farm. And once again, the farmer answered, "Maybe it is . . . maybe it isn't!"

And so it goes. It would help for us all to understand that, on the face of things, none of us know what is good and what is bad. Maybe we all need to adopt the farmer's attitude of "Maybe it's good . . . maybe it's bad." In truth, when things do not look right to us, they may actually be "perfect" in the Grand Scheme of things, and vice versa. I guess the key is to follow one's heart and do what one does and then sit patiently and watch and listen . . . watch and listen . . . watch and listen.

Ram Dass has said many other things that relate to this matter of self-righteousness and one is particularly relevant to my experience during the MX interview. He suggests that the minute we are born into this world, we go into "somebody training." That "somebody" includes many levels—our physical appearance, our emotional makeup, the roles we choose to play (teacher, wife, mother, doctor), our beliefs, our sun signs, and so on. These are our "story lines" at a party—how we identify ourselves.

Most of us go through life identifying only with these "lower" aspects of ourselves. Yet, if you think about it, these are the human dimensions that cause us to remain separate from one another. This is the level of our differences. Ram Dass suggests that there is more: there is the level of the Spirit or the Soul (or the Higher Self), where we lose our separateness and become connected as one. He says this is the level at which we can look into someone else's eyes and say, "Are you in there? Far out! I'm in here!" This is the level at which you can see another you, but in a different package. *If we can find a way to connect at the level of the Higher Self, we can always surmount our differences at the lower levels of our being.*

The question is: "How can we women begin to incorporate these ideas into our relationships with men?" We can begin by seeing that our self-righteousness, anger, judgments, expectations, and all the rest of the conflicts with our men take place at the lower levels of our being. As we find ways to transcend to a higher plane of being, as we remind ourselves to jump up to the level of the Higher Self, we then begin to see men in a different way.

From the level of the Higher Self we are *all* beautiful. From the level of the Higher Self, *we are all the same!* It is at the level of the Higher Self that we are able to keep our hearts open to the struggles and joys that we all share by virtue of the fact that we are all human beings. This is the place where it is impossible to remain numb to the beauty inherent in our own or another being. We must learn how to transcend the petty ego and jump up into a higher plane if we want to experience loving relationships.

When we are locked into the lower levels, the level of our belief systems, we are blind as to what lies beyond the walls we have created around ourselves. For example, if we have high walls around a belief system such as *men are insensitive,* we can see nothing but our belief, no matter which way we turn, as follows:

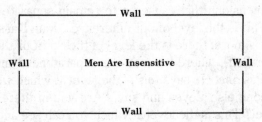

As we transcend to the level of the Higher Self, we can stand above and see beyond our own limited vision. In this way, we begin to dilute the rage that our blinders have created, as follows:

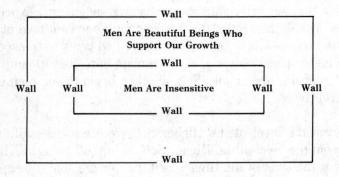

When we reach the level of the Higher Self, we can see men as people who enhance our lives. Men are insensitive is now combined with the reality that men are beautiful beings who support our growth. Look at how we've expanded our vision! Remember that having belief systems is part of the human condition. There is nothing abnormal about growing up with blinders. The game in life is to learn how to take off the blinders.

In effect, when we take off our blinders and incorporate other viewpoints into our vision, we become bigger. Robert Fuller was asked by an interviewer, "Is there a better game than war?" Fuller responded that there is war and there is peace, but there's another game that is more fun. It's called *completion:*

". . . completing ourselves through each other by incorporating into ourselves the empowering truths that other people embody and exemplify."[6]

The nature of it is "finding what you love in what you hate." We might have some negative feelings about men, but if we can remember what it is we love, we can hold our "hate" in its proper subordinate place. Fuller also says:

"The minute you find what you love in someone else, you're bigger yourself, and stronger; you're more powerful. That will be, I think, the meaning of power in the twenty-first century. It's power that comes from the completion of self, from the incorporation into your behavioral repertoire of the other person's (or culture's) secrets."[7]

This is a very important statement indeed. We women are at a point where we need to drop our swords and realize that we have pushed away one of our biggest resources when it comes to self-growth: men. In so doing, we have denied men one of their biggest resources: women. Much of what we have to learn in this big wide world can be taught to us by men once we get off the position that we know it all, and vice versa. We make it more difficult to become whole by severing relationships with those who hold secrets we need to learn in order to complete ourselves.

In this sense, giving up our position is not about surrender or yielding, but rather about becoming whole. As I described in Chapter 1, relationships in the past were "complete" in the sense of:

$$\tfrac{1}{2} + \tfrac{1}{2} = 1$$

We can now begin to teach each other how to become truly complete and create the healthier and more powerful formula of:

$$\tfrac{1}{2} + \tfrac{1}{2} = 1 + 1 = 2$$

Before there was one . . . and then there were two! Miracle of miracles! We can thus begin to see each other as mentors. We need to incorporate into our vocabulary, "Please teach me about this" and "Thank you for showing me that." When we ask with love in our hearts, we will get answers that enrich our body, mind, and soul, answers that will make connection on both a practical and transcendent level much easier to attain. What a valuable resource we provide one another!

It is clear that a battle won from the position of self-righteousness is a hollow victory indeed. Not only do we end up hating our men, but we end up hating ourselves as well. As with any of our seemingly negative patterns, self-righteousness can be a wonderful teacher if we remember to pick up our mirror whenever self-righteousness rears its ugly head. There will always be a part of us that is insecure, hence self-righteous (don't let me mislead you into thinking that you can "cure" it forever), but when we know what questions to ask ourselves in the face of our self-righteousness, we will come out winners in the end:

What am I afraid to hear?
Why am I feeling so insecure?
What part of me is not feeling OK about itself?

We might not always come up with answers immediately, but we can learn to say to ourselves:

"I'm good enough, whether you agree with me or not . . . and so are you. I'll listen to you carefully because you may have something to teach me. Thank you for showing me the possibility of another way."

If we can say this to ourselves, even if we are not believing it at the time, we will find ourselves relaxing and becoming more comfortable with the situation. I suggest you memorize it and use it when appropriate. Eventually you will condition yourself to believe it.

There also will be times when you are faced with someone else's self-righteous behavior. You can be of great service to that other person if you learn to transcend to the place within yourself that can see the other person's pain and you can silently communicate to them:

"You are beautiful."

"You are enough."

In that kind of loving and compassionate space, many barriers will be broken down easier than you can ever imagine.

It is essential to the happiness of our relationships that we learn to deal with our self-righteousness. It helps to remember that while self-righteousness can be delicious at times, the down side is mammoth: it hurts men and makes them our enemies instead of our friends; it keeps us from moving forward; it keeps us from liking ourselves; and, for many of us, it results in our picking partners who make self-righteousness easy—alcoholics, drug users, "babies," workaholics, and so on. (And then we sit around wondering why there aren't any good men out there.)

With all this in mind, remember that there is only one time when it is absolutely appropriate for you to have the last word. That is when the last "word" happens to be "I LOVE YOU"!

We have now looked at four of the biggest barriers to love: anger, unrealistic expectations, judgment, and self-righteousness. There is still much to learn:

- How do we use our mirror when it comes to burning issues such as intimacy and trust?
- How can we become more loving of ourselves?
- How can we have more loving relationships?
- What does the world feel like through the eyes, heart, and soul of a man?

Read on!

"Mount Palitana" Affirmations

I am a beautiful being who has much
to contribute to this world.

You are a beautiful being who has much
to contribute to this world.

I love all of who I am.

I respect who I am.

I respect who you are.

We can think differently and both be right.

I am learning more and more every day.

I respect your point of view.

I listen and I learn.

I look at you with love in my heart . . .
despite what you say.

I see me in you.

I see you in me.

At the level of the soul, we are the same.

I see in you what I need to learn.

I surrender and I let go.

I want to love more than I need to be right.

I open up to hear what you have to say.

I love you.

6

WHY HE'D BE CRAZY TO OPEN UP!

Perhaps one of the biggest complaints women have about men is in the area of intimacy. "Why can't they open up?" is a common cry. When I began teaching workshops about intimacy, I was pleasantly surprised to see the large number of men in attendance. It was clear that they knew they had a big problem opening up and were eager to learn how to change their behavior.

Many of the women, on the other hand, had a different motivation for attending. They were eager to change, not their behavior, but that of their men! They were convinced that *they* didn't have an intimacy problem. As the class progressed, however, they began to realize that they needed help in this area as well.

Before I go any further, let me give you my definition of intimacy:

Intimacy is the feeling we get when we mutually open our minds and hearts in total acceptance of each other to truly hear what the other is saying and feel what the other is feeling. At its best, it is the sense of human connection at the level of the soul.

Study this definition carefully, phrase by phrase, and keep it in mind as you read this chapter. As you are well aware, it has little resemblance to the communication that goes on between most men and women today!

In his moving book, *Two Hearts Are Better Than One,*[1] Bob Mandel coins the word *into-me-see* as his way of looking at intimacy. This fits the above definition. To be open is to allow the other to see who we are, and to share what is deepest in our mind and soul.

Given these definitions, can we women point to people in our lives with whom we have this kind of intimacy? For most of us the answer is definitely yes: with our female friends. The level of connection that many of us find with each other is sublime. And why not? After all is said and done, we have all walked the same road in terms of our experience of being a female in our society.

For the most part, I can look at any female stranger, and despite the exterior appearance, I know, consciously or unconsciously, her internal conflicts, her insecurities, and much more. At some deep level, we all understand where the other is coming from, despite differences in the way we handle what we have been taught.

My closest friends and I have reached the point where we seldom judge each other, even if we don't always see eye to eye on a given issue. We accept the fact that we all have human frailties and know that we are all doing the best we can, even though we haven't quite reached perfection.

When my friends make suggestions as to how I can improve something in my life, I listen attentively. Even if I don't agree with their advice, I show appreciation for their caring, and vice versa. It should be noted that for many of us, this kind of communication was not prevalent prior to the women's movement. But in today's world, many women have found soul-mates in their "sisters."

Because of this deep female connection, a frequent cry among women is, "If only I could find a man who communicates with me the way my women friends do!" In this thought lies the basis of a very inaccurate assumption under which women have been operating:

> If we can feel so close to our female friends and not to our men, then obviously something must be wrong with the men.

While we might want to believe this conclusion—and after all, it does sound logical—the truth is that it doesn't hold up under close inspection. Furthermore, it is a powerless conclusion. As I discussed earlier, any time we blame the other sex for what is wrong in our relationships, we give away our power and abdicate responsibility for doing anything constructive to improve the situation.

The path of power lies in once again picking up our mirror instead of our magnifying glass, and asking ourselves if there is anything that we are doing to make the situation worse than it need be. Yes, men have difficulty opening up, but are there any barriers to intimacy that we are responsible for creating? I asked my female students to really look at this question with an open heart and see if they could find anything in their own and other women's behavior that would inhibit intimacy with the men in their lives. The following is the list they came up with, the length of which surprised us all.

How We Create Barriers to Intimacy

1. Our expectations are unrealistic.
2. We are not really open to men in the same way we are open to our female friends.
3. We don't always want to hear the truth . . . and the men know it!
4. Many of us prefer closed men and choose accordingly.

5. We judge what they say . . . and don't say.
6. We want to fix everything for them instead of just letting them tell us what is on their minds.
7. We often demand intimacy for unhealthy reasons.
8. We are too frightened of losing our identity to really let any man in.
9. We are competitive and need to have the last word.
10. We don't "see" their attempt to connect when it doesn't fit our picture.
11. We are confused about many issues and often send mixed signals.
12. We talk too much!
13. We often can't be trusted with what they tell us.
14. We are often truthful but not always honest about our motivations for being truthful.

I was impressed with the insight that this list represented for the women in the group. You might even be able to add a few more items to the list as a result of your own experiences.

In any case, it will be helpful to enlarge and clarify each of these statements so that you can get a better grasp as to how these behaviors stop intimacy dead in its tracks. While you might not identify with all the ideas presented, embrace those which hold a grain of truth for you and begin to turn around your behavior.

Again, while our tendency is to resist our own responsibility in the matter, our power lies in learning more about who we are and changing what doesn't work. Remember to keep in mind that I am not saying men do not need to work on this area of a relationship, or that women are to blame. There is no blame. There is only looking at ourselves with the understanding that we can do much to improve communication with members of the opposite sex, particularly with those who mean the most to us. Remember to keep a smile on your face, it helps to lighten up!

How We Create Barriers to Intimacy

1. Our expectations are unrealistic. The truth is that, generally speaking, men do not know how to open up with women, or anyone else for that matter! It isn't that they don't want to; they simply have not been trained to be open in the same way women have. There are a number of studies to back up this difference between men and women.

For example, in *"Intimate Strangers,"* Lillian Rubin describes a study of 200 men and women.[2] Two-thirds of the men in the study could not name a best friend. Of those who could, the best friend *was likely to be a woman.* (Does that surprise you?) In those rare instances when men named men as their best friends, they did not have intimacy in their sharing. They shared activities, but they could not discuss their feelings.

Three-quarters of the women in the study could easily mention a best friend, and *it was always a woman.* Even those women who were married picked a woman as their best friend. Their friendship involved not only activities, but self-revelation, nurturing, and emotional support. Given this information it follows that, *in terms of friendship and sharing, women are more important to men than men are to women.*

There are other studies that back up the idea that men are not as open with their feelings as are women.[3] Men are trained to be strong and silent, and most are very good in the role for which they've been trained. This does not make them bad or wrong, they are just good learners.

If men are not trained to communicate intimately with others, *why do we expect it?* Men won't open up because they have been taught that in order to survive in the society in which they have been raised, you keep your feelings to yourself. Very little has changed over the years. Men will stay that way until it's safe to let it all out. Certainly in terms of our society and in terms of the attitudes of both men and women today, it still isn't safe for a man to be open. Openness is still equated by too many with weakness, homosexuality, dependency, and other characteristics thought of as "unmanly."

Hence it's our expectation that is unjustified and is the cause of much of our unhappiness. A teacher of mine once told me, "Susan, if you want chicken soup, start with a chicken, not a veal chop." If you want real depth of verbal communication, look to a close female friend, a support group, or even a platonic male friend who feels freer to talk with you than your mate (for reasons I will mention later). The message here is to stop expecting to find it from your mate. If you find it, that's great, and I don't want to imply that there are no men who are open, but don't make it one of your expectations.

What you also might not understand is that *most men don't want to be emotionally closed.* Believe me! Both my professional and personal experiences have shown me that men desperately want to communicate with us, as well as with members of their own sex. Many express much loneliness and frustration because they are not comfortable communicating openly with anyone. When in trouble, they often have no one to talk to.

As frustrating as their silence may be for us at times, there has to be a place within our heart that takes us beyond our own wish to connect and allows us to see their frustration, rather than being the unloving critic who only sees someone who is "broken" and needs fixing. Because of our own insecurities, we take men's inability to communicate with us so personally, when in fact, with few exceptions, they don't communicate particularly well with anyone! Also, we look at them as deficient, when in fact the deficiency lies in our society and the way little boys are raised.

I am married to a man who is relatively quiet and introspective. In the beginning, I had a problem with his quietness. But as soon as I dropped my expectation that he communicate with me in the same way as my female friends, our relationship was transformed. I know his lack of openness is nothing personal.

He grew up in an English boarding school and was trained to survive by hiding his feelings. I also have learned to focus on the many other ways in which he makes me feel loved and supported. And isn't that what it's really about, anyway?

I know so many women who measure the soul-mate quotient of their men by the level of their verbal intimacy. To them, Mr. Right is that special someone who will reveal a magical depth of spiritual communion in the form of intense discussions about their deepest feelings. Unfortunately, this idyllic picture of the soul-mate is very hard for some women to give up, and, as a result, they are often alone. I don't even know if this kind of soul-mate exists or not; I seriously doubt it. In any case, I'm glad I didn't wait. Instead, I took the advice of someone who said that the likelihood of our finding our true soul-mate is very remote, indeed, but that we should take delight in knowing that we are with someone else's! Amen! I don't know whose soul-mate my husband Mark is, but I am thankful they didn't find each other. I feel blessed that we found each other instead.

2. We are not really open to men in the same way we are open to our female friends. As my students and I reflected on conversations that we have had with our female friends, we realized that the nature and content of these discussions differ greatly from those with the men in our lives.

We noted that basically our "female" discussions took one of two forms. We either moaned and groaned about life in general, paying particular attention to the shortcomings of our men, or, on a healthier note, we used our friends as sounding boards to help us work through problems we seemed to be having in our lives relative to men, work, or whatever. We listened to suggestions they made and thanked them for their help. "I feel so much better after talking to you," is a common utterance between females.

We then noticed that our discussions with men are quite different. The content of these discussions must obviously be altered since so much of what we talk about with women has to do with men. (They should only hear what we have to say about them!) Not only is the content of our conversations different, but our reactions to what they tell us are different. We noticed that when men gave us the same kind of feedback as we get from our female friends, we generally did not thank them for their help. We did not feel better. Instead, we found a need to defend our position and prove ourselves right. Their suggestions tended to be taken as a personal assault and, in retaliation, we set out to show them how messed up their lives are.

For example, one of my students was crying to her second husband about how upset she was about her relationship with her daughter. When her husband tried to tell her where she might improve the situation, she answered with, "Who are you to talk! You haven't spoken to your daughter for two years." She acknowledged that if a female friend had given her the same suggestion, despite what was going on in her friend's relationship with her daughter, she would have at least listened to what her friend was saying and thanked her for her ideas even if she didn't agree with them. It's no wonder that men often keep quiet instead of offering helpful suggestions.

Another reason we don't open up with our men in the same way we open up with women is that we are more dependent on our male relationships and therefore want to be seen in the most favorable light. With our female friends we are more likely to laugh at our foibles, our insecurities, our shortcomings. We trust our women friends will accept us unconditionally.

It stands to reason that the less dependent we are and the more secure we feel about ourselves, the more honest we can become in a male–female relationship. But until we gain that inner security and self-love, we will remain too frightened to reveal the truth about ourselves to the men we care so much about.

The truth is we are not really intimate with the men in our lives. We don't open up as fully or in the same way to men as we do to women. One of the men in my class lamented, "I was married for years and never knew what the heck my wife was thinking!" You can bet her female friends knew exactly what she was thinking! But most of us cannot as yet share that honesty with the men we love.

3. We don't always want to know the truth . . . and the men know it! One of my male students said that the reason he can be more intimate with platonic female friends is that there is no fear of reprisals. The truth is that women do not want to hear anything negative from their men—particularly in the area that they are most insecure.

One of my students brought the message home beautifully:

My husband owns his own business, and whenever he would share with me the problems he was having I would try to tell him how it was all his fault that he was having problems. Finally he said to me, "I see you don't want to deal with the problems I'm having at work. I'm not going to tell you anything anymore." I was insulted that he didn't want to tell me anything. And then one day I came to the realization that I really can't handle it. I don't want to hear it. I don't want to know. I just want him to tell me that everything is just great and the money is coming in. I'm aware of it now, but I'm really ashamed of the truth.

I assured her that there was nothing to feel ashamed of. Many financially dependent women feel the same way. I suggested that a healthy response to his statements might be:

I really get scared when you tell me that, because I feel so dependent on your ability to make money. So if I'm not receptive to your problems, please understand I'd like to be. I'm really working on feeling more secure.

I have a male friend who is an attorney. The deep, dark secret he kept from his wife was that he wanted to be a writer. She was dependent on him financially and he knew that she was threatened by his desire to be a writer and possibly leave his job. He purchased a word processor which he put in his basement and worked long hours into the night on his secret passion. He told her he was working on his cases, just work that he brought home from the office.

When he wanted to talk about his passion for writing, he called me. I asked him why he was afraid to tell his wife. He said he didn't have the strength to deal with her lack of encouragement and the put-downs that would ensue. I said, *"Feel the fear and do it anyway!"* It's better to have a more honest relationship even if there are reprisals.

He eventually did tell her and, indeed, she did put him down with such statements as "You could never make a living at writing!" and "Who told you you could write, anyway!" All these comments, of course, reflected her own insecurity. Her own fear kept her—and still keeps her—from opening her heart to the fact that because of the commitment he feels for her, he is not doing what he really wants to in life. She doesn't even notice and acknowledge that she is free to pursue anything she wants because of his willingness to support her financially. How sad for both of them.

When I made a career change a few years ago, my husband most willingly supported me financially. During that time, I found my old insecurities about money creeping in. As my new career became more and more financially successful, he could freely discuss any worries he was feeling about his business and I was able to be totally receptive. Obviously, on many levels:

Security and intimacy go hand in hand.

To demonstrate, let me create a scenario in which a man comes home from work and reveals that he is really scared because he grossly underestimated the budget in one of his projects. This mistake could cost him a great deal of money. Which of the following responses would lend itself to greater closeness and intimacy?

Insecure woman: "Well, why didn't you research it more thoroughly? You should know better than that! You've been in the business long enough. How could you make such a stupid mistake? We really can't afford it! How could you have been so careless?"

Secure woman: "Hey, don't worry so much about it. You'll find a way to work it out. And even if you made a mistake, so what! Everybody makes mistakes. We'll manage. We always have and we always will. I have all the faith in the world that whatever happens, we'll find a way to handle it. Not to worry. Hey, come here and give me a hug. I love you."

Same situation. Two different responses. The first woman is unwittingly an enemy to her man's self-esteem; the second is a friend. If you were a man, to which woman would you choose to reveal your feelings?

There are other situations when we really don't want to hear what our men are feeling. We all laughed when one of the women in class admitted that if she heard a burglar trying to enter her home, she really wouldn't want her husband to tell her that he was scared and didn't know what to do. What she would want is for him to act bravely, tell her to stay where she was, and calmly go fight the burglar single-handedly. Also, some, not all, of the women acknowledged that they didn't really want to know if men felt trapped in the relationship or were attracted to other women. And so on.

Despite what some of us would like to believe, men are not

fools. They know when it is safe to rock the boat and when it isn't. Most of the time, it isn't.

4. *Many woman prefer closed men and choose accordingly.* To complicate the matter even further, I was surprised to learn that some of my female students, especially the younger ones, were not turned on by open men. As young as they were, they felt that these men were wimpy and soft, even effeminate. These women were still victims of the "strong, silent" stereotype. As a result, they always chose men who were closed and then complained about the situation.

Interestingly, the older women had lived through too many negative experiences with the strong, silent type and were ready to be with men who were softer and more open and loving. To them, a really strong man is one who can let his vulnerabilities show and not be frightened by them.

But it was clear that manliness for many of the women was still equated with strength, not vulnerability. These women stated that they didn't want to feel like a mother to their men, and that's how it felt when the men opened up with them. It's significant that the women didn't feel like a mother when their female friends opened up to them. They saw that as sharing. What we concluded was that many of us were still looking for a father figure or a prince charming, both symbols of indomitable strength.

In any case:

Until we, as a unified body, create the critical mass that prefers warm, soft, delicious, and open men who are comfortable revealing all of who they are, men will continue to be "manly" and closed. They would be crazy not to be!

It is clearly up to us to change our tastes in order to make it safe for men to be open with us . . . or choose to be happy with men who are closed.

5. We judge what they say . . . and don't say. I have noticed that in the area of verbal intimacy, men are damned if they do and damned if they don't. If they do talk, many are judged on what they talk about and how they talk about it. If they don't talk, they are judged as being closed and hostile.

I remember a time when my friends and I constantly put men down for talking with each other about business, sports, cars, and so on. We felt so superior. I used to scoff at my male friends' attempts to communicate with their children or their parents. "Pathetic. He hasn't seen his father for months, and all they can talk about are the football scores!"

But when I learned to open my heart, I realized that, given who they were, their communication was perfect. This was their way of connecting, of sharing, of feeling close. Who was I to judge? But judge, I did . . . for many, many years. And today I listen to so many women exhibit the same criticalness I once felt.

Thankfully, there were many teachers in my life who taught me the error of my ways, who taught me to stop judging and to start loving. As a result, my intimacy with Mark has dramatically improved. The truth is:

> When we stop judging, men will begin to trust that we are on their side. When they have that trust, they can begin to open up.

No one is going to open up to you if he doesn't feel you will support who he is. He'd be a glutton for punishment if he did. Men do not like to always be told that they are inferior when it comes to communication, or anything else for that matter. Just like us, they want to know that it is all right to be who they are.

The more we acknowledge and support the beauty within our men, as we do with our female friends, the more they will want to be intimate with us.

Just as importantly, *as we support their beauty, our once criti-*

cal eyes begin to see only the beauty! And the circle of abundance in the relationship is begun. There is something about focusing on what is wonderful in life that makes life wonderful. So it is in looking at our men. Therein lies part of the answer to the frequently asked question, "Where are all the good men?" Beauty *is* in the eye of the beholder!

6. We want to fix everything for them instead of just letting them tell us what is on their minds. While it is natural to want to help our mates when they open up to us about problems they are having in some area of their lives, it usually isn't wise to do so. My career is about helping people when they open up to me, so it is quite natural for me to want to solve any problem my husband is having. I've learned to stop doing this.

In the first place, I usually don't know enough to assess the situation properly, especially when it comes to issues dealing with his career. Also, my advice is sometimes tied up with personal considerations or insecurities; hence I am not as objective with my husband as I can be with a student or a friend. And finally, when I give him advice, I tend to be disgruntled if he doesn't follow it!

So how do we respond when our men open up to us? We listen. We empathize with statements such as, "I understand why that would be upsetting to you." If they ask for our advice, we recognize their individuality and simply say, "I can't speak for you, but if it were me, I might try this . . . or this. But we are all different, so you really have to do what feels right for you." We encourage with statements such as, "I trust it will all be fine. Not to worry! Whatever happens, you'll handle it!" We let go and recognize that if they don't follow whatever advice we have given, it is nothing personal. Everybody has to follow their own instincts. If things don't turn out the way they want, we soothe them with the thought that life is a learning experience and as long as they have learned something for the next time, all is well.

This happens to be one area where men are benevolent culprits. They are even more compelled than we are to be fixers, since that has been their assigned role and many feel very inadequate when they can't solve our problems. However, once again, it is to the benefit of all concerned that we first and foremost alter our own behavior . . . not theirs.

7. We often demand intimacy for unhealthy reasons. There are many of us who have a deep fear of being without a man. Alone in life, we experience varying degrees of emptiness, loss, and despair. When we have these painful feelings, we desperately seek out another person to fill us up and make the pain go away. We find, however, that this "fix" never fixes; it only masks the pain.

I attribute these painful feelings to what Dr. Roberto Assagioli, the father of psychosynthesis, calls "Divine Homesickness," a condition that is created when we are, often unknowingly, out of touch with our own center, our own essence. We truly *are* lost. We've drifted far from our own inner Home.

This Divine Homesickness has a powerful effect on our expectations in terms of intimacy. Because of our need to connect, silence can be excruciating when we are in the presence of another person. Hence, when our men are quiet, because they are reading, involved in their own thoughts, or whatever, our sense of isolation is activated. We sometimes can feel lonelier with someone than if we were actually alone!

What results is hurt, disappointment, and anger, sometimes rage, that the other person is not filling us up. And the judgment begins. We are convinced that a different man would better fill our needs. We try changing our men, yet the pattern goes on. Ultimately, we become convinced that men in general are terribly deficient when it comes to filling our needs. In this way, the stereotypes are born.

Many of my female students identified with this feeling. One reported that her way of dealing with the void was to start a fight about something. Anything was better than the silence! Even though there was no intimacy—only frustration and anger—at least there was connection. Another student reported that her boyfriend wouldn't even react to her attempts to pick a fight. The more he remained self-contained, the more vicious her verbal attacks became—anything to get a reaction. She said it was a wonder he didn't kill her!

You might be wondering why men seem to tolerate silence better than we do. Some don't. But many men have been trained to hide so many of their feelings, that, generally speaking, they are more comfortable going within themselves. In fact, our need for constant verbal exchange can put them on unsteady ground since that is not an area in which they feel proficient.

On a happier note, there are many of us women who have learned or who are in the process of learning how to connect with that wonderful place within, and to us, being alone can be a joy. No need for the radio, the television, or the telephone. We have learned that silence can be wonderful whether we are alone or whether we are with someone else.

It takes a real commitment to learn how to make that essential connection with our inner selves. And once we do, a constant vigil is necessary. There are so many forces that seem to pull us away from our center. We get caught up in these externals— our possessions, societal expectations, need for status and power, and relationships, to name a few. We must learn to be conscious of when we are straying away from our inner sense of peace and power. We can't look to someone else to hear those silent screams. Once we can answer our own cry for help, we need never feel lonely again.

8. We are too frightened of losing our identity to really let any man in. A new breed of woman has emerged in recent years—the no-need woman. In our desperate struggle to pull away from our dependency needs, many of us have become independent to an extreme. Having worked so hard to stand on our own two feet, we are petrified of falling back into old patterns, and as a result we begin closing off that part of ourselves that has normal human needs.

We notice that whenever we get involved with a man, old dependency patterns emerge. Once again we find ourselves waiting by the telephone, losing our focus on our career, seeking his approval, and so on. Panic takes over and we close our hearts to the person we have begun to love. This is often the time in which we cause the end of the relationship, either by bolting or by becoming so hostile in the relationship that he decides to leave.

What makes matters worse for the no-need woman is that underneath that independent exterior, her need for love and nurturing begins to mount, and she has to work harder and harder to maintain her independent stance. Consciously or unconsciously, she always has to be on guard to protect her new-found strength.

One woman in my workshop remembered an incident that typifies such a woman:

I remember crying one night about something that had transpired with my son. My boyfriend, who didn't have a clue as to what was the matter, came over to comfort me. He said, "Put your arms around me. Let me hold you. Tell me what's the matter." I sat there crouched with my arms crossed and locked around my chest. A truck couldn't have pulled my arms apart. I simply couldn't let him in. I realize now that underneath all my pretense at independence, I really wanted to open up my arms and let in his love. But I was so afraid of needing anyone that I felt I would literally die if I released my arms and let him in. It was as though my very survival were at stake. It wasn't until many years later when I attained a strong sense of self-trust that I could allow someone in with the confidence that I wouldn't let him take me away from myself.

One of my students adopted her independent stance as a result of watching how her parents related:

I've never been a very dependent person. My mother is dependent, however. My parents have a fairly decent relationship, at least on the surface. But I hate what I see in that relationship. I see my mother as very dominated by my father, and I would never want a relationship like that. As a result, I'm a very self-sustaining person. And as you speak about letting someone in, I find all kinds of fears coming up with me. I would love to be intimate, but to me, that's terrifying.

When we take the stance of the ultra-independent woman, we are constantly pushing men away. We don't admit to our friends, or even ourselves, how much need lies within. To accept love and nurturing is too terrifying because it reminds us of the pain of helplessness . . . the pain of the Child-Within. Perhaps our isolation is a necessary step to where we want to go. Sometimes we must exaggerate new behavior until it becomes second nature. We can then relax a little and let go of the defenses. In that sense, our extreme independence can be looked upon as part of a healthy progression.

It is clear, however, that until self-trust is firmly established, our hearts will remain closed. And when we close our hearts to men, because we are determined to show them and the rest of the world how strong we are, intimacy is impossible. If we cannot admit to normal human needs, we cannot be intimate.

9. *We are competitive and need to have the last word.* As a past master of self-righteousness, I know this barrier to intimacy very well. There is no question that our need to be right gets in the way of our listening to what the other person is saying. We are so intent on proving our point that a simple discussion

can escalate to a major battle, or, depending on the man, can shut him up entirely.

As I discussed earlier, those of us who are still very insecure about ourselves have a frantic need to validate our point of view. The more inferior we feel, the more self-righteous we become. It requires a great deal of work on our self-esteem before we feel strong enough to eliminate our defenses. It is very difficult to have an intimate relationship with a wall!

10. We don't "see" their attempt to connect when it doesn't fit our picture. Most men really do want to connect with us, even though it is often difficult on a verbal level. They attempt intimacy and closeness in many other ways, although we may not not recognize it as such. I asked the men in my class to tell how they express intimacy to women. Here are some of their responses:

Sex

Gifts

Touching

Listening

Spending time with them

Talking about the day's events

Taking care of them

Telephone calls

We often do not recognize that all of these are attempts at closeness. In fact, sometimes we push men's attempts away, especially in the area of sex. For example, one female student complained that every time she and her boyfriend have a fight, he gets sexually aroused and wants to make love. Her usual response is, "Don't touch me, you animal! How could you want to make love when we are in the middle of a fight!" I pointed out to her that this was simply his attempt to be intimate with her. The upset that arguments bring is often very painful and confusing to men. Since they often have difficulty getting close through words, they sometimes resort to sex, which they associate with closeness. One man in the group smiled and reported that his wife deliberately creates fights because she knows at the end of it is sex. As men sometimes use sex to communicate, women sometimes use fights to communicate. Anything to connect!

So you see, men attempt closeness in many ways, but we sometimes get hung up on form. *We don't focus enough on what men do for us, but rather on what they don't.* As a result, we feel scarcity in the relationship instead of the abundance that is often there.

11. We are confused about many issues and often send mixed signals. This is a time of transition. We are giving up an unhealthy way of relating to ourselves and others and searching for one that is more satisfying. Transition, however, brings with it confusion. As I described in Chapter 1, I believe that this confusion is simply part of the process of becoming clear; but when we are confused, we certainly are not sending clear signals—to ourselves or to anyone around us. In fact, very often we lie to ourselves. In trying to become strong, we deny the human need for bonding and nurturance, and in trying to find someone to take care of us, we deny our inner strength. Either way, we are left confused as to who we really are.

Even more confused are the men who want to make us happy. This is the time for the damned-if-they-do-and-damned-if-they-don't syndrome. "Don't you think I can take care of myself!?!" At the same time, consciously or unconsciously, we become hostile when we feel we are not being taken care of. Our behavior can be crazy-making!

Until we are more sure of who we are and what we really want in life, our signals will continue to be mixed, making it very difficult for men to approach us on an intimate level. This isn't good or bad, it just is. It doesn't mean we have to have it all worked out before intimacy is possible; but it does mean we have to reach the point where we can take responsibility for our own lives and realize that when we are confused, it has to do with us, not them. At that point, when we are free from judgment, we can at least begin to share our deep confusion and concerns with the men we love instead of blaming them for everything that is wrong in our lives.

We can begin the challenging task of self-exploration with some journal work. In a notebook, begin creating endings to such statements as:

I hide from myself the fact that . . .
I hide from you the fact that . . .
What scares me most in life is . . .
What makes me happiest in life is . . .
What I am most confused about in life is . . .

Spend at least a half hour on each statement and write whatever comes into your head, even if it sounds silly to you. As you keep writing, you will soon get past the rational mind that blocks what is going on inside. Work with your journal regularly so that you can begin to chip away at those secrets carefully kept.* We will have to be patient with ourselves until this kind of honesty shines through. It will then be possible for us to ask in a more direct way for our needs to be met. Intimacy requires bringing out the essence of who we are. Without a clue as to what is going on with us, intimacy becomes very difficult.

---

*Journal writing can be very satisfying and revealing. You might want to investigate journal writing workshops in your area.

---

12. We talk too much! Oh, yes! Women can be wonderfully verbal beings. So wonderful that it is difficult for the less verbal among us to get a word in edgewise! One of my students gave the following account of her experience with, as she put it, "my big mouth":

> In the beginning of my relationship with Joe, I thought our conversations were wonderful, until one day I realized that I was always giving a monologue! I decided to stop talking so much (which was not easy for me to do) and see if it left him any space to say something about what was going on with him. In the beginning, he was uncomfortable with my new quieter stance and kept asking if there was anything wrong. I assured him there wasn't and told him I realized I did most of the talking and didn't leave him any room to open up to me. He said he loved to hear me talk. I told him I loved to hear him talk, too. It took a while, but soon he began to open up. And the more comfortable I get with silence, ironically, the more he opens up. Now it's a much more even exchange.

Some of us women have an incredible need to fill in the space when there is a moment of silence. We have to learn to put a zipper on our mouths in order to allow the less verbally assertive men to speak. This isn't to say that the reverse doesn't occur as well. Men, too, have been known to take over conversations, but in truth this is more comfortable for us than their being silent, as we feel less isolated when there is noise of any kind in the room.

13. We often can't be trusted with what they tell us. As I've already discussed, we are much more open with our friends than men are with theirs. This includes our being open about *their* "secrets." "You mean you told Jeannie what I told you!" And indeed we have told Jeannie what he told us! Little is sacred in terms of what we tell our friends. And the men sense this. Therefore, they tend to be cautious about what they communicate to us. Men simply are not comfortable sharing what is going on with them, sometimes even with their closest friends.

This was vividly brought home to me when I was dating Josh, a very verbal but emotionally closed man. One Saturday afternoon, when Josh had gone to the market, Al, one of his best friends, called to say hello. Al and Josh had been friends for twenty years and spoke to each other almost every day. So it was natural for me to tell Al the truth when he asked the question, "How's the relationship going?" The truth was that the relationship was not going very well. Later, when Josh came home, I told him to return Al's call. He asked what we had talked about, and I repeated our rather brief conversation. Much to my surprise, he blew up. "How dare you tell him anything about what is going on between us! It's none of his business!" I then realized that as close as Josh and Al were as friends, they never really discussed what was going on in either of their lives.

Certainly this was not the case with my friends and me. We all knew exactly what was going on in our relationships and most everything else in our lives. At that moment, I felt great sadness for Josh as I realized how alone he must have felt going through life revealing himself to no one. I, on the other hand, drew great comfort and support from the fact that my friends and I shared so much of our lives with each other.

The important point, however, is that when men fear that what they tell us is not going to remain within the realm of the relationship, it stands to reason that they will be more cautious about what they reveal to us. Hence, if we want them to open up to us, we will have to have more respect for their need for privacy.

Also, men have complained to me, personally and professionally, that what they say to us is often later used against them in heated moments. It's as though we collect ammunition to bring out when an argument ensues. Men often marvel at our incredible memories. When they can't even remember saying certain things, we can remember the date, time, and what each of us was wearing! Again, what this signals to our men is that they have to be careful in what they tell us. It is clear that for intimacy to occur, men will have to trust that what they tell us will not be held against them at a later time. We have to learn to keep our remarks to the subject at hand, instead of bringing up old "evidence" from the past.

14. *We are often truthful, but not always honest about our motivations for being truthful.* One of my students came up with her own definition of intimacy: openness without trying to control. In true intimacy, it is necessary that our only motive be to share with someone the essence of who we really are. But in fact, this rarely is the case. I have noticed that, with our men, most of our "honesty" comes out when there is something bothering us. "I'm just telling you how I feel!" Very often our honesty is really about manipulation and control, or about hurting or putting someone down.

One student, who was working very hard on saving her marriage, said she thought she was her husband's best friend until she really started to look at what she does. Under the guise of honesty, she often was brutally hurtful. She told us:

> While what I told him was true, my intent in telling him was not to communicate, but to damage his ego. If I think about it, why would he ever want to tell me anything? I can be such a devastating person for him to talk to because I want to tell him all the things about him I think are terrible. Who needs to hear it? I'd hate him if he did the same thing to me. Only a masochist would want to be intimate with me. Someone who loves punishment!

I pointed out to her that her awareness as to what was going on was the first step in changing it. I also warned her not to be so hard on herself. It's true that when we take that first look in the mirror, we sometimes can be horrified in what we see. Once again, we must remember that we are all doing the best we can. When we behave in a way that lacks integrity, it is because of our own insecurities and fears. It follows that our next step should be to get to work on improving our sense of self.

In the meantime, we must continue to stay aware. And when we start the attack, we must be able to understand what is going on. It would be helpful at those times to say, "For some reason I'm feeling very needy right now. That's why I am attacking you." That awareness opens the door to intimacy. At least this opening allows your partner to say, "What is it that you are needing right now?" If we simply attack, the whole exchange ends up in a huge fight, which totally masks what is really going on.

I could go on, but I think that by now you have the picture. If we want to be more intimate with the men in our lives, we must learn how to be true friends to them, just as we are to our female friends. In any conversation with a man in your life, you need to ask yourself the following questions:

If I were talking to my best friend, what would I say?
If I were talking to my best friend, how would I react?
If I were talking to my best friend, how would I listen?
If I were talking to my best friend, how would I empower?
If I were talking to my best friend, how would I be loving?

Then do it with the man in your life. It's letting somebody tell you who he is and you being there to support him as if he were your best friend. It's opening your heart and recognizing that this is someone who is doing the very best he can. As we begin to transform our behavior by focusing on the fourteen points mentioned above, little by little, step by step, we can begin to change the patterns that create separation. And who knows? Maybe a soul-mate lies within that man behind the mask!

Intimacy Affirmations

I am opening up to the best within me.

I am a loving and accepting person.

I listen and I hear.

I open my heart to receive.

I am becoming more confident every day.

I am creating a beautiful relationship.

I love who you are.

I see the beauty within you.

I support who you are.

I have all that I need within me.

I am your best friend.

I am my best friend.

I am on your side.

I am letting in your love.

I accept we are both doing the very best we can.

I am sending you thoughts of love.

I choose to be happy instead of "right."

7

BUT YOU PROMISED!

When the most wonderful man I had ever known lied to me about something in his past, I was devastated. The incident in his past didn't bother me; his lying about it did. Though the relationship was still new, I was sure I had finally found a man whom I could trust with all my heart . . . and, then, to find out that he was a lying creep! It was almost too much to take!

His cries of "I was afraid I'd lose you if you found out" only seemed to make my disdain grow. I self-righteously accused him of being a pathetic coward. My hurt and disappointment were so intense that I almost ended the relationship on the spot. Thankfully, experience had taught me not to make such a rash decision in such an agitated state.

Over the next few days, I despaired with the realization that I could no longer trust him completely. My rage was uncontrollable at times. And so was my sadness. After all, if he deceived me once, he could do it again. How could I love someone I couldn't trust? Haven't we been taught that trust is one of the most important ingredients of a relationship?

Another disturbing question lurked in the depths of my despair. He really was an incredibly wonderful person. I knew he cared deeply. I knew our relationship was important to him. I knew that in the depths of his being, he really wanted what was best for me. I asked myself, given all this, if I couldn't trust him, who could I trust? My moment of enlightenment came when a voice from within answered, "probably no one!"

I really didn't want to hear that. The implications were too upsetting. If total trust was one of my conditions for a relationship—and it was—I would probably be alone for the rest of my life. It wasn't that I thought I couldn't survive on my own. I knew I could. I had for years, very successfully and very happily. But I was then at a point in my life where I wanted to create a loving relationship with a man and eventually remarry. Hence, I had some serious thinking to do about my attitude about trust. Maybe if I could change my thinking, I wouldn't have to change my man!

I first asked myself, "Why do so many of us feel such a sense of betrayal when our men don't tell us the truth? Why the incredible hurt?" It occurred to me that maybe our emphasis on trust tends to be a bit overdone when it comes to our men. From them, we expect truthfulness 100 percent. Maybe expecting 100 percent of anything from another human being is asking for trouble. Maybe our clawing at this notion of trust with such tenacity is self-destructive and relationship-destructive.

I then asked myself, "Do I expect 100 percent trust from everyone in my life?" My mind immediately went back to the time my children were very young. They lied all the time, blatantly. Nothing subtle about them. "We did *not* break the ashtray; the turtle did!" I even considered recording their lies for posterity, they were so clever.

Yet with all their lying, I never stopped loving them. Trying to be a responsible mother, I pointed out the evil of their ways. Underneath, however, I chuckled to myself with the understanding that kids will be kids. They will do anything to protect themselves. It has finally occurred to me that, like it or not, *adults will be kids as well.* While they look all grown up, their egos are sometimes stuck at the level of the playpen. They are often frightened of losing something they value and, at such times, may tell a lie or two to protect themselves.

I then looked into my mirror and asked, "Mirror, mirror on the wall, who is the most honest of us all?" The mirror responded that it was probably some little old lady in the heart of Kansas, but it certainly was not me! The mirror found me out. Yes, I had told a few lies in my time to save my hide. And had I told Mark *everything* about my past? Indeed I did . . . well, except for those things I didn't want him to know. And although I tried valiantly, I could not come up with any great "spiritual" explanation for my lying. I finally had to admit that I was simply playing the same game as he had played—self-preservation.

The mirror revealed something else. If the truth be known, I was feeling a definite sense of relief underneath all my self-righteous rage. I think it had something to do with freedom. I had been working very hard to approach this relationship with an unnatural degree of perfection. It was beginning to feel oppressive—like a life sentence. It's very limiting when you try to be perfect. My discovery of his lie let me out of my self-imposed jail, and it allowed me to be human as well. I don't mean this in a "Now I can lie, too" sense, but purely in the sense of, "Hey, we all make mistakes." Trying to maintain impossible standards for ourselves creates an intense feeling of being trapped!

Maybe total trust—or total anything—is not within the bounds of reason. Why couldn't I summon up the same understanding I felt for my children or myself when the man in my life lied to me? I guess it has to do with a basic insecurity that many women experience.

We look for wholeness through our mates; hence, not only are we afraid of being abandoned, but we are also afraid to leave. Our fear of abandonment creates our need to possess and control. Our fear of leaving creates our need to have the "perfect" man so that we won't have to leave. No wonder we become enraged when we have been lied to: we feel a loss of control *and* we realize he isn't perfect.

One comical result of the kind of insecurity I'm talking about is that it causes us to desperately look for a guarantee, often in situations in which a guarantee is impossible. The wedding ceremony offers a perfect example. There are people marrying for the second or third or more times still uttering the words "until death do us part." Are they serious? Haven't they learned by their own experience that life doesn't work that way? Wouldn't it be more honest for them to say that they will love, honor, and . . . whatever . . . until it doesn't work for them anymore, however long that may be? But who wants to ruin their marriage ceremony with truth? We all want the guarantee.

Even with my awareness of all this, my own need for security still prompts me, every now and then, to ask Mark stupid questions such as, "Will you love me forever?" Being sensitive to my needs, he obliges with a tender, "Of course I will." Music to my ears, even though I'm subliminally aware that it would be more honest for him to tell me, "At this moment I feel I will love you forever." He needn't even add the logical sentence that would follow. "Who can predict what the future holds?" This is honest. That I can trust . . . but do I really want to hear that? Absolutely not! I want the guarantee, even if it is a "lie."

If insecurity is at the root of our unrealistic expectations, the answer to the problems relating to trust is self-evident. It lies in getting to the place deep within us all that understands that there really is no one we totally can trust . . . except ourselves. I don't mean trusting ourselves to never tell a lie; I mean trusting ourselves to handle whatever anyone else does to us. The bottom line is this:

> The only thing we can safely trust is our ability to handle whatever anyone says or does to us!

Really emblazon this thought in your mind. For in this kind of thinking lies our sense of inner peace. No longer do we have to control the actions or thoughts of the men in our lives. No longer do we have to feel outraged or betrayed when they change their minds. Whatever happens relative to the people in our lives, we will be able to handle it.

Aside from our peace of mind, there are definite advantages to this kind of thinking. In the first place, we can breathe a sigh of relief knowing we won't have to retreat to a convent for the rest of our lives. And while this new attitude may take a little romance out of our lives, we shouldn't feel disillusioned. On the contrary, we can feel wiser and in much better control of our lives and our relationship. The mere debunking of the fairy tale expectation of perfect trust creates a healthier and more compassionate way of relating. When we really trust ourselves, the fear goes away . . . and what's left is the love.

As for me, I guess I'll always want Mark to tell me he'll love me forever. It does sound divine. But my heart will rest a little easier knowing I don't have to hold him to it. We are a race of imperfect individuals, and while he is a beautiful person, he is, after all, human.

To keep it in the realm of the fairy tale: my prince has gained back a few characteristics of the frog, but frogs are really lovable once you get to know them. Now that my mirror has revealed my own froglike tendencies, I realize that I would not really be compatible with a fairy tale prince. So, you see, everything works out just as it's supposed to; not necessarily how we imagined it, but exactly as it's supposed to.

At this point, you might be feeling that I have been dealing much too lightly and superficially with the issue of trust. So let's get "heavy" for a moment. I know that there are trust issues that carry very deep emotional scars—issues such as a mate leaving or infidelity. These kinds of events can be devastating and invariably create deep pain within us. Can the same principles apply? Can we learn to look at these situations in a way that won't wipe us out? Indeed we can.

Maxine felt totally betrayed and devastated when her husband of twenty-three years left her for another woman. Her reaction to the situation was fairly predictable and understandable: "That creep! I gave him the best years of my life. I trusted him and look what he did to me! I'll never trust another man as long as I live." All her "friends" rushed to her side and supported her in her outrage. "That animal! You poor thing. How could he do such a thing to you!" (Notice the "victim" mentality.)

What could they have told her instead that might have eased the pain and humiliation she was feeling and helped her to open up her heart? They could have suggested that instead of feeling betrayed she might realize that her husband shared a very large part of his life with her; twenty-three years is a long time. A lot of people never have that kind of loyalty and continuity in their relationships. It was now simply a time for both of them to move on to a new beginning. Her friends might have pointed out to her that he brought her a lot of joy in those twenty-three years (or why would she have stayed!).

After her pain had subsided somewhat, they might have told her that it would be very healing to work on letting go of her anger so that she could ultimately come to thank him for the things he gave to the marriage.

They could have told her that she has a beautiful life in front of her and that while it doesn't feel like that now, there is light at the end of the tunnel. They might have pointed out the many stories of women who have been in similar situations and who have grown enormously when on their own after so many years. Their sense of self-esteem flourished as they unleashed their own power. Most were thankful that they were given the opportunity to discover a new love in their life—themselves.

They could have told her that she had unrealistic expectations about "forever"; that when he originally said "forever," he really meant it. But human beings sometimes change their minds. We have always been told that "nothing lasts forever." So why do we expect that relationships are an exception? Even if the relationship is blissfully happy, one partner has to die eventually. We must always be prepared to be able to stand alone. We cannot trust "forever." There is only now.

After many years of bitterness, someone finally did tell Maxine all these things, and thankfully she heard. Only then was she able to deal with her hurt and humiliation and release her anger toward her ex-husband. And her new life began.

I don't want to minimize the anguish that this kind of experience can have on a person. A mourning period is an important part of the process, and saying good-bye is never easy. We must, however, go through the pain facing forward instead of backward, knowing time heals our wounds. "This, too, shall pass." When we go through our pain facing backward, we are caught in the quicksand of hopelessness and longing. We want what was, not what could be. But we can't go back, no matter how hard we try. It is better to turn around and go forward.

A dear friend of mine, Bobbie Probstein, wrote a very moving book about her odyssey from excruciating pain to a sense of inner peace after Larry, her husband of twenty-eight years, left her for another woman. She aptly titled the book *Return to Center: The Flowering of Self-Trust.*[1] The center is exactly where we all must return in order for us to open our hearts. The book describes the magical and sometimes painful spiritual path that Bobbie followed and the wisdom she garnered from a number of very wise teachers as she struggled to let go of her rage and her "victim" role after Larry left.

At one point she asked one of her teachers, "How do I give up my fantasies of getting back together, as well as giving up the man I loved and trusted with my life?" His answer:

> You do it by letting go of the need for a future that has a shape you know, and you do it by letting go of the past and what it was or was not. You become a child again—tender and loving and vulnerable and creating and daring, and you do this by letting go of everything that is not real.[2]

And what is *not* real for all of us are our fantasies about what other people are supposed to be in our lives.

Bobbie's story has an interesting twist. At about the time she let go of her "forever and ever" fantasies and began looking forward to the unseen adventures of life that lie ahead of her, Larry asked if he could come back. She didn't know the answer to that immediately, but eventually said yes. They didn't "go back," however. They began anew. Their relationship is very different this time around. Larry has joined Bobbie on her "return to center" pathway. He has been transformed by what he is learning about himself and the world around him. And as for their future, I can't improve on Bobbie's words:

> How did we come to this wondrous point in our lives? That we are here is enough. Perhaps the pain cleansed instead of soured us, for we live each day in appreciation of the other, rarely dwelling on the past, and planning for a future in which we continue to share our love and bounty in an ever-widening circle. I dare not ask if it will linger: to demand that it does would be to destroy its precious fragility, like a bubble burst by a poking finger. We teeter on the brink of new discoveries, of falling into old chasms, and walk the Way hand in hand.[3]

I often ask myself if I could similarly reunite with my husband after he had been involved with another woman. I honestly don't have the answer to that. I would hope that I could find the same kind of forgiveness that Bobbie found. What is clear, however, and what keeps me feeling peaceful, is the absolute trust that my life would go forward no matter what happened in my marriage. I love Mark more than I have ever loved any man, yet I know I am whole without him. The freedom in that kind of certainty is awesome! This isn't to say that I wouldn't mourn the loss if the relationship ended. It is only to say that I know I would get to the other side and go on to live a beautiful life.

Ironically, that certainty has come about as a result of my first marriage having ended and my discovery of the magnificent vistas that lie on the other side of the pain. I felt very insecure in my first marriage. Strangely, my divorce laid the groundwork for my being able to feel much more secure in my present marriage . . . another reminder that it is all happening perfectly even when it doesn't feel like it at the time.

Infidelity, even when our partner does not want to leave the marriage, is a challenge to our keeping an open heart. Again, our reactions are a matter of choice, and our perceptions determine our choice. If we perceive our mates as human beings who won't always follow our script, we can keep an open heart. If we have fairy tale expectations, our hearts can be easily broken and it is hard to "fix" them again.

This doesn't mean we have to stay in a relationship that does not serve our well-being. It does mean, however, that if we understand we are all human beings doing the best we can, including our mates, we can leave the relationship with a much more open heart, thus taking a lot of hurt out of the healing process. Again, our ultimate security in life comes from that inner knowing—that inner trust—that whatever choice we make, our lives will work just fine.

I might add that there are those who choose partners "knowing" they are going to be unfaithful. Their sense of denial is so strong that they avoid all the signals. One of my students married someone she had found in bed with another woman just weeks before their wedding. While he begged forgiveness, claiming it was just his last fling before their marriage, no one believed him, except her.

Now, three years later, she came to me complaining bitterly that her husband is having an affair. I asked her why she was so surprised; she had already caught him in one infidelity before they married. Further, he was married to someone else when he began dating her. She had deluded herself into believing that it would be different with her, but on a deeper level she had to know what she was getting into. She made the decision to marry knowing he had a problem being faithful to one woman. It wasn't that he was a bad person; he wasn't. He simply had a lot of problems about self-worth that he had to work out. Obviously, he still hadn't worked them out.

This isn't even to say that she shouldn't have married him; no one can be the judge of that. The marriage might have been exactly what they both needed on their path toward self-discovery. Sometimes we need to tread murky waters before getting to the other side. Sometimes we need to repeat the same patterns over and over again until we get it right. So rather than complain about him, I asked her to see if she could take responsibility for the situation and ask herself why she chose to marry him in the first place.

As she looked within, a lot of her own "frog" qualities came to the fore. She began to see the many lies she had told herself . . . and ultimately him. The truth was that she did know what she was getting into, but she married him anyway for a variety of "survival" reasons. She married him because he offered financial security and she was tired of living on her meager salary. She married him because she didn't feel like starting all over again with another man. She married him because her biological clock was running out and she wanted to begin a family. She married him because everyone had been invited to the wedding and it would be too humiliating to cancel. She married him because she was afraid she wouldn't find anyone else. This is not to say that she didn't love him; but in this case, love was not the determining factor in the decision she made to marry him.

As she acknowledged all these truths about herself; her anger toward him began to diminish. She was unhappy about her own behavior in the matter, but, in time, even that dissipated as she came to terms with her "dark side." She still loves him but decided to leave the marriage realizing that his need for other women was not OK with her. What was important is that she left with an open heart and they remain good friends. Embracing her own humanness allowed her to deal with his.

Given all I have said, I believe there are certain basics of trust that need to be there for a relationship to flourish and for our hearts to remain open. Clearly they are not the "he can't ever tell a lie" variety. These basics are as follows:

I trust that you care about my well-being.
I trust that you do not want to hurt me.
I trust that you respect my feelings.

And the ultimate in trust . . .

I trust that I will be able to handle
whatever happens in our relationship.

With this trust, we need also to have understanding.

I understand you are a human being
and not always perfect.

I understand that sometimes your own needs
get in the way of your caring about my well-being.

I understand that you really are doing the best you can.

With this kind of trust and this kind of understanding, our hearts can remain open and we can rest a little easier.

Given that we are with someone who fills the basic trust requirements (and if you are not, why are you there?), how do we pull ourselves out of the destructive traps of mistrust that seem always to be lurking? What can we do to relax and let go?

There are times when my jealousy (a definite sign of mistrust!) gets the better of me. This is my clue that I am feeling a definite lack of self-trust. At these times, I notice I act the most obnoxiously! It's hard to keep my Chatterbox from going on incessantly when I am feeling noncentered. What has helped to center me and take away my neediness during those painful times of insecurity is to put my relationship in perspective relative to the rest of my life.

I know that when I am feeling the most insecure about my relationship, I am making it the only thing in my life, as follows:

WHOLE LIFE

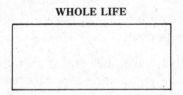

Relationship

If my relationship disappeared, my life would look like this:

WHOLE LIFE

Empty. Black. Bleak. Feeling like this, it is no wonder I feel frightened about losing my relationship and allow myself to experience such negative emotions as jealousy and mistrust. Yet there is another way of looking at my life that takes away the desperate feeling. (One of the clues you have of this feeling of desperation is that you are "plugged in"; that is to say, you can't seem to stop harping on an issue.)

Whenever I feel this way, I make myself focus on the abundance I have created in my life. I have my loving family and friends, my work that nourishes me, the alone time that I treasure, and so on. I can then see my life as looking like this:

WHOLE LIFE GRID

Relationship	Alone Time	Family
Friends	Spiritual Growth	Contribution
Playtime	Personal Growth	Career

What a difference! Now I see a full, rich life. My relationship is only one part of my life. If my relationship disappeared, my life would now look like this:

WHOLE LIFE

	Alone Time	Family
Friends	Spiritual Growth	Contribution
Playtime	Personal Growth	Career

Yes, there is an empty space in my life, but I wouldn't feel wiped out. When my first marriage ended, I didn't see my life as full and rich. Now I do. I've created it that way. With this in mind, I am able to center and remind myself that I have created *my own universe* and I am not dependent on anyone else's. I can then say to myself:

Mark is a very important part of my life, but he is not my whole life. I trust he has my best interests at heart. I also trust that if I lose the relationship for any reason whatsoever, I will go on to have a beautiful life.

After I repeat this to myself a few times, I begin to relax and let go and realize that whatever happens relative to my relationship, *I will handle it!* I also remind myself that, while relationship is one of the most important areas of my life, I have meaning and purpose in the other areas as well, and I renew my commitment to participating fully in all parts of my life.

You will notice that I have a box in the grid called "contribution." This is the area of your life in which you ask yourself, "What can I do to help the world?" When we participate in helping others, we experience the sublime joy of connectedness and inner beauty. Make this category a must in your grid. When you are feeling empty about your life, you are not in touch with the fact that you make a difference. By simply reaching out, you eventually live into the feeling.

Another process that works really well for me when I am feeling insecure is as follows:

Close your eyes and in your mind's eye, simply stand up tall and cut the imaginary umbilical cord that destructively ties you to men in your life. See yourself as strong and whole. Really get in touch with that feeling of cutting the cord and standing proudly and lovingly on your own.

Our insecurity is, I believe, only our primitive fear of truly leaving our childhood behind and being on our own. We all want the security of being attached to someone else who will save us. But when we cut the cord and see ourselves standing on our own, we get in touch with our own power. Our fear is greatly diminished, and we can become loving and trusting once again.

Perhaps a more dramatic way of seeing the cord is to see it around our necks. Unless we cut it, we will strangle ourselves to death, especially when it comes to our emotions and our spirit. Take a deep breath and feel the infusion of life when you don't have that self-imposed shackle around your neck cutting off your life!

Close your eyes and try this process right now. Cut the cord to whatever you are feeling attached to in your life and breathe a sigh of release.

It is important to see that other person as standing strongly on his own as well. Often we feel guilty when we cut the cord, as though our mates couldn't stand on their own unless they were attached to us. I know it is a blow to our ego to realize that our significant others can survive without us. The truth, whether we want to hear it or not, is that our mates certainly can make it on their own. If they choose to be miserable as you stand on your own two feet, it is important to realize that they have made that choice. Ultimately, they will learn from the experience. We are responsible to our mates, we are not responsible for them. It is demeaning to them to think they can't make it on their own.

When the situation is reversed and our mate mistrusts us, we must show them how to stand tall and be on their own as well. There are many professionals who, contrary to popular belief, feel that men are more dependent on women than the reverse. Often a man's refusal to get too close is simply his way of protecting himself from becoming overwhelmingly dependent on a woman. When this dependency need flares, men find themselves just as unable as women to cut the cord.

If you are with someone like this, you might find yourself feeling smothered. Sometimes it is necessary for your mutual growth to leave such a relationship and find someone who can stand on his own two feet emotionally and spiritually. It is only when two people are whole that they can grow and love each other with open and trusting hearts. This doesn't mean that we can't look to each other for help during difficult times in our lives: that's the beauty of having a partner. What I'm talking about here is that basic foundation of wholeness and self-trust so necessary in a loving relationship.

As you read this you might be thinking, "Well, you must not love your man as much as I love mine. I'd go to pieces if I ever lost him!" Remember not to confuse love with need. Love in its highest form means being able to let go and allow your mate to learn and grow in whatever way he has to . . . as you must. I will talk more about this later.

You already know that letting go is not an easy thing to do. As I said earlier, there is nothing "easy" in this book. Growing into a confident woman who totally trusts herself relative to the man in her life is a lifelong process. At times we will get lost. That's the only guarantee I can offer you! When I am feeling lost, I remind myself that at that very moment my self-trust is at a very low ebb. I then haul out my bag of tools, in the form of the exercises provided in this book, to help me get in touch with my Higher Self. And I flourish in the feeling of being whole—and trusting—once again.

Trust Affirmations

I trust who I am.

I know everything I need to know.

I'll handle whatever happens in my life.

I set you free.

I set myself free.

I am strong and I am whole.

I am cutting the cord.

My life is rich and abundant.

My life has meaning and purpose.

I make a difference.

There's always more.

I am in control of my life.

We are all doing the best we can.

My self-esteem is growing every day.

I learn from all my experiences.

I am creating a beautiful life.

There is only now.

I let go of the past.

I am moving forward in my life.

I trust the future.

8

THE MAN BEHIND THE MASK

"I hear "equal" all the time, and I don't know what that means. I don't want a woman to be my equal. I want a certain amount of control. I want my masculinity. I don't know what the rules are anymore. I know I'm uncomfortable and I struggle with the rules. She wants a piece of the action, and I'm willing to give her whatever I deem is OK for her piece of the action. It's OK as long as I don't continue carrying my terror about her being better than I am, or having control of who I am. It all stops when the change is so radical that I give up my nuts. I don't want to give them up. I will never give them up!"

"I really feel that my wife is my equal. What's important to me is my growth, and who contributes to that, and vice versa. I want a woman to tell me I'm full of shit if I'm offtrack. While I'm living on this earth, I'm going to have all this conflict and insecurity going on inside myself . . . the searching. I'm with a beautiful woman who is struggling just the way I am, just as every other human being is. I'm happy that we are just walking the walk and talking the talk together. And for me, that's where it's at."

T wo men, each providing us with an insight into the depths of their feelings. Within these two statements we hear the fear, confusion, searching, struggle, hope, and love. Men, too, are going through difficult times, but most of us don't really have an insight into their feelings. We tend to believe that men have it easy, but they are going through the upset of transition, just as we are. In order to help us open our hearts, I felt it was necessary to include one chapter in which men speak for themselves.

For many of the "voices" that speak to you here, I owe a debt of gratitude to a men's self-help group in Los Angeles who invited me to be the first woman to attend one of their meetings. Aware of the subject of my book, they were willing to open up to me in order to to promote a better understanding of the issues with which men are struggling today.

Before I let the men continue to speak for themselves, let me set the stage by telling you that this group is just one of many that are springing up all over the country. They mirror the support groups that many women have been attending for years. The groups exist to provide communication, growth, self-knowledge, friendship, feedback, and support. While tempers sometimes flare, the spirit is one of love and understanding. They are usually led by a different group member whenever they meet. This particular group has been meeting for almost two years.

As I walked into the meeting room, I felt a bit nervous. I had attended (and conducted) many women's and mixed groups before, but never an all men's group. I decided to play the role of "a fly on the wall" and simply listen. I must admit that keeping my mouth shut for three hours in such a tantalizing situation was probably the hardest thing I've ever done in my whole life!

The fifteen men sitting around the massive marble table ranged in age from their mid-twenties to their fifties. They were all heterosexual—some were married, some were living with

women, and some were alone. They talked about many things—
their fear of losing their looks, their health, their sexuality, their
careers, as well as their relationships with parents, children,
and, of course, women. I was moved by it all. Space constraints
preclude my including all that they had to say, so I have chosen
those statements that relate specifically to the spirit of this
book. Note the rainbow of feelings they express—from powerless to powerful—in the following excerpts:

"Six years ago, I got mad and I got divorced. She stepped
on my toes. I hate when women come on with their
strength. She confronts me. Rattles my cage. I don't like
it."

———

"I can't digest the idea that I'm with a woman who's my
equal. It's just incomprehensible to me. As my wife
becomes stronger, I feel as though I am vanishing, disap-
pearing; my territory is getting smaller and smaller. I don't
know who I am anymore or who I'm supposed to be. When
I feel a territory infringement, I ask myself, "Why do I feel
so weak?" I know it's weakness at the base of my needing
to have control. I feel as though a woman, child, home,
should all fit in the flanks of my arms. (He stretches out
his arms.) That's *my* territory. I can't seem to see it any
other way. When my wife talks about being really equal,
it feels like an assault on a cellular level."

———

"I'd guess I like a strong woman versus a wimp. A strong
woman who tells it like it is. But I can't help but notice that
there is such a deep anger inside of me. The fact that I need
them makes me angry—deep, deep, deep inside of me—
that I need these women (banging his fist on the table) and
they have so much power. I try to be nice and sweet and
patient and twentieth century and, damn, I don't like it!"

———

"Under the rage is the hurt and pain. I'm trying to surrender. I get something from control, but I lose so much. I lost all my other relationships before this one. After a while I got bored, tired. I had to choose to surrender. As I surrender, it gets scarier and scarier and scarier. Yet, I'm feeling better. There's something that's happening. I'm able to say, "You got your own things to do? That's OK." It's not as important as before for her to want to spend every waking moment with me. I'm going for it and it feels good. Love is real power . . . more powerful than control. Before I didn't understand this. It's scary, but I'm feeling better. The more I attempt to control, the more I lose control."

"This is funny to say, but it is the truth and it's scary as hell to say it. Part of me likes to be depended upon; it gives me a role to play, an identity. But now, I don't want a woman to search for her happiness in me. God, that really scares me to say that. I guess that's because I'm letting go of a very old and familiar tape. I would like a woman who really loves me and is not searching for her life's happiness in men."

"The stronger the woman, the better. I don't want to protect or take care of anyone. Just the idea of that really scares me. I don't know if I have the capability to do that, especially financially."

"In the past, I enjoyed having relationships with women who were dependent on me. It's great for a while, but then it gets really lonely because they're not there to share with you in that place of power that you really want to be. To avoid loneliness, one has to be with someone who can share that place of power with you. And I can now recognize when a woman feels powerless very early on in the relationship . . . and I end it immediately."

"It's funny, in my own evolution, I thought the natural bent of man was to be the protector and take care of. Now when a woman says she wants to be taken care of, that scares me. I don't understand it as a mature role for any individual to take. Who takes care of anybody anymore? Adults should be able to take care of themselves. That's not a role I want to assume anymore in life."

"What I like about my new relationship is there seems to be equality. I like a strong woman, and the stronger she is, the more she can give me feedback and validation . . . and vice versa. I don't want to always protect someone, because it begins to feel like I'm carrying around this baggage, and you know what it does? It gets less interesting for me. It gets really boring."

"I've discovered in my relationship that control is nothing. It is meaningless. Zero. It doesn't mean anything to have it. It enhances nothing."

"This is the first time in my life I'm beginning to feel what love really means. It means trying to get along with another human being. I don't have anything going on in me about her crushing my balls and territory. I'm inviting her in and she's inviting me in. I get so much from her validation of "You are a beautiful man, I love you, I care for you, I want to do things with you." She appreciates what I give to her. I give her validation, too. There's a real melding. Maybe I'm crazy, but what I see happening is that I get a lot more done when I am not angry. In the beginning I objected to her independence. I had to get in touch with the rage I was feeling. And what I finally realized was that under the rage was this enormous hurt. All my hurts from the time I was a kid. Boy . . . then the tears. And I'm looking at this woman that I really care about and she's looking in my eyes and she moves over and puts her arms around me when she sees I am desolate with no balls. And she gives me back my balls, if you know what I mean."

———

"We all know on some level that our happiness does not come from someone else and our full acceptance doesn't come from someone else, so I ask myself, why have a relationship? (laughter) The answer I've come up with is that I am trying to discover my most holy self—the person within me that could laugh, cry, and love and not lash out, out of unconscious living. I want to live out of consciousness. I want a partner who has the same desire for herself, for her to be also on a journey to discover the holiest part of herself. For me, it's important that we have that mutual feeling and therefore we can be partners in helping each other arrive there. I want us both to be discovering all that we are."

Pretty amazing stuff, isn't it? The fifteen men in the group represented a very wide range of feelings about women and the women's movement. For those of you who may feel put off at any of their comments, don't be. If you had been there firsthand, you would have seen the poignancy and pain of their struggle and their genuine desire to understand what was going on within them.

It is significant and not surprising that those who admitted feeling less powerful as men were having the hardest time seeing women as equals. These men saw their masculinity as being tied up with their playing the dominant or care-taking role . . . this, of course, being the flip side of women still expecting "to be taken care of." Others, who felt more secure, had begun to enjoy relating to women as equals. They realized that, while it was scary treading on new territory, there was much to be gained from having a partner in life. For these men, the re-visioning process had already occurred, and what they once saw as acceptable and "normal" in relationships no longer was. Some had traveled even farther down the Path of self-discovery and were able to see their relationships in a very spiritual and transcendent way.

While some of the men felt good about their relationships with women, others expressed disillusionment, the same kind of disillusionment I've seen in so many women. It is a given that confusion and upset is to be expected in an age of transition. Still, the pain that these men were feeling was so tangible, it moved me to tears.

Listen:

"I see the world as a messed up place. I know that's a projection of the fact that I'm a messed up guy."

"I don't know what the words mean—equality, femininity, strong woman, ego, control, power. It's all bullshit—we're all hurting inside."

"The other day I made a few meager attempts at affection with a woman I have been dating and was called a seducer. Suddenly there was this string of profanity about what shits men were. Where does one go from there?"

"I go to so many activities, yet I'm not hooking up with anyone very deeply. I'm going home alone. I keep myself busy and I'm always interacting with people . . . but I'm not really relating to anyone. All this socializing keeps me from confronting the profound sense of loneliness I feel. (As the tears roll down his face.) Maybe the answer is to go home and be alone and delve into what I'm about. But I think I'm too frightened to do that. I think I'm too frightened of the pain. (Tears running down many of their faces.)"

"I feel a sense of hopelessness in terms of relationships. I'm surrounded by so many relationships that don't seem to be working. So much hurt going on all the time. I'm thinking a lot of what I do in relationships is about filling my needs and that's why none of them have lasted. Most of the women I've chosen have not been willing to be vulnerable. Why am I choosing these women? Maybe the problem is I have such needs and I don't know how to fill myself up and I lay it all on women. Somehow I expect them to fill me up and I choose women who can't. I haven't found my way out of that. I want to be loved and adored like everyone else. I want to laugh and play and be intimate. Of course I want that. I know there are women out there who fit the bill. The question for me is what am I doing that is not allowing me to be with a woman like that?"

"I was with two female friends this weekend who got into this heavy fight. I said very little. I realize that I'm not man enough to speak up with women. I always assume a lesser role. I can't ask a woman for anything. I won't take the chance of their not giving it to me. That would feel like too much of a loss."

"It scares me to get involved in a relationship. I'm very needy. I didn't realize how needy I was. Neediness to me is suffocation and when someone comes toward me, I get this icky feeling I'm a victim and they are taking over. I like being a kid and swapping roles and hanging out and being sloppy and not being judged and being told that "I love you and I like who you are. You're a good person. You have a good heart." We all want to laugh and play and be totally accepted as people. Can I give it to myself? Can I give it to another person? Hell, that's what I want! I want to be totally accepted. What can we do to get it? What can we do to accept ourselves?"

"So many women I know say they want love and communication. But that's not what I see. I see that they want rejection, they want to be used, they want challenge. It seems like the most remote thing for them to really experience meaning and communication. It doesn't have much reality for them. They would rather have all the drama and the illusion, the mental abuse. I've always admired those who connect on another level, but I have rarely experienced it."

———

"I've always wanted approval from women, so it's real interesting that I picked a very critical woman in my ex-wife. Here I was wanting approval, and all I got was lectures. I was very provocative and messed things up. I could have behaved differently to get approval . . . so my behavior was incongruent with my goal of wanting approval. . . . It replicates the behavior of my father. I saw what he did to avoid intimacy. Part of me feels that if I don't go all the way into intimacy, the hurt will be less. I avoid intimacy in my attempts at new relationships. I back away with excuses. So it becomes a tremendous push–pull—a cycle of dissatisfaction. How do I get out of it? If I could be more honest, more vulnerable, more sharing, more open, more crying, learn to express sadness and let any woman know I am desperate for intimate contact, and it's real hard. (Tears) Right now I'd rather be alone than be hurt and it's sort of giving up . . . 'cause I could see myself being alone for twenty years."

You will notice that despite the stance the men took, very few blamed the female sex. So much of the sharing was about looking into themselves to find out the answers to their problems.

As the meeting came to a close, I asked the men if they had any particular message that they wanted women to hear. I hope I can convey the depth of emotion that was released in the room.

———

The men spoke slowly, quietly, and with great intensity of emotion. Many had eyes filled with tears.

"I want to walk 'within' a relationship rather than lead or follow."

"When I walk up to a woman that I would like to get to know better, know that I bring my fears of rejection with me. If you indicate to me that you are not interested in me at first glance, I walk away and lick my wounds. Please take a deeper look."

"I want a woman to be able to share my sadness. Some of the best nights I spent with my friend were when I could just lie in bed and cry. And she would just lie there and hold me. She didn't ask why. She just let me be. I often cried when I thought of my friend of ten years who died. (Tears on his and other faces.) He was my best pal. She knew the pain I felt. When I was with her it was really OK for the tears and the pain to come up. I've never had that with a man. I don't feel comfortable being held by a man and crying. That doesn't feel right for me. It's just with a woman that it's OK."

"I love to cry in a woman's arms also. I think it's related in some way to my needing to be nurtured by my mother. And I think we continue to search for that. But it's an illusion because they can't be that for us . . . no one can. I don't really expect it any more. That's a sign of growth."

"What we are looking for is balance. Women started out looking for control. They take control and they sit there in the position of control and are unhappy with it. It looks like we need to learn to be fluid and dance with each other instead of creating a boxing match."

"The most important thing I would say to women is to be women. And find out what that is fully and not throw away the strength of the willow to hang on to the strength of the oak. Women have their own innate power. For millennia women actually ran the planet. They controlled everything, but they did it subtly and softly by giving and shaping and moving . . . not by feeling they had to confront. I would like to tell women they have the strength. They have the power. But they need to have it coming from their own inner self—from their own femininity."

———

"I would like to tell women that I've been treated like a sex object on many occasions, and it feels just as bad for me as it does for you. I get a headache. I get sick. I go through all the same avoidance tactics. I don't like to have to perform. We are all human beings. We need to find the balance."

———

"The deepest and most important thing beyond the fun and games in a relationship is a sense of honesty and truth about what we each are feeling about any subject. To have that solidness, that basis, that rock . . . that if I'm doing something you don't like, you'll tell me. I don't have to second-guess you. And I want the freedom and agreement to give my truth that way also."

———

"I want to be a source of pleasure. I don't want to be the only source, but I want to know I bring you pleasure."

———

"I want women to know that we like them better than they like themselves. And we need them more than they can understand. I feel all of us are searching so deeply for the secret of how to make a perfect relationship. We don't have training. The species isn't trained. But eventually we'll grow up and get it right."

———

And I know he's right. We will get it right, as long as we continue to "walk the walk and talk the talk" together.

I pointed out as they finished their final go-around that since some of us have found beauty and joy in relationships, it is not an impossible dream. One of the men responded with, "Yes, but isn't that the exception to the rule?" I answered, "First it's one, then two, then 100, then 1,000, then 1,000,000, and on and on and on." But the process has begun, and certainly many of us do see a light at the end of the tunnel.

So ended a magical evening for me. Had you been there, you would have loved every man sitting before you, even those who might have been in conflict with what you hold deepest in your heart. Their pain and their struggling is no less real than yours or mine.

While you have just heard the words of only fifteen men, they certainly seem to me to reflect the feelings of the male population at large. I have heard the same sentiments expressed in a multitude of ways in all my workshops and in all my research on the subject. For a more in-depth look at men's feelings, there are a number of books on the subject. My favorites include *Why Men Are the Way They Are, The Hazards of Being Male, How Men Feel, Secrets Men Keep,* and *About Men.* [1] I implore you to read these books, as they will help dispel some of the commonly held illusions we hold about men, which in reality have little basis in truth. Here, in brief, are a few to think about.

Some Common Illusions about Men

Men feel powerful. No, in terms of feelings, men belong with women in the category of the weak! Because we women have experienced ourselves as powerless, we have made the erroneous assumption that all the power *must* have gone to the men. Where else could it have gone? I assure you, it was *not* to men.

Psychologist Herb Goldberg describes the male position in this way:

> The male in our culture is at a growth impasse. He won't move—not because he is protecting his cherished central place in the sun, but because he *can't* move. He is a cardboard Goliath precariously balanced and on the verge of toppling over if he is pushed even ever so slightly out of his well-worn path.[2]

Of course, there are some men who do "move": those who are feeling the most secure about themselves. Others, who feel powerless, are not dealing well at all with the changes that are occurring.

Physical violence is evidence of men's disdain for women. No, it is evidence of men's sense of powerlessness. The more we put men down, the more powerless they will feel. Physical violence is also created by our expectation that our men be tough. Sam Keen has this to say:

> "The more the identity of the male is rooted in the warrior ideal, the more a society will degrade women and cast the relationship between the sexes as a form of warfare."[3]

It follows that we have to begin to define masculinity by warmth and compassion instead of by whether he is the captain of the football team!

Men are the privileged sex. I certainly don't see it that way! While men make more money in the workplace (and this inequality needs to be corrected), we, at least, have the right to work (and we make a damn good success out of it!). Society has not yet approved the flip-side "right" of a man to stay home and be with his children. And many men would love to do so. While there are those who are courageous enough to make this choice, they receive a great deal of scorn from the outside world. In other words, women have made greater strides in the workplace than men have in the home.

Many men feel the most pain in regard to their lack of "privilege" when it comes to their children's custody. What many women don't understand is the deep despair that men often feel as they lose rights to raise their children after divorce, even when the wife is the one to leave. Fortunately, more women today are agreeing to joint custody, sometimes allowing the children to live with their fathers. While this prospect is still horrifying to many women (and men!), it has been very freeing to others, in some cases clearly benefiting the children. It also has given children a new kind of model upon which to live their lives.

On a related matter, women have the ultimate right in all matters of bearing children. A man cannot impose his will one way or the other. If he wants a child, a woman can deny him that wish. If he wants a pregnancy terminated, a woman can deny him that wish . . . and then demand that he pay for the support of the child. Not much privilege here!

Taken to its extreme, men are born into a world where they are expected to die in battle, if need be, protecting women and children. Why? Are their lives less valuable than ours? Are they really *less* equal than we are? Of the 57,000 names on the Vietnam War Memorial, all but eight of them are men's.[4]

I think ultimately we have to acknowledge that:

Being a woman carries with it many inequities and being a man carries with it many inequities. They are just different inequities. It's time we got off the position that men have it easy. They don't!

Men don't want commitment. The truth is that most men are eager—some desperate—for commitment, but, in today's world, many are often fearful of the implications. Sociologist Warren Farrell points out that:

> When commitment is associated with diamonds and mortgages, promises of love can feel like promises of payment.[5]

Another of the reasons men fear commitment is that they feel our expectations—financial and otherwise—seem to have increased, instead of decreased, as a result of the women's movement. They are frightened they can't fit the bill. When I asked women in my workshops, "If you were a man in today's world, would you be eager to commit?" very few of them were willing to answer "yes."

How can men become more secure about making a commitment? Commitment should stem from caring instead of neediness, for a start. One of my students told me:

> I was living with a woman last year, and my father passed away and I had to go back to New York. She called me and was terribly upset that I hadn't called her and told her that I loved her. And there I was in the middle of burying my father. Right then and there, I knew that was it. There's no room for me to deal with that kind of insecurity on a full-time basis.

When our neediness forms the basis of a relationship, most men know there is no way they can ever please us. They are smart to run the other way.

What else would men need to feel safer in terms of commitment? They would also like to feel appreciated. They would like to be acknowledged as very special in our lives. They would like to feel a heart-to-heart caring, one that is not born out of neediness. They would like to feel *loved*.

Men treat women as objects. Of course, many do, but the implication is that women do not treat men as objects. (Talk about the disowned self!) The truth is that *all insecure people treat others as objects.* They must in order to survive psychologically! Insecure women see men as breadwinners, caretakers, fix-its, security blankets, sex machines, adornments, and so on . . . *not as people.* The more closed our hearts, the easier it is for us to forget that men have feelings just as we do. Many of us still expect men to approximate the traditional masculine model, and that's about as much of an object as you can get! I recently saw advertised a course for women entitled "How to Marry Money." There is no mention of a man, only money. Need I say more?

Men have a double standard. Yes, some men have a double standard, and again this assumes that women don't. But one brief look into the mirror reveals that we do. I winced when I read an article recently telling women what to do with freeloaders in their lives—defined as "those men who always seem to forget their wallets." The article warned that the prime targets of these freeloaders are women who make more money than the men do! I ask you, in the interests of equality, shouldn't women who make more money than their men be willing to pay, or at least contribute to, the tab? Certainly in the past our stated reason that men should pay was that they made more money than we did. Doesn't the reverse apply? There are also many situations involving children and lifestyle where we can see evidence of our double standard in action.

Men do not want to see women succeed in the marketplace. While some men still feel threatened by women's success in the job force, many would love to have some relief from traditional masculine burdens. If they are feeling difficulty, it is because of their insecurity.

"Most of us identify our masculinity so completely with our work and our traditional roles of dominance that we start to feel unmanned—which is to say, we start to lose our identities, ourselves, our very humanity when women show that they can do the same work or exercise the same power."[6]

Again, as the re-visioning process takes place, this kind of resistance will be harder to find. More and more men are admitting the incredible relief they feel as women bring in money to help support the household.

The nurturing of children is biologically determined to be a woman's role. No, men can be as nurturing as women. In fact, in many cases men are far better nurturers than their wives. (Certainly, this was true about my ex-husband and myself!) Thankfully, this myth is slowly being replaced by a new reality: *Men can be great mothers.* Largely because of the women's movement men are beginning to claim their "motherhood." One man talks lovingly about his new role:

> It has freed me most as a parent. I am, among other things, a fairly good natural mother. I like the nurturing role. It make me feel good to see a child eat—and it turns me to mush to see a four-year-old holding a glass with both small hands, in order to drink. I even enjoyed sewing patches on the knees of my daughter Amy's Dr. Dentons when she was at the crawling stage. All that pleasure I would have lost if I had made myself stick to the notion of the paternal role that I started with.[7]

Whatever one thinks about the artistic quality of such movies as *Three Men and a Baby, Mr. Mom,* and *Kramer Versus Kramer,* these movies are helping men to get in touch with the nurturing part of themselves that has so long been disowned. As I write this book, I am aware of the birth of a new magazine for men called *Single Dads,*[8] which mirrors many women's magazines about parenting. We can also see evidence of the re-visioning process as more fathers' groups emerge, and as more men request flexible work hours, corporate day-care centers, and time off from work to spend with their children. Fathers are becoming proper parents instead of work machines. And what a great picture this is for our young! The sooner our sons and daughters understand what true equality looks like, the sooner we will see equality between the sexes. This thought might help dispel our fears about going out to work and sharing the parenting with our husbands. (You might notice that just as men do not want to give up their stronghold in the workplace, many of us often resist giving up our stronghold in the house. It hurts for us to realize our husbands make just as good mothers as we do!)

Men are only interested in themselves. The truth is that most men want to make their women happy; they see that as their role. Hence they feel very powerless when their women are unhappy. They see themselves as failures. Journalist Anthony Astrachan says it beautifully:

> "Most of us truly want the women in our lives to be happy. Many of us have come to realize this means they must have personal autonomy, including economic freedom. Some of us want to overcome our fear of female power. Some of us want relief from traditional masculine burdens. We therefore struggle to welcome change."[9]

Women are more dependent on men. Not necessarily so! As Michael Blumenthal puts it:

> "I still haven't quite grown used to the new sense of my initial unimportance (or, at least, neutrality) in the eyes of women, to the fact that they can (and do) live very well without me or other members of my once-benighted kind. All the studies I've read on the subject, in fact, suggest that, of the four possible heterosexual categories (married

men, single men, married women, single women), single
women and married men tend to fare psychologically the
best, married women and single men worst. What this
might say about who "needs" whom the most I leave for
you, gentle reader, to decide."[10]

Since the women's movement began, more women than men
initiate divorce, and the men are finding themselves lost at sea.
As women are discovering how much they *don't* need men, men
are discovering how much they *do* need women. And many find
it frightening. Since men rarely share their feelings, they cannot
find solace in their friends as women can. Consider this: divorced males have an annual death rate that is more than three
times as high as divorced females; suicide and alcoholism is
much higher in unmarried men. There is much evidence to point
out that a man suffers more. Hence it is understandable that men
worry about our becoming financially independent. They worry
we won't need them. It would seem that if we want to keep our
growth from hurting men, we must let them know they are
needed for things other than money . . . and back it up with
constant appreciation.

These are just a few illusions to whet your appetite. Reading
the books I have suggested will give you much more breadth and
depth of understanding about the reality of men's feelings today.
If you had many "yeah buts" going on in your head as you read
through the list, remember that "yeah but" is your signal that
you're looking in the wrong place. It's once again time to pick
up the mirror and put down the magnifying glass. Remember:

Pointing a finger is a powerless act—the only real power
lies in taking control of our reaction to whatever life hands
us.

And speaking of power, we've talked much in recent years
about the battle between the sexes. I think if we looked a bit

closer we would notice that it's hardly a war at all; it's more a one-sided attack of women on men. This is not to say that some men haven't picked up their arms. Some have, but generally speaking it has been our battle. As I discussed earlier, it was perhaps a battle we had to wage in order to get a sense of our own power.

But the power that comes from warlike behavior is very limited, indeed. War precludes love, and it is only through love that we will begin to understand what real power actually feels like. I hope the voices of the men in this chapter have created an opening that will allow us to move forward to a more loving place, one that will signal the beginning of the next step in the women's movement—*women loving women, women loving men.*

What this means in practical terms is that we need to end any warlike behavior. Men are not our enemy. They are just human beings doing the very best they can at this moment in time— given their understanding of who they are in this Universe. In their own way they are trying, just as hard as we are, to find their rightful place of dignity in the Grand Scheme of things. At times this task can be awesome.

One thing I do know for certain is that most men like women and are more interested in connecting than separating. They need women and do not want to fight with them. I recently read a letter written to a Toronto newspaper from a man who expressed his hope that, as men's groups surface, they avoid other-gender bashing that is evident in some feminist groups. He had just been sold a button at an Ottawa woman's conference that read "The only good man is a dead one."

I hope that button makes you as sad as it makes me. We have to be aware of how badly we hurt men by our attacks. I know, I know! Sometimes their behavior makes us want to hurt, maim, and kill. There are some very awful men out there, no doubt about it, and we often want revenge for all the "injustices" that they perpetrate. But it's time we put it all in a proper perspective. The reality is that there are good men and bad men, there are good women and bad women. Men and women come in all types. We cannot generalize and make all men out to be bad. They simply aren't. In fact, the horrendous behavior of some men makes other men cringe with embarrassment and guilt, just as the horrendous behavior of some women makes us cringe. It helps to keep in mind that when someone—male or female—behaves badly, it is their own pain that is yelling out. This doesn't excuse their behavior, but it does help to soothe our hurt.

Ultimately, even when we feel pain, we have to learn to have compassion. Through compassion we can heal our aching hearts . . . and theirs. Compassion allows us to see how much we hurt men with our male-bashing . . . how much it hurts a man to be handed a button that says, "The best man is a dead man" . . . how much it hurts a man to see our "self-improvement" magazines filled with such articles as "How to Wipe that Jerk Right Out of Your Mind."

Perhaps it would be a greater incentive for us to stop the attacks if we understood that our putting men down is hurting us more than it is hurting men.

While we might get a good laugh from our clever slogans, the laugh is really on us. Why? Because:

It kills our sense of self-worth to hurt other people.

I believe we are all on this earth to learn how to manifest our inherent beauty. I suggest that one of the ways we can speed the process is to become very conscious and responsible about all that is said in the name of "woman." For example, as we read our women's magazines and find such hurtful material as I described above, let the editors know that we no longer feel comfortable with this kind of hostility toward men. Let them know we want to spread the language of love, not the language of hate.

Don't mistake me . . . I love women's magazines! I think they have contributed much to help us get a handle on our lives thus far. But we now need to direct them as to what "the next step" in the women's movement is all about—*women loving women, women loving men*—so that we stop the above kind of male-bashing from occurring.

This also applies to the male-bashing books, television shows, movies, and so on that point the finger at men. By devouring the negativity they feed us, we convince the media into producing more of the same. It's a vicious cycle!

We need to be more accountable for what we say about men, even if it means disapproval from those around us. We must take on the responsibility of creating love for men and not disdain. In so doing, we create a greater love for ourselves. In so doing, we train ourselves to become more compassionate beings, which feels really wonderful. I don't think compassion comes naturally. It has to be learned.

And what really is compassion? Merle Shain describes it beautifully:

> "Real compassion is a strength born of a shared weakness, a recognition of a common humanity, a way of healing the wounds of separation by making connections. And it contains an acceptance of the fact that even in their deepest being, everyone is helpless and would welcome love from us."[11]

Read it again . . . and carefully. Compassion gives us strength in the understanding that we all have our weaknesses, and there is nothing inherently "bad" about that. It is part of our common destiny. When we attack others, we deny our oneness with humanity. Hence, in attacking others we kill a part of ourselves.

I believe that when we "kill" our men with heartless attitudes and behavior, we also kill a part of ourselves. Psychological numbing is death to our soul. By learning to respect and honor ourselves as we open our hearts to others, we form the basis of a new kind of revolution, the kind of revolution that could abolish war forever. I believe women have that kind of power.

We women are capable of generating a whole new kind of energy in this world, one that is capable of tearing down walls between "enemies" instead of building them. Once we understand how important we really are, we won't take our actions in the world so lightly. We will realize that *equality is nothing without responsibility.* That's the only combination that works—equality *and* responsibility. I implore every woman reading this book to understand that each and every one of us has the capacity for making a positive difference in this world. The time to start is now. It all begins the moment we decide to become more loving as human beings.

As we open our hearts to men, we begin to discover our own inner beauty, inner strength, and inner light.

Which brings us to the nitty-gritty of this book: *owning our own magnificence.*

9

OWNING OUR "MAGNIFICENCE"

OWNING OUR MAGNIFICENCE: a pompous-sounding phrase indeed! Yet say it a few times and note that it makes you stand a little taller and breathe a little deeper. What does it actually mean? As I define it:

> To "own our magnificence" is to know in our minds, to feel in our hearts, and to reflect into this world our inner beauty, inner strength, and inner light.

Hardly a pompous thought at all, but rather one that is spiritual and giving in its essence. *It is about loving ourselves enough so that we can project our loving presence onto all those around us.*

Clearly, some of us are more in touch than others with the good "stuff" that lies within; but all of us, at times, have doubts as to whether we are good enough, beautiful enough, strong enough, or lovable enough. Self-doubt is another one of those intrusive human foibles that we can't seem to escape. However, we can learn to smother it with love whenever it threatens to get in our way!

I'd like to report that I have an instant smother-it-with-love remedy up my sleeve, but I don't. I have my share of self-doubts, like the rest of you. But I've made some pretty big leaps in confidence in recent years, and my intention is to share a few of those insights with you in the hope that you can begin to see the light within and reflect it onto a very needy world.

I can hear some of you now:

"What is she talking about? I picked up this book in order to find a new boyfriend, and I end up reading about projecting my light onto a needy world! Give me a break!"

Trust me! It makes perfect sense that there is a strong correlation between finding a healthy nourishing relationship and being in touch with our own inner beauty. Have you noticed that those who project light into this world draw light into their lives, and those who project dark clouds into the world draw dark clouds into their lives? I noticed that the number of loving men who were drawn to me increased in direct proportion to the amount of loving energy I projected. And now that I am married to a very wonderful man, that loving energy helps keep our relationship healthy.

As you move forward on the Path to wholeness, the first thing I would like to suggest is that, when you finish this book, go back and read it again. While the focus of everything I have talked about thus far appears to be about loving the men in our lives, the key to our success really lies in self-love. *The very act of picking up the mirror instead of the magnifying glass can be considered one of the most loving things that we can do for ourselves.*

It is only through self-searching that we can begin to find our way to the best part of who we are: our Higher Self. When we are filled with a feeling of inner emptiness (Divine Homesickness), it is because we have lost touch with this inner Home of all our sublime virtues—creativity, intuition, trust, love, joy, inspiration, aspiration, caring, giving—everything we, in our heart of hearts, would like to experience.

Then, after you reread the material, I'd like you to think about what you usually do after reading a self-help book. Is it your practice to put the book back on the shelf and say to yourself:

"That was really good. That made me feel better."

. . . only to discover that the initial high wears off in a matter of days? Or do you say:

"That was really good. Now, how can I take the suggested exercises and make them part of my daily routine?"

One thing I can guarantee you is that no teacher, whether in the form of a person, a book, a tape, or a workshop, is going to do the work for you. The teacher can only give you tools. Then it's up to you. Lessons of the Heart (Heartwork) involve learning, but they are really meant to be lived into over time. There is never an end to the lessons and the learning. Sometimes we grow weary. Yet, if we can see it all as an adventure, we can actually begin to love the process.

What makes the Journey to the Higher Self exhilarating is the constant discovery that we are more than we think we are. This is the bliss of self-awakening, and for us to be self-awakened is what "consciousness" is all about. This, of course, suggests a new ending to our favorite tale, "The Sleeping Beauty"!

With that in mind, let me suggest that you start your own brand of Heartwork by creating a workbook that allows you systematically to do the exercises I've included throughout the chapters. *Feel the Fear and Do It Anyway* also has a myriad of exercises designed to make you feel more loving and more lovable. These exercises can be included in your workbook as well. Some of my readers have told me that to keep themselves motivated they have started their own self-help groups, using the exercises as the basis of their meetings. So if you have trouble motivating yourself, create your own self-help group!

The following are a few additional ideas and exercises to add to your workbook. I've touched on some of these topics earlier in the book, but I feel they need some expansion as they apply to the subject of this chapter. As always, hold on to what seems right for you and let the rest go.

A Few More Tips
On the Road to the Higher Self

Play the game of Act-As-If. An important tool that you can begin using immediately is the familiar game of Act-As-If. This is a trick you play on your negative mind, the Chatterbox, that allows you to live into a more loving feeling about yourself. The way you begin to own your magnificence is to Act-As-If you already owned it and were already projecting it out into this world . . . despite what your Chatterbox is telling you. One of the main questions in your life becomes:

If I really owned my magnificence, what would I be doing?

If I really were in touch with my inner beauty, strength, and light, what would I be doing to reflect it onto this relationship? Make a list and then do it! Onto this family? Make a list and then do it! Onto this job? Make a list and then do it! And what would I be doing for myself? Make a list and then do it!

Let's take relationship as an example. If I really were in touch with my inner beauty, strength, and light,

I would write him a letter telling him how much I appreciate his being in my life.

I would make my own plans when I know he will be coming home late so that I don't put pressure on him for working long hours.

I would incorporate a program of positive affirmations into my daily routine so that I would constantly be reminded of the blessings in my life.

I would take workshops and read as many books as I could about creating a love that works.

I would act more responsibly about money so that the financial burdens wouldn't all be on him.

I would shut up when I begin judging him and ask myself, "What am I not doing for myself that I am expecting him to do for me?"

I would praise him, instead of putting him down, in front of our friends.

And so on . . .

Then I would go ahead and do it! Your lists should be revised often to accommodate what is going on in your life at any particular moment in time.

The great news about the game of Act-As-If is that you don't have to wait until you feel magnificent to project your magnificence into this world. Acting-As-If serves your purpose just as well! While it all sounds terribly immodest (and our mothers warned us not to become conceited), its implications are glorious:

To come from a place of self-love is to act in a way that has integrity, compassion, caring, respect, kindness, and appreciation of all humankind . . . and that includes one's self.

So when we ask ourselves, "If I really loved myself, what would I be doing?" you can be sure that the answer has within it virtues that will benefit all concerned. On the contrary, those who are filled with self-loathing will act in ways that are selfish, hurtful, and cruel. Self-love carries with it the characteristics of abundance . . . self-loathing carries with it the characteristics of scarcity.

Talk yourself into loving yourself. I am a firm believer in the power of positive self-talk. In *Feel the Fear and Do It Anyway,* I've outlined a "Beginners' Intensive Program for Positive Thinking," which is a ten-step program that can be incorporated daily into your regular routine. I have also included in this book many examples of affirmations—one of my favorite positive thinking tools. The instructions in the index tell you how to use them. It is important that you understand that *you don't have to believe the affirmations you are saying for them to work.* This is an extension of the Act-As-If principle, only this time it is Talking-As-If. The words themselves create a whole different energy pattern in your body. Trust me!

The power of positive words and thoughts are just now being appreciated in the world of sports and medicine. Thinking beautiful thoughts (even if we don't believe them at first) affects our health, the way we function in this world, and certainly our relationships.

There are whole books written on the subject of positive thinking and positive self-talk. I am on my knees begging you to immerse yourself in the subject until you have incorporated positive thinking exercises into your routine. They truly are powerful tools for creating a life that works. I have seen incredible transformations in people (including myself) when they have learned how to become positive thinkers. Remember, *like attracts like.* When you are positive, you draw positive things into your life. When you are negative, you draw negative things into your life.

There is no doubt that owning your magnificence is constantly to affirm that you are a beautiful being and that your life matters . . . and to live accordingly.

Pay attention to how far you've come. Not only is it important to pat our men on the back for their wonderfulness, but we have to pat ourselves on the back as well. During one of my workshops, I asked my students to write down, in the space of five minutes, fifty positive things about themselves. The response of two of the women was very telling. Of the sixty people in the room, only one was able to come up with the fifty items and only one was able to come up with none! Can you imagine the difference in the way each of these two women interact in the world? Where would you fit on this scale of zero to fifty?

One thing I can assure you is that:

When we don't give ourselves credit for what is good about who we are, we set ourselves up for a feeling of inner emptiness that no man, however he may try, can fill up!

The tendency is for our negative Chatterbox to pay attention only to how far we have to go, not how far we have come. One of my students recently said to me, "I'm so stuck when it comes to men. I don't know what's wrong with me. I'm hopeless." I asked her to think back two years and see if she has made any growth in her life during those two years. She thought about it for a moment and replied, "Yes, I guess I have. I've really healed my relationship with my father, and I got myself into a career that I love, and I really became committed to exercise and good food, and I now notice many destructive things that I do in relationships that I never noticed before . . . I guess that's growth." She continued on in this vein for a while, and I asked her to write down everything she told me and keep it as a reminder that she is growing every day of her life . . . although she forgets to notice. When she left the session, she was glowing. All it took was a little noticing.

Take out your newly created workbook and do the same exercise. Write down all the ways you have grown in the past two years. From this day forward, commit to writing down all your *wins,* which I define here as anything you create, no matter how large or how small, that makes you feel better about yourself.

Examples of wins are that you signed up for a workshop, that you complimented someone, that you did twenty minutes of exercise in the morning, that you called a friend to thank her for being in your life, that you picked up a piece of litter on the street, that you stopped the car to watch the sunset, that you noticed something you were doing that was destructive to your well-being and committed to changing it . . . and so on. These are all wins. Instead of putting yourself down for being stuck, begin relishing how much you have moved forward.

Be patient with yourself. Not only does our Chatterbox forget to tell us how great we are doing, but it further chastises us for moving at a snail's pace. It is only over time that we drop a lot of our excess baggage and truly learn the lessons of love. We are not born awakened in love, although there are those who would disagree with me about that. I believe we are born to be takers (in the beginning we must take or we will die), and one of our lessons in life is to learn how to be givers. Sam Keen shares my sentiments when he says:

"We age in order to become lovers."[1]

That puts a new perspective on aging, doesn't it? Time is healing. Time gives us perspective. Time is not our enemy, it is our friend. While I haven't reached the point of growth at which each new face wrinkle thrills me, I can honestly say that I wouldn't want to go back one single day. When I think about the learning that has taken place throughout my life, I realize that I have never been more loving to myself or others than I am at this present moment in time. Why would I want to go back? I can only anticipate how much more loving I am going to be in ten years, twenty years, forty years! I always maintain that by the time I am ninety . . . wow!

When you find yourself on that desperate treadmill of impatience, the only thing you need to do to calm yourself down is to affirm lovingly to yourself:

There is plenty of time. And despite what my Chatterbox (or anyone else) is telling me, it is all unfolding perfectly.

Let there be no self-recriminations, no regrets—nothing but the healthy sense that you are on a Journey and each day brings new awareness that allows you to become a more complete and loving human being.

Learn to love "the older woman." Speaking of aging, I couldn't let this chapter go by without noting the mental torture we women put ourselves through when it comes to the aging process. Talk about disowning our magnificence! Since the likes of Linda Evans and Joan Collins, we've made a little progress in appreciating the fifties-looking-like-thirties as opposed to appreciating only the twenties, but we still have a long way to go!

We allow our glamour magazines to parade thirteen-year-olds (yes, thirteen-year-olds!) before our very eyes as a model of what we are supposed to look like. I recently heard the head of a modeling agency state that the purpose of the beauty product sell is to create a world of glamour and illusion . . . a world that "doesn't exist, but in the minds of the public, it does!" Talk about following the "impossible dream"! I talked earlier about the re-visioning process. Instead of being re-visioned to like ourselves better, we are being re-visioned to like ourselves less!

I heard a thirteen-year-old model explain in a television interview that the reason advertisers prefer thirteen-year-olds is that, by the age of sixteen, pores start showing up on camera. What's wrong with pores?!? They are important in maintaining our health! They allow our body to breath! The irony of it is that most men would like us to look more natural. I'm married to a younger man, and I can assure you that my talk about plastic surgery is not music to his ears. He likes my wrinkles . . . it's me who doesn't!

We have to stop blaming the men for preferring younger women. Some do, some don't. What is significant is that *we* prefer younger women! I suggest that every one of us write to our favorite women's magazines and ask them, please, in the name of humanity, to allow pores to appear on their pages! Explain to them lovingly that they are part of the problem of dissatisfaction that we feel about ourselves today. If we don't complain, it is our fault that this is happening.

Tell them it's not that we have anything against advertising. We don't. One of our most pleasurable pastimes is shopping. All that we are requesting is that advertisers create a "sell" that makes us see the beauty inherent in *all ages,* including the pores, wrinkles . . . the whole package. Believe me, I'm sure they can come up with some great innovative products. Just as surely as we have been "conditioned" to believe that only youth is beautiful, we can be re-visioned to believe that aging is beautiful. It is really true that beauty is in the eye of the beholder . . . where else would it be?

Magazines are powerful. They can create self-fulfilling prophecies. If we are fed only articles about glamour, beauty, competition, and manipulation, that is what we will strive for. We need a new image, one of depth, caring, commitment, and love. Let's ask our magazine editors to become co-creators in helping us to re-vision an image of women of which we would truly be proud—inside and out.

Just as we can shift the mindset from loving short skirts to loving long skirts, we can shift the mindset from a youth-oriented to a getting-older-is-great society. Let's go for it! Let's adopt the attitude of the absolutely gorgeous Helen Hayes who says:

Remember, age is not important unless you are a cheese!

Participate in the process of external change. One way for us to get a better sense of self is to participate in what is happening externally. We remain powerless if we stand by helplessly wishing the world would be another way. In keeping with the theme of this book, we certainly must all continue to pay attention to the issues of the women's movement. We have all benefited by the women's movement, even if we are sometimes turned off to it.

There are many inequalities that still exist for both men and women in our society. We must fight for what we believe in— only this time with the weapon of love, instead of anger. As Alan Cohen says:

> "Now is our time to speak . . . through words, through pottery, through housecleaning, through right business, through silence, through every avenue our heart guides us to walk for the sake of creating a new world."[2]

As we build a new world, don't deny today's reality. This falls in the area of "stop being a victim." Interestingly, one of the definitions of a victim is "a person who is deceived or cheated, as by his or her own emotions or ignorance."[3] We do it to ourselves when we let our emotions or ignorance override the truth of what is happening in the world today. And what is happening in the world today?

As I discussed earlier, we are in the middle of a huge shift in consciousness. We haven't as yet figured out exactly what we want equality to mean. Until we do, traditional role assignments will often prevail—women will more often than not find themselves in charge of the home and men will find themselves the primary breadwinner.

This means that all your wonderful premarital agreements of

sharing the raising of the children and tasks of the household could fly out the window when it comes down to the crunch . . . and the crunch is usually signaled by the birth of a child. It is more than likely that your mate will be too frightened to stop the male push for financial betterment, and it is likely that you will be too frightened to tell him to stop the male push for financial betterment. It is also likely that your guilt will keep you from asserting your demands and acting in a way that makes sure he keeps to his agreement and you keep to yours. This reality is slowly changing, and I have seen cases where men and women do share equally and lovingly in matters of money and care of the house and children. But as yet, this is not the norm. Be responsible for understanding this before you decide to have children.

Understand also that if your mate goes along with your ideas about equal rights, *you* might not like the new arrangement. I heard one woman lament that she had a strong wish to stay at home and take care of her six-month-old son, but her husband reminded her of their agreement to share in all matters of money, the home, and kids, an agreement she had insisted upon before they got married. To make matters worse, she made more money than her husband. So, quite logically (and fairly), he suggested that he stay home and take care of their son, something that he, being a very nurturing man, would also love to do. I do hope this couple will pioneer a new pathway for themselves in which both will have time for work *and* time for their child. I've seen it successfully done with other couples. It requires that each open their heart to the feelings of the other and solve the problem with love and empathy instead of anger.

Other women feel frustrated when they find themselves in the opposite role of sole caretakers of their children, financially and otherwise. Again, in the spirit of self-love, we must take responsibility for our decisions in life. I always ask my students—men and women—who are contemplating having children, "Would you be willing to raise that child on your own—100 percent?" If they say no (which is usually the answer), I strongly urge them to wait until the answer is yes. We need to be aware, *not angry,* that this is a world of high divorce rates and frequent nonpayment of child support, and we need to be willing to accept this reality *before* a child is born. To take responsibility is to speak, to write down, and to hold close to your heart the following words:

> I want this child and I feel privileged to take the responsibility of its well-being, whether help is there or not. I will always find a way to protect and nourish this loving soul— despite what happens to my mate. I will not be a victim. I made this choice and I will be totally responsible for the consequences.

Feel the integrity and strength in this statement, as opposed to the whining sound of:

> I never would have had children if I thought he would leave me! It's not fair that I am stuck with the kids and he's out there free as a bird!

We shouldn't condone a man (or woman) who abdicates responsibility, but rather make ourselves feel more in control of our own lives and proud of the decisions that we have made.

We must also take the responsibility for understanding that if you make the choice to stay home and take care of hearth and children, you will lose ground in the world of work. That is a fact. All the outrage in the world won't change that. And from a business standpoint, that is the way it should be. Unless you keep your skills honed, you are of little value to a would-be employer. If a man stayed home and looked after the children, he, too, would lose his place in the work force. This is not a sexist thing. Of course, men don't usually stay home and look after children. At this point in time, most men would not be comfortable with that arrangement nor would we, since we still look to men as the primary breadwinner.

If we choose to opt out of a career and stay home with the children, it is important to recognize that today's world requires a new kind of full-time motherhood. It requires that we integrate future goals with our present roles. It requires that we keep our skills honed, that we avail ourselves of educational opportunities, and/or that we become entrepreneurial in our thinking and actions. It is self-loving to know, come what may, we will be able financially to take care of ourselves and our family if need be.[4] Not to prepare ourselves for this possibility is irresponsible. We might have the greatest husband in the world and have no intention of ever getting a divorce. This doesn't preclude the possibility that he could die, or become ill and need us to step in and help out. Men have reported to me what an incredible burden it is to know that if anything happened to them, their wife could not financially step in. This isn't to frighten you. On the contrary, it is to empower you. Some of the most frightened women I know are those who feel they couldn't make it financially if anything happened to their husband. A pretty powerless position indeed!

It is important to remind you once again that getting off the victim position is also to refrain from asking the two most powerless questions I hear women ask:

What about the men?

Why do we have to change?

Why is it up to us? Because if we are sincere about our equality and liberation, then who else would it be up to? As Colette Dowling puts it:

We have only one real shot at "liberation" and that is to emancipate ourselves from within.[5]

Equality is more than anything a state of mind. We are already equal. Oh, yes, there are issues for both men and women that need to be worked on . . . and it is happening. *But the real problem is that we don't feel equal. We feel second-class.* When we feel second-class, we act second-class. And when we act second-class, we are teated second-class. The real work to be done is internal. Owning our magnificence is also owning our equality. So, why do we have to change? Because if men change, that is great. But their changing has nothing to do with our feeling better about ourselves in the core of our being. That's why we have to change!

Honor who you are. As I touched upon earlier, honoring the self and stepping into equality requires a certain clarity about what we want and acting in a way that is consistent with our desire. It means acknowledging what is true for us despite what men or other women judge to be good or bad.

I also mentioned the film *Three Men and a Baby* as being a breakthrough film in showing "macho-type" men as nurturers. What mustn't go unnoticed is the breakthrough way two women in the film were portrayed. The grandmother refused to take the child off her son's hands even though he implored her to do so, and the girlfriend of one of the three men refused to be put in the role of babysitter for the child. In honoring who they were and not trying to make brownie points with the men, the women were able to support the men's discovery of the nurturing part of themselves, while maintaining their own integrity. What they learned to do was to say no. Not out of hostility, but out of integrity.

I must say that I am absolutely amazed at how difficult women find this to be. For example, I am a person who hates to cook and clean. For the twelve years between my two marriages, I always went out for dinner or brought food in and hired someone to clean my apartment. I certainly intended never to change this arrangement, even if I got married. Hence, very early into any new relationship, I would let it be known that "I don't cook and I don't clean." When I tell this to my female students, they gasp that I had the courage to do that. As one woman put it, "But you lose brownie points if you say you don't cook." (Ironically, this was a woman whose primary focus was on her career!)

In order to honor ourselves, we have to stop worrying about losing brownie points that make us lose ourselves.

We can't sell out anymore and complain that we are not equal. We must be who we are and maintain a confidence that we will find someone who loves the whole package. Not wanting to cook or clean . . . or not wanting to be a career woman . . . or whatever else we do or don't want to do . . . does not make us a bad or undesirable person.

The answer to honoring the self is to figure out what you really want and then live your life accordingly. We must make sure that we are not so needy in terms of relationship that we sell out our own heart's desire for a little security. Our grid of life must be filled with all sorts of wonderful things. We must believe in our own strength and not hold back because we think some man won't approve. This doesn't imply we need to be hostile to those who expect other than what we want to give. It only means we have to be clear and confident.

Self-love requires that we love our femininity. It is time for us to stop apologizing for our womanly traits. They aren't a sign of weakness. They are beautiful to behold. Many of us have been so wrapped up in emulating men that we have lost much of our own essence. As a group, we haven't as yet truly acknowledged just how grand the female of the species is and just how much we have to contribute to this world. While some of us have much bravado about women being the superior of the species, our actions and reactions belie our rhetoric. It's time we acknowledge *we've got what it takes!*

If you haven't seen the film *Yentl*, please do. It is a lovely story about a woman who, after rejecting her own femininity because of cultural restrictions imposed on women, ultimately sees the beauty of womanhood (thus, of herself) through her friendship with another woman. She sings (as only Barbra Streisand can) the following:

> She's mother, she's sister, she's lover, she's the wonder
> of wonders, no man can deny, so why would he change her.
> She's lovely, she's tender, she's woman . . . *so am I.*

And so are you. No matter how else you define yourself, underneath it all you are *woman.* It's time that you claim the beauty that being a woman implies, with words and with actions that come from deep within our hearts. We must stop apologizing for, but honoring, who we are and make our presence in this world count for something wonderful.

We must also begin to encourage the female energy in our men and not consider them weak when they allow themselves to be warm, soft, and nurturing. There is magnificent strength in warmth, softness, and the ability to nurture. If you've got it, flaunt it—male or female! For too long, male energy has been dominant. Most men would agree that the world needs more balance. Whether we want the responsibility or not, the fact remains that what we do with what we've got will be a contributing factor to the future of our wonderful little planet.

Fall in love with your power. As we accept our femininity, we must also develop our power. Many women reject the word "power" and in so doing reject our true capacity to love ourselves or anyone else. If we don't feel powerful, we feel fearful. If we feel fearful, our life becomes a Greek tragedy instead of a love story. Keep in mind that when I speak of power, I don't speak of manipulation of the outside world. Rather, I speak of our ability to touch that part within that knows there is nothing to fear . . . that part that allows us to react to what is going on around us with confidence, integrity, and compassion. That is real power.

Power also implies adulthood. We don't think of children as being powerful in the sense that they can take care of themselves. Unless we reach the point where we *know* that we can take care of ourselves—emotionally and financially—it is impossible to act as a responsible and loving adult. As Merle Shain so charmingly puts it:

> Unless we pick up our power and grope our way to adulthood, we will always want.[6]

Picking up our power and behaving as an adult implies many of the things I have already discussed, including the concept of equality. The truth is that to be equal is very scary and uncomfortable during the transitional period. A transitional period is a time for self-renewal. It requires that we detach from our vision of our mate as Daddy and take ourselves seriously.

We have to make our choice. Are we going for equality 100 percent or are we going to remain protected children? There doesn't seem to be any middle ground. We either feel equal or we don't. To feel equal we have to act equal. Acting-As-If is the essence of creating what we want.

If you choose to stay home and raise the children, and lately that is something that takes courage, then jump in 100 percent, feeling just as first-class and equal as any other woman or man out there. If you choose to get out there in the work force, then jump in 100 percent, feeling just as first-class and equal as any other woman or man out there. When in doubt, keep repeating to yourself one of my favorite affirmations:

> I am powerful and I am loving and
> I have nothing to fear!

Learn the secret of "having it all"! Somewhere in the process of writing this book, a new meaning of "having it all" has become clear to me. Let me explain: Much of the impetus of the women's movement was to create for women that great freedom in life called *choice.* But what does choice mean? By definition, choice implies taking one road or the other, not both! Yet, also by definition, having it all implies that we don't have to make any choices at all! Hence, logically we can make the frustrating conclusion that having choice means we can't have it all! What a revolting development this is! We have been unwittingly driving ourselves crazy trying to live two totally incompatible concepts.

By not accepting the fact that the choice of one option precludes us from another, we experience our hard-won blessing called choice as a feeling of loss instead of gain.

Read it again. Some dilemma, isn't it? Choice implies not having it all, just as much as no-choice implies not having it all. You can't spend all your time with your child *and* have a career. You can't have a career and a child *and* expect to have a lot of free time. You can't want your husband to become rich *and* spend a great deal of time "playing" with you . . . and so on. So how can we ever have the feeling of "having it all" . . . or can we? You'll be happy to know that I've come up with a solution that works for me.

We can change our experience of most things in our life by changing our perception. With this in mind, I've created a new definition of "having it all" that allows us to "have it all"! Here it is:

Having it all really means accepting our choices and having no regrets about the road we didn't travel.

This isn't to say that we can't change any of our choices if we decide to travel another road. We simply accept our new direction as one more choice we have in life and go merrily on our way.

As I stated earlier, *you can have anything in life, but you can't have everything.* And this is true. But by being content with our choices, we can now affirm with joy and satisfaction:

> I don't have everything, but I do have it all!

I've been feeling a sense of having it all lately, and obviously I don't have everything: I work hard, therefore I don't have much leisure time; I got married, therefore I don't do what single people do, and so on. Yet I feel I have it all. What creates the feeling now, when I didn't have it earlier in my life, is simply a sense that my life is abundant and filled with blessings. I've come to realize that:

> There's nothing else to "get" in life but that feeling of
> abundance and blessing, despite the choices we have made
> in life and despite the circumstances we find ourselves in.
> Once we have that feeling, we, indeed, "have it all"!

Having worked with the poor in New York City for ten years, I knew so many people who had nothing from an objective standpoint, yet seemed to "have it all" when it came to their participation in their community and the joy they got from so many aspects of their life. They didn't feel they were "missing" anything. I also know some multimillionaires who look like they "have it all" but are always searching for something to fill up the emptiness.

A nun was once asked if she would like to have had a child. "Oh, yes," she replied. Her interviewer then asked her, "Then you regret becoming a nun?" "Oh, no," she replied. "I love my life, but I have always realized that there are so many different kinds of experiences one can have in life, and we can't experience them all. Yes, I could have had a child, but I chose this and

I feel peaceful and content in my choice." To me that truly is the meaning of "having it all"! Perhaps one of the most self-loving things we can do for ourselves is to affirm daily as we write our fifty items in our Book of Abundance:

My life is abundant. I *already* have it all.

Create a Higher Life Purpose. Many of us think of purpose in terms of acquiring externals—money, children, relationship, a sexy body, owning a home and car, and other worldly things. You may have noticed that while external goals often bring us pleasure in life, they do not, in and of themselves, fill us up. More often than not, our question becomes, "Is this all there is?"

The way out of the "is this all there is" syndrome is to choose a Transcendent or Higher Life Purpose. A Higher Life Purpose is the product of your Higher Self, not the Chatterbox. While the Chatterbox is always screaming hysterically, "Get! Get! Get!" the Higher Self is always gently nudging you on with "Give! Give! Give!" Hence your Higher Life Purpose is about living your life from a perspective that is bigger than your life, and it has a quality of outflow rather than acquisition.[7] I love the following quote of John Powell:

I doubt that there has ever been one recorded case of deep and lasting fulfillment reported by a person whose basic mindset and only question was: What am I getting out of this?[8]

I spent much of my life asking this last question and somehow never really felt good about myself despite the fact that I "got" a lot. I gave a lot, too, but underlying all my giving was the question, "What am I getting out of this?!?" Sound familiar?

When I realized I was feeling dissatisfied with my life, even though I had achieved a lot, I knew I had to try something new. The old one wasn't working. It was at this point that I adopted the Higher Life Purpose approach instead of the lust and greed approach, and it has made an incredible difference in my life. Three of the Higher Life Purposes I created for myself at various times over the years are:

To learn and teach about love.

To open my heart.

To focus on giving instead of getting.

Believe me, in the beginning, it was all Act-As-If. I hadn't a clue as to what giving was really all about. But I persevered! With these noble goals in mind, this not-so-noble person tried (and often failed) to make all my choices in life consistent with my Higher Life Purpose. In the beginning, it was really difficult, as I was so accustomed to take from the Universe instead of to give. Much of the time I forgot that my Higher Life Purpose even existed, and even when I remembered, it was hard to give up my former myths about survival:

I don't care about learning and teaching about love. I just want to make money!
I don't care about opening my heart. That jerk really made me angry!
It'll be a cold day in Saudi Arabia when I help her out. What's she done for me lately?

Ah, yes, my magnificence just came shining through! Thankfully, I practiced and practiced and practiced and practiced (and am still practicing), but slowly the good stuff started to filter in and made me understand for the first time in my life the meaning of the phrase "heaven on earth." What happens to my sense of well-being when I remember to think from my Higher Self and act accordingly is nothing short of a miracle!

I always know when I'm back into an old pattern. I begin to feel frightened, withholding, angry, judgmental, and every other unmagnificent feeling you can think of. When I pick up the mirror, I realize the angel has fallen and has once again become attached to the acquisition of money, success, power, or some other thing "out there." I then have to remember to play the game of Switch and transcend to where I can see the world in terms of my new Higher Life Purpose . . . and peace reigns once again. The more I use the messages of the Higher Self, the less I lose myself to the cruelty of my negativity. It takes a constant awareness, which, of course, is why the exercises are so important.

Make no mistake: If you make relationship or career or material gain—or anything external—the purpose of your life, you will always make yourself a candidate for mental torture. Even if you succeed in getting what you want, you will live with the fear that you will lose it.

It is only through creating a higher life purpose that we earn peace. It is our gateway to the Higher Self. It is the key to finding our own magnificence.

Now that we understand about Higher Life Purposes, how do money, relationship, career, family, and other worldly things fit into this picture? In at least four ways:

1. We live in this world, and it is in this world that we need to participate. While we learn our most important lessons from the Higher Self, we then need to shower what we learn onto everything and everyone around us. For example, our Higher Self teaches us about love. We then need to shower this love onto our relationships, our careers, our children, our community . . . even our houses and cars. Did you ever see a house and a car that weren't loved? Pretty pathetic, indeed! Loving every-

thing in our lives creates an inner sense of abundance of the beauty that surrounds us, that "having it all" feeling I just talked about.

2. Without the challenge of the external world, our internal lessons would have a hard time being learned. We must brush against the externals to push through the barriers our old conditioning has set up for us. For example, what better way to learn the true meaning of giving than to brush against conflict in a relationship! A relationship provides opportunity after opportunity to practice our "giving" skills when our "getting" appetite is at its most voracious. In fact, in a relationship, the opportunities for practicing our Higher Life Purpose never cease! Seen in this way, there's no such thing as a bad relationship, only a useful one.

This doesn't mean that the hurt is not present while we are going through one of our "lessons," and it is important that we allow the pain to be felt and released. But when we look for the value to be gained from our experience, the sting is taken away and we become a discoverer instead of a victim of external circumstances. With this shift in attitude, we make life an adventure instead of a heartache.

One student asked if we weren't just conning ourselves with this kind of attitude. I answered, "No more than we are conning ourselves when we see ourselves as victims." I believe there is no objective truth—it's all about how we perceive it—and some will perceive it in a way that supports their aliveness and others won't. It's truly a matter of choice. So why not choose to think in a way that brings you peace instead of misery? Makes sense to me!

3. Higher Life Purposes affect our external world in still another way. When we have a Higher Life Purpose, our neediness diminishes to an extraordinarily low level. Did you ever notice that when you aren't needy, everything somehow falls into your lap? And when you are desperate, the world seems to

be looking the other way? I was amazed to find that when I stopped focusing on money, relationship, career, and so on, as my primary goals in life, they all fell into my life!

To have a Higher Life Purpose is not to deny oneself of the "gifts of the gods"; it is simply not to make your joy and satisfaction in life dependent on them. I love money! I love being in a relationship! I love having a successful career! And as long as I do not expect these things to create my joy and satisfaction, my life works.

4. Having a Higher Life Purpose is also the key to letting go of attachments. For example, if we want children and are afraid the biological clock is running out, our Higher Life Purpose helps us to understand that the problem is not the biological timetable, but our attachment to the idea of having children. If we can let go of the attachment, there is no upset. Attachments are unloving to the self. They bring you pain.

If your Higher Life Purpose is about becoming a more loving person, you would see that you could become a more loving person whether you have a child or not. There are millions of ways to express your love in the Universe. Your Higher Life Purpose is transcendent and takes you to a lighter plane where you have a much grander perspective. Wanting to have a child becomes a want instead of a desperate need. *Wants* are always easier to handle than *needs!* From the perspective of the "lower" self, everything is a big deal. From the perspective of the Higher Self, it's flowing and easy. From the perspective of the Higher Self, you can say:

"I want children and if I have them, that's great! If I don't have children, life offers many opportunities to give and to love. I look forward to the Journey, wherever it takes me."

Nothing heavy. We realize that it is all simply part of the Journey.

How can you incorporate the idea of a Higher Life Purpose into your life? First, you have to choose one. Don't get too heavy about it! You will notice that all Higher Life Purposes are reflective of the same governing principle—*Love*. You can adopt one of mine if you choose. Some other possibilities are:

> To own your magnificence and reflect
> it into this world.
>
> To learn and to grow.
>
> To move from a position of pain
> to one of power and love.
>
> To create a more loving world.

It's important that you create a Higher Life Purpose that feels right for you at this moment in time. You can add and edit as you go along. The way you use your Higher Life Purpose is as follows: Whenever a choice comes up in life, ask yourself:

"Which decision or action would be a demonstration of my Higher Life Purpose?"

The answer to that question is one that only you in your heart of hearts can make. For each of us, the answer would be different. It is important that you don't punish yourself when your choice runs contrary to what you know would best serve your Higher Life Purpose. By definition, that would be unloving, and based on the "lower self purpose" of "I have to be perfect." Your Higher Life Purpose is meant only as a guide, not as a jail sentence. You will find that by simply keeping it in your awareness, you begin to live into your Purpose . . . little by little, step by step. You don't have to force it! Write it out and put it in a number of observable places so that it will be there as a constant reminder. But let it work its own miracles.

It's important that I tell you not to make the goal of "happiness" your life principle. There are many great thinkers and feelers who, in their wisdom, tell us that you don't become happy by pursuing happiness. As Rabbi Harold Kushner tells us:

"You become happy by living a life that means something . . . I suspect that the happiest people you know are the ones who work at being kind, helpful, and reliable and happiness sneaks into their lives while they are busy doing those things. Happiness is always a by-product, never a primary goal."[9]

Wherever your journey takes you, commit to living as a source of love and light. Actually, this could be one of your Higher Life Purposes. We don't have to look very far afield to understand that the world is in a very shaky place right now. The unrest that we see is a reflection of the fact that so many of us have strayed from our loving center. We need to find our own inner guiding light to love so that we can begin to transform, not only our little place in the sun, but that of the rest of the world as well.

Understand that everything you do contributes to the pot of energy that defines the world. Always ask yourself, "Am I contributing loving energy or unloving energy?" I believe every one of us wants to be a source of strength and love.

We all have the power to touch the lives of others around us. We can always find ways to give of our magnificence. When you see virtues in others that you wish you had, know that you have them. It is simply a matter of accessing them. No matter how bleak you may feel about yourself, you can begin to fill yourself with light by very simple loving acts. To help a child across the street, to comfort a friend who is in pain, to make a beautiful dinner for those you love, to help where help is needed in your workplace, to stand up for what you believe in—to say no to violence and yes to love, in whatever arena you find yourself.

Loving acts raise you to the level of magnificence. I love Mother Teresa's wonderful line, as told by Marianne Williamson:[10]

> There's no such thing as great deeds, only small deeds done with great love.

We get there by Acting-As-If we really count. It doesn't work to say, "When I feel better about myself, I'll go out and help the world." No, it is the reverse: "I'll go out and help the world, and then I'll feel better about myself."

We don't possess energy . . . we are energy. And we can change that energy from negative to positive. The Light is always there. It's only our inner enemies that block the Light. With a little help from our mirror-mirror-on-the-wall we can discover what these inner enemies are and separate them from our Essence.

> Liberation is really about letting the light shine through. It has nothing to do with men, money, power, or anything else that is external. It is purely about the light . . . purely about the light . . .

With that I will move on with you and your magnificence and show you how to use it to create a powerful new kind of relationship.

Affirmations for Loving the Self

I am filled with a vibrant living force.

Everything I need to know is within me.

I count my blessings.

I am in control.

Whatever happens in life, I can handle it!

I love the challenge.

I can feel success pouring into me.

I have the force within.

I am valuable.

I can find support whenever it is needed.

I am on a fascinating journey.

I have so much to give.

I am a responsible person.

I am powerful and I am loving.

My life is unfolding perfectly.

My life has meaning and purpose.

I have the power to bring dignity into my life.

My life makes a difference.

I am filled with beauty, strength, and light.

10

GIVE ME A HIGHER LOVE!

Reflections at the End of a Marriage

We thought one got married and lived happily everafter;
  We didn't know that relationships require hard
    work . . .
We thought it wasn't any good if we had to ask for what we
    needed;
  We didn't know that no one is a mind reader . . .
We thought all our needs should have been filled with our
    marriage;
  We didn't know what our most important need was—a
    sense of self . . .
We thought our becoming one made us whole;
  We didn't know two whole people were necessary from the
    start . . .
We thought he had to be strong and take care of her;
  We didn't know we were supposed to take care of each
    other . . .
We thought it was disloyal to grow as an individual;
  We didn't know how stifling too much togetherness could
    be . . .
We thought that when the other grew, it was a threat;

We didn't know we were good-enough, and shouldn't feel
  threatened . . .
We thought money would make us secure;
  We didn't know that security meant knowing you could
  make it, with or without money . . .
We thought those who went for help were weak;
  We didn't know that everyone needs help . . .
We thought the other wasn't giving;
  We didn't know we weren't taking in . . .
He thought I was happy;
  He didn't know how frightened I was . . .
I thought he was happy;
  I didn't know how frightened he was . . .

We didn't know . . . We just didn't know . . .
  There was so much we didn't know . . .

Susan Jeffers, 1972

O ne day, not long after my first marriage ended, I was sitting at my desk reflecting on what went wrong and, in a moment of inspiration, wrote the preceding poem. Then, with the bitter-sweet sadness that always accompanies the end of an era, I tucked it away and went on with my life. As I was rummaging through a drawer recently, the poem resurfaced. I sat down and read it after so many years, once again reminded of the destructive misconceptions that propelled us, and so many others, into such unnecessary disharmony.

Today, destructive misconceptions clearly still abound. One has only to look at the number of miserable relationships to realize that most of us still don't have a clue as to what a nourishing relationship looks like. Instead we've become used to the ones that take away all our joy. It's as though relationships don't feel good unless they feel bad. And no wonder! Look at the stories that are held up before us as romantic models of love.

Romeo and Juliet, for example, is still referred to as "one of the greatest love stories ever told." (It was obviously the prototype for that ever-popular song, "I Can't Live Without You!") With all due respect to Shakespeare, it really should be considered one of the *sickest* love stories ever told! It is the ultimate portrayal of dependency, and, as we all know by now, dependency is not love. To top it off, those two silly kids had so little sense of their own possible contribution to this world that they chose to end their lives. Do you think that if they really were in touch with their own beauty, strength, and light, the story would have ended the way it did? No way!

Had they not chosen to take the coward's way out, the story would have had a predictable ending, given their age and level of maturity. It would only have been a matter of time before Juliet started asking such questions as:

"Why art thou fifteen minutes late arriving at the balcony tonight? Doth a new maiden capture my lover's eye, per chance?"

Eventually her sad little inquiries would turn hostile, and you would hear something like this:

"Why art thou so late this midsummer's eve? Doth thou not thinketh I have better things to do with my time than waiteth around for you?"

(A Shakespeare I'll never be!) They probably would have broken up a few months later, when one of them decided that the other really wasn't filling their needs and there must be somebody else out there who could make them feel more special. So much for Romeo and Juliet!

While I jest, I realize that this kind of intense, all-consuming attachment is the kind of love that we all dreamed about as children. It is the kind of love we searched for when we got older and, in many cases, thought we had found when we said our marriage vows. And it is the kind of misconception about love that has created a divorce rate that is well over 50 percent!

Obviously, passionate attachments have nothing to do with meaningful love. Perhaps they're God's way of perpetuating the human race. Like animals in heat, we cling together in a blissful state convinced that *this time* it's going to last forever . . . until we wake up one morning and wonder what we ever saw in the other person, anyway!

No matter how unreal we know passionate attachments to be, we nevertheless seem to be caught unaware when they occur. We call it "falling in love." I've learned that the best thing we can do when Cupid strikes is to pray we get through it quickly so we can pick ourselves up and finally get to that place where a more sustaining kind of love can begin.

Unfortunately, having only been exposed to the nonsustaining attachment, most of us wouldn't know a sustaining one if it hit us in the face. One woman told me, "I was seeing a man who was really very wonderful, but I broke up with him because I didn't hear any bells ringing." I told her that if she ever did hear bells ringing, she should immediately make an appointment with an ear specialist. Ringing in our ears is not a healthy state of affairs.

At this point, you might be thinking I'm very cynical when it comes to love. On the contrary, I'm really high on love and I consider my relationship with Mark to be one of the best I've ever seen. I also happen to be a romantic and so is Mark; that is, if being a romantic means constantly doing loving things for one other. Yes, I'm high on love, but I'm not high on attachment anymore. Let me explain.

By the time I met Mark, I was in my forties, and for the first time in my life I was truly feeling a sense of wholeness and power. Although I wasn't against having a relationship, I didn't "need" a relationship. I was happy. I was independent. I had many friends. I had a great family. I loved my home. I had a great job. I was contributing to my community. I dated a lot. I was learning how to connect with my Higher Self. As a result of the fact that my "grid" was so full, I was a full-filled person. I had gone beyond the point in my life where I was defined by a relationship.

Also, by the time I met Mark, I wasn't looking to "fall" in love. I was looking to "rise" in love. I had already learned through much experience that "falling in love" was simply a practical joke Cupid plays on the innocent Child-Within. I was onto all his little tricks and refused to be duped yet again. So whenever I experienced a strong attraction to some enticing "stranger across a crowded room," I knew it was my signal to find the quickest exit. I had enough of childish love. I was ready for something meatier. I was ready for a lover who was first and foremost my friend. Enter Mark!

You might have wondered why I would even want to bother with a relationship if I was feeling so whole and independent on my own. And that's a good question, indeed. In the first place, a truly loving relationship feels wonderful, sometimes sublime. It makes life sweeter and easier in many respects. It gives you great joy to be able to make your mate's life a little brighter, and it feels blessed to take in the love that he brings to yours. As one of the men so beautifully stated in an earlier chapter, there's nothing more divine that having someone there "to walk the walk and talk the talk." We share the Journey together. And as far as I'm concerned, there's nothing more sacred than that.

There is another important reason to be in a relationship:

A relationship is the best training ground for learning how to open your heart.

As many of you have already discovered, nothing brings up the truth of unresolved dependency better than a relationship. Many women (and men) are out there making it on their own and seem to have made that psychological leap into adulthood.

Yet the minute they get into a relationship, the Child-Within emerges from the hidden depths. While it creates obvious havoc in our lives, the Child-Within is better handled on the surface than hidden in our unconscious, where the damage is much more lethal, controlling us in a multitude of subtle and twisted ways.

Because of the pleasure that can be derived, the joy that can be given, and the self-knowledge that can be gained, I am very much in favor of relationships, especially the loving kind. But what does a really loving relationship look like? How do we go about creating a love that really works? S. Kriyananda tells the wonderful story of a famous sculptor in India who was asked by an admirer how he was able to create such a magnificent shape of an elephant out of a piece of stone. The sculptor replied, "It was easy. I simply cut away everything that didn't look like an elephant!"[1] Using this magical piece of wisdom as a model, I've learned that:

The way we create a loving relationship is to cut away everything in our actions and feelings that doesn't look like a loving relationship!

I understand that this process takes a lot of time and possible heartache and you may be impatient. I'm sorry to report that no shortcuts that I know of have as yet been devised. Sometimes it takes many relationships—boring, volatile, oppressive, depressing, unhealthy, painful, or whatever—before we can cut away enough of "what doesn't look like love" to allow the true picture of love to emerge. And sometimes it takes many years of drama in one particular relationship to get to that place where it looks like love.

As long as we're aware that it's all part of the "whittling" process, we should never feel that the time is wasted. Each experience, positive or negative, brings us closer and closer to the "look" of love. Hence, no matter how awful a relationship appears to the naked eye, take heart—there is always something to gain.

I was once in a relationship that from the outside looking in resembled a combat zone. None of my friends could understand what I possibly could see in this man who was possessive and consuming on the one hand and the master of the put-down on the other. Truthfully, I couldn't understand it either. Breaking up and getting together was the story of our lives. The drama was awesome!

Then after four years of warfare, the day came when I could allow him to spout his put-downs without becoming a raving maniac. I was able to respond simply and without attachment:

> "Thank you for sharing your feelings, but I like the way I am. Would you like another cup of coffee?"

I also was able to recognize that it was only his own insecurity that was making him behave in such a negative way. While it took me four years, I finally did learn that I didn't have to allow someone's opinion to take away my sense of self. I also learned that his put-downs were nothing personal, (although it sure felt that way at the time!). They were a reflection of the way he felt about himself.

With these two powerful lessons in hand, I was able to lovingly let go of the relationship and move on—having cut away still another part of the picture that didn't look like love. I was ready to "graduate" to the next level. Have you noticed that if we don't learn our lessons, the Universe hands us the opportunity to learn them over and over and over again . . . until we get it right? So if you wonder why you are always drawing the "wrong" kind of man into your life, you can now understand that he is the "right" kind of man to teach you what you need to learn. This is why I love to call all the men in our lives "practice people." They evoke such questions as . . .

Why am I drawing such negativity in my life?

Why am I remaining in this relationship?

Why am I not feeling secure?

Why am I not appreciating his kindness?

Why do I want so much attention from him?

Why do I feel abandoned when he takes an evening to be
with his friends?

Why do I expect him to pay for everything?

Why do I pick on him?

Why does he make me so angry?

Why do his put-downs upset me so much?

Each question leads us closer and closer to opening our heart, which ultimately is the key to creating a blissful relationship in our lives. The adventure goes on and on and on. No matter how hard we work to manifest the ideal relationship, there's always more to learn. We're all lovers-in-training.

I've written the following guidelines to what I call a *Higher Love* to help your training program move along a little more quickly. Please understand that they are an ideal toward which we can strive. I know of no relationship that comprises all of these ingredients all of the time. Our fear and insecurity sometimes get in the way. As you may have heard me say before, "Even the Buddhas have their days!" So in no way are you ever to put yourself (or anyone else) down for acting in an unloving way. We're *all* doing the best we can!

I suggest that you read the guidelines over and over again, simply absorbing the *spirit* of what is being communicated. Then hold that *spirit* within your Heart and trust that you have within you everything you need to know to create the kind of love you seek. With that in mind, let me show you what a higher love looks like through the eyes of just one other lover-in-training:

Guidelines to a Higher Love

1. A Higher Love begins with a love of humanity. I was once speaking to a woman who was bereft because her latest boyfriend had departed from the scene. She sobbed to me that she had so much love to give to the world and nobody to give it to. I pointed out to her that there were millions of people who desperately needed and would welcome her love, but she didn't understand. Until she does, it is doubtful that she will draw the kind of love she wants into her loveless life.

A Higher Love is part of a Grander Plan of loving. The more we succeed as a "lover" in the world outside our relationship, the more we will succeed as a "lover" inside our relationship. The more we succeed in putting love and harmony into our outer world, the more we will succeed in putting love and harmony into our inner world. Our life has to be about creating a context for love which touches *everything* and *everyone* that comes into our sphere of being . . . and that, of course, includes men.

2. A Higher Love focuses on essence rather than form. A Higher Love focuses on the larger picture, not the everyday specifics. It notices that this is a loving and caring man. It does not focus on the fact that he forgot to take out the garbage. It notices the blessings he brings into your life. It does not focus on the fact that he forgot your birthday.

We can apply this same principle of choosing essence over form when we put in our "order" for someone new to come into our lives. We create a picture that emanates from the Higher Self that simply affirms:

I am creating a healthy, nourishing, and full-filling relation-ship.

rather than:

I am creating a relationship with a tall, blond, blue-eyed man who makes $200,000 a year and drives a Porsche.

You may get the man, but you may not get the healthy rela-tionship. The Chatterbox and the Higher Self are very different, and they often pay attention to very different things. Your Soul could care less if he has blond hair or not, or, for that matter, if he has any hair at all! Your Soul only sees another beautiful Soul who would love to have us love him.

Once we start to pay attention to essence rather than form, you will notice that the number of possibilities for relationship increase dramatically. It's not that more men materialized over night; it's just that from the Soul's perspective, lovers abound!

3. A Higher Love is about learning. A Higher Love includes most of the same "lousy" ingredients as unenlightened love: anger, self-righteousness, expectations, judgments, fear, and all the rest. The only difference is that *a Higher Love uses negative feelings as keys to self-discovery, not as a way to put down our mates.*

I know we sometimes get tired of the fact that our life is about constant learning. There are times we feel hopelessly stupid and wish the day would come when we finally get it right! Whenever I start to feel this way, I remind myself of what J. G. Bennett has to say about learning:

My own belief is that the ability to learn is so precious a quality that it cannot disappear from the perfected man. To be able to learn is to be young and whoever keeps the joy of learning fresh in him remains forever young.[2]

A new secret to eternal youth! The day we stop learning about ourselves and our world around us is the day we spiritually die. Why would we want to throw our youth away?

4. A Higher Love is not about drama. This doesn't mean that drama doesn't sometimes appear in a loving relationship, but it isn't about drama. After being exposed to the likes of Romeo and Juliet for so many years, we are indeed conditioned to believe that love *is* drama! When things are going along peacefully, we miss the thunder and lightning that give us a sense of excitement. As a result, when we are experiencing sweet, supportive, gentle love, it doesn't feel like love!

When we are focusing only on externals, this need for drama is understandable. Everything out there ultimately becomes boring when it becomes familiar enough, which explains why passionate attachments soon lose their passion. We then go looking for someone or something else out there to excite us once again. But when we are looking into the mirror instead of the magnifying glass, relationships are *never* boring. This doesn't mean that boredom doesn't come up in a higher love. It does. But when it comes up, we simply pick up our mirror and ask, "Why am I bored?" And we discover it has nothing to do with our men.

Stewart Emery described boredom as "hostility without enthusiasm."[3] The hostility is about the fact that we are not creating our own inner world of excitement and we are waiting for our mates to create it for us. The remedy for boredom is to ask ourselves the important question: "If I really owned my magnificence, what would I be doing right now?" . . . and *do it!* As we make ourselves less boring, our mates appears to be less boring.

As long as we are showering love into the relationship and into the world, we will never be bored. There's too much to do! We become involved in a new kind of drama—the kind that loving acts produce within the deepest part of our Soul. Here the drama is mind-blowing, but it is the drama of bliss, of expansion, of light, not of agitation and disharmony.

5. *A Higher Love is intentional.* A Higher Love is governed by an active thought process. It is something we pay attention to. It is conscious. Marianne Williamson tells the story of a beau who hurt her badly, then told her, "I never consciously intended to hurt you." She responded with:

> "I know you never consciously intended to hurt me. The problem is that you never consciously intended to love me!"[4]

Williamson brings up a point that is essential for us to understand: The natural process for things left unattended is deterioration. Have you ever seen a house left unattended for a number of years? It is a sad sight. It's not as though anyone intentionally meant to destroy it; it's just that no one intentionally meant to preserve it.

In like manner, the world is becoming an unloving place, not because people are consciously intending for it to be unloving, but because people are not consciously intending for it to be loving. We don't get up every morning and say, "I'm going to add negativity to the world today." The problem is that we don't get up each morning and say, "I'm going to make this a better world today." When we don't put conscious intention into it, the natural state is for it to deteriorate. This same principle applies to our relationships.

I have learned that when we put conscious intention into love, a chain reaction occurs that keeps the love increasing and increasing and increasing. As soon as the conscious intention stops, the process begins to reverse itself. So:

> In order to keep love alive, we must consciously intend to shower it with all the magnificence we can muster!

6. A Higher Love is constantly activating love. Once we get our intention awakened, we need to take the next step and *make it happen.* As we whittle away what doesn't look like love, we begin to actively throw the ingredients that do look like love into the pot. If we see appreciation as part of love, we begin expressing our appreciation to the one we love. We do not wait to be appreciated first. If we see touching as part of love, we begin the activity of touching the one we love. We do not wait to be touched. If we see gift-giving as part of love, we begin thoughtfully choosing little gifts. We do not wait to be given to. Particularly if we feel we need something from someone, we give that something to them. And thus we learn the feel of love!

I am in total agreement with others who teach that our main "craving" in life is not to be loved, but *to love.* By acting the part, we become the part. Every day we need to ask ourselves:

What am I doing to keep love alive?

Some of us have the words "I love you" dripping from our lips. *But "I love you" means very little if you are not being a loving person to the person to whom you are saying "I love you"!* This is the classic case of setting a banquet table and not bringing him any food. It's only as we act lovingly will we know love. *We* are the source of our experience of love, not our mate. In one of his workshops, Werner Erhard asked a wonderful question:

If love is scarce, who isn't creating it?[5]

His audience got the point. You can't go after love without loving. Just as owning our magnificence is acting out of our magnificence,

Owning love is acting out of love. It doesn't depend on anyone else.

Remember, motive is critical. Many "giving" activities are not about giving, but "getting." I know women who knock themselves out giving to their men (and vice versa), with one motive in mind: to quench their desperate search for approval. This is not love, it is barter!

Remember also that sometimes our mates have a harder time expressing their love than we do. That doesn't mean the love isn't there. It just means that their expression of that love is constrained by their earlier experiences. If we can be mindful of the contributions they make to our lives and be ecstatic about the expression of love, no matter how small, that is there, perhaps we can make it safe for their bound-up expression of love to be released.

There are other times when our mate is incapable of loving or taking in love even in a bound-up way and may even throw our gift of love back in our face. *This doesn't mean that we stop our habit of loving.* I'm not talking about being a doormat here. People who own their magnificence are never doormats, but they are in touch with other people's pain. They may decide to leave the relationship and find someone who can enjoy their gifts, but they leave with an open heart and a wish that the troubled Soul they are leaving will soon find his way. They say to themselves:

I choose to be a loving person. I do not choose to be a person entwined in a hateful game.

I have heard so many women say they have to play it "cool" to keep men in their lives. A Higher Love says it is important for you to be the person you love to be and draw into your life someone who loves you best that way.

A Higher Love says stop playing games and losing your Soul just so you can keep someone in your life!

7. A Higher Love invites touching but not attachment. This is a tough one for most of us. In our society, we think love *is* attachment. Yet I know my relationship with Mark is healthiest when I am not feeling attached. Attachment creates neediness, and neediness takes away our ability to love. Attachment also creates dissatisfaction. We are not meant to be a child forever. The direction in which all human beings inherently are drawn to travel is toward what Jung called "individuation"—toward becoming our own person.

> When we cling to another, we can't become our own person; we become their person. We fall into disharmony with our own inherent need to grow.

I think that, on an intellectual level, most of us understand and agree with our need to become our own person. But when it comes to applying it to our relationships, there appears to be a mental block! I once told my students that I love Mark more than I have ever loved any man, and yet I know if we were parted tomorrow, my life would still have meaning. That doesn't mean I wouldn't grieve the loss and miss him terribly, but the day would come when the tears would stop and I would once again feel life pulling me forward. They couldn't understand how you could *really* love someone and feel you could live without them. (There's the Romeo and Juliet influence once again!) I told them that there were relationships in the long ago past when I did feel almost suicidal at their breakup. I realize now that they were relationships that had little to do with love. They had to do with the desperation of a lost Soul.

> There's an irony in the fact that the less you need someone, the more you are able to love them.

Many of us already understand the self-destructiveness of attachments. Hence, becoming attached is not necessarily one

of those things we consciously intend to do. It sometimes just
"happens" at those times when we feel safe in the arms of
someone's love. The feeling of safety soon disappears as the
familiar signs of attachment begin to emerge—fear, jealousy,
possessiveness, disappointment, expectations, and so on.

There was a time when these feelings of attachment signaled
to me that it was time to end a relationship. My fear of falling
into the dependency I felt during my first marriage was enormous. After leaving a multitude of relationships, it dawned on
me that at times, dependency needs *always* surface in a relationship! But instead of running away, we simply need to recognize
what is happening and quickly take out our little bag of tools that
guide us back to our Higher Self, which, as we know, is our place
of strength, beauty, and love.

You may ask with sadness in your heart:

Are we never to allow ourselves to fall into the safety of
a loved one's arms and the delicious respite that "two
melding into one" allows?

Oh, yes, for a moment, an hour, a day or more . . . but always
with the knowledge that the surrender of self can only be a
temporary thing. Strangely, the more secure we are within our
Soul, the more we can allow those moments of "falling" to
occur. We are at peace with the inner "knowing" that we will
soon pick ourselves up again and connect with the safety and
respite that a feeling of Inner Oneness also allows.

8. A Higher Love requires a higher trust. I talked in an earlier
chapter about trust within the relationship. There is a more
transcendent kind of trust we need to have in order to allow our
relationship to flow, the trust that:

Whatever future direction our relationship takes is the
gateway to our highest good.

What this means is that we, with our limited vision, cannot see far enough into the future to know the experiences that would best teach us what we need to learn. For example, when I look back at all the broken relationships, I can now see that they were perfect conduits for leading me to the wonderful place I am today. As they were occurring, it was hard to see the exquisite order of it all, but I certainly see it now. I've come to learn that there seems to be a Higher Wisdom that knows far more about relationships than I do!

As a result, I approach my present marriage much differently than the first. I planned for my first marriage to last forever. My plan, however, conflicted with a Higher Plan that decided it would last sixteen years. Looking back, the Higher Plan was conceived with far greater wisdom . . . for both of us! I don't think of forever anymore. I live with the "knowing" that my present marriage will last exactly as long as it is meant to last. That could be a year or a lifetime. While I would prefer that it would be forever, I'm now willing to do what I can to nurture and enjoy it, at the same time, letting go of my picture of forever. The peace in that kind of trust is wonderful!

Having a Higher Trust also allows me to better understand the concept of living in the now—living moment to moment—instead of living twenty years from now. I love and appreciate him *now!* I take in all the love he has to give me *now!* I savor every moment that we are together *now!* With this attitude, I am much more aware of the beauty in the relationship *now.* I don't put my enjoyment on hold, looking forward to the grand Paradise that waits ahead of us . . . sometimes later . . . when we have more time. I create present moments of Paradise for myself just by acknowledging the beauty that is there *now!* And I don't presume to have the wisdom to understand what is best for both of us in the bigger picture.

This principle works not only in relationships, but in every aspect of our lives. As long as we remember to operate from this place of Higher Trust, our life flows as smoothly as a mountain stream. Whenever we try to block the flow, instead of going with it, we succeed only in knocking our heads against the rocks and giving ourselves a great big headache . . . and an even bigger heartache! On that I can speak with highest authority!

9. *A Higher Love is committed.* Commitment means that we will participate 100 percent full out in making our relationships the best they could possibly be for however ·long they may last, whether it is a week, a year, or a lifetime. No holding back! I often wonder why so many of us are holding back. Could it be that we are saving it for that elusive soul-mate who is only a dream away? Don't wait! Give it away *now!* All of it! When we open the floodgates of our love, the supply is endless. And if, in the end, it doesn't work out, we will know that we did our best (which is wonderful to know), and we will remember that not everything is meant to be "forever."

How does marriage fit into commitment? Personally, I'm all for it. For years I was convinced that marriage was no longer a necessary formality for me, especially since I didn't want any more children. After I lived with Mark for three years, I changed my mind. I realized that I was playing the same game that I played with all my other relationships; the game was called "one foot out the door." Because I was never quite sure where the relationship was going, I was really never "there." I was always making plans in my head as to what I would do if the relationship ended, and I went to every party checking out the room . . . just in case. I decided that I needed to go one step further in the way of commitment in order for me to step inside and shut the door behind me. And for me that step was marriage.

I am also a strong believer in the magic of vows—marriage or otherwise—which today many couples are creating on their own. A few months ago I attended a magnificent wedding. While many aspects of the ceremony were traditional, at one point, our friends faced one another and, in their own words, told of their appreciation of the other's beauty, strength, and light. They recently told me that, when in the course of everyday living, they begin to lose sight of the magnificence that brought them together, they make a practice of playing the videotape of their marriage and the gates of love are released anew.

We are friends with another couple who repeat their vows at the end of every month. They have been doing this for over twenty years, and when you are in their presence, you would think they were newlyweds. In a sense they are. Mark and I have reaffirmed our wedding vows each year for the three years we have been married. In the "ceremony," we include our appreciation of how much the other has added to our life during the previous year. We do this in the presence of friends, which seems to add even more meaning for us. Two years ago, we and five other couples got together and created a magical evening in which we all reaffirmed our vows. Can you imagine the loving energy in the room as one couple after another renewed their commitment to each other? It was perhaps one of the most memorable evenings of our lives.

I do not in any way mean to say that commitment requires marriage. There are committed relationships without marriage and there are marriages without commitment. Individually, we have to judge which arrangements better serve our present needs. The essence of commitment is simply that we honor our agreements in whatever form they take and that we love, respect, care for, and support the growth of the beautiful person over whom we have been privileged to be given guardianship.

10. A Higher Love is light. A Higher Love requires that we keep a sense of humor. You must admit that in our struggle for wholeness, we do some pretty funny things when it comes to our relationships! If we can laugh about it all, instead of taking ourselves so seriously, we can greatly lighten the weight that we sometimes carry as we struggle along on the Path toward wholeness.

I've been privileged over the years to be in the company of

some very enlightened couples. The one quality that stands out among all of them is their ability to laugh at themselves and invite you to laugh with them.

This lightness allows us to understand that our human foibles are not bad . . . and we can be loved, not in spite of them, but because of them.

11. A Higher Love is uplifting. A Higher Love understands that as guardian over another person's feelings, we need to lift them up spiritually when his own belief in himself falters. The beauty of it all is that as we offer inspiration to our beloved, we inspire ourselves. Conversely, when we drag him down, we drag ourselves down as well. Inspiration could mean a number of different things to different people. To me, it means the following:

It means, when our loved one doubts his beauty, we remind him how beautiful he is.

It means we encourage him to stretch and grow, even if we fear he will "grow" away from us.

It means we stretch and grow in order to become a support instead of a burden.

It means we applaud when he is succeeding. We don't begrudge him success, despite how unsuccessful we may be feeling at the moment.

It means we applaud when he isn't succeeding and we let him know that "it's all happening perfectly."

It means "I depend on you sometimes and you depend on me sometimes." Our support is reciprocal.

It means we don't buy into dependency, but encourage him to stand on his own two feet. Sometimes this requires tough love!

It means that as we cease being the victim in our own lives, we encourage him to cease being a victim in his as well.

It means that first and foremost we are his friend . . . and
  we treat him accordingly.
It means we don't seek happiness from him, but for him.
It means we protect the wounded child within him instead
  of making it bleed more than it is already bleeding.

You get the picture. Keep in mind that supporting someone
doesn't mean doing it for him . . . or insisting he does it your
way! Since we are all the blind leading the blind, we cannot
always know that our way is the right way.

Nourishing the growth of our mates is sometimes a scary
proposition. We fear that if they grow "too much," they may
leave us behind. One thing I can assure you is that the likelihood
of their leaving is far greater when we try to stop their growth
than if we try to encourage their growth. If we are the ones who
are helping them to feel great about themselves, it is doubtful
that they would leave. Would you?

12. A Higher Love asks that we open our hearts to men. A Higher
Love asks that we warm the part of us that hasn't allowed us
to treat men in a loving way. We need to understand that under
whatever mask a man chooses to wear, there exists a person
who really wants to please women, particularly his mate. When
he isn't succeeding, it's only because his (or our) pain and fear
are getting in the way. I believe that:

One of the most precious gifts we can give men is to let
  them have the experience of "making it" with us.

One way to do this is to constantly acknowledge their gifts:

You are contributing so much to my life.

You are a beautiful person.

I learn from you.

I feel supported by you.

I feel blessed by the way you love me.

We say these things, not only in private, but in the presence of other people. Nothing will make our men (or anyone else) feel more special than your validating them in the presence of other people.

It's time we gave men a break. Their hearts ache to be acknowledged. I recently told a male acquaintance of mine the subject of this book and he broke down and cried. What we don't understand is how much men are starved to hear us say:

"Hey, you're OK in our book!"

I know that deep within our hearts, under the pain of our struggle to become whole, we hold the precious understanding of how much men have contributed to our lives in their roles as friends, mentors, lovers, fathers, sons, and husbands. Indeed, we have much to be thankful for as a result of their presence in our lives. So let's consider today the beginning of a new kind of love . . . an aware love . . . an adult love . . . that allows us to appreciate the myriad actions men take to show us how much they care.

I know for many of us this is still an angry and frightening time and it is, indeed, difficult to open our hearts. If this is still true for you, I implore you to keep working to uncover your own magnificence—your own beauty, strength, and love—trusting that the day will soon come when you can look into that mirror-mirror-on-the-wall and see only love.

Harold Kushner cites a wonderful quote from the Talmud, an ancient collection of the works of the rabbis of the first five centuries:

In the world to come, each of us will be called to account for all the good things God put on earth which we refused to enjoy.

As far as I am concerned, one of the great things God put on earth for women to enjoy—body, mind, and soul—is men . . . will you refuse this gift? And will you refuse to share with men the huge amounts of love that you hold locked inside your heart? Remember, that if on the last day of our lives we can answer "yes" to the question, "Did you warm the world with your love?" we can be at peace with the knowledge that our lives had meaning . . . and that the world is better off for our having been a part of it.

I may be a dreamer but dreams do come true, and . . .

I foresee a day in the not-too-distant future when the collective opening of our hearts will occur, and it will be as though the floodgates of dawn have opened wide apart showering the world with the blood-red warmth and glow of the sun . . .

En masse we unleashed our anger . . .

En masse let us *now* unleash our love . . .

APPENDIX A
Affirmations

The positive affirmation is a very effective form of self-talk, which, when used regularly, can help you to become a more powerful, loving, confident and peaceful person.

What exactly is an affirmation?

An affirmation is a positive statement that something is *already happening.*

For example:

I am now creating a healthy relationship.

Note that even if there is no man in your life at the present moment, this affirmation is appropriate. Affirmations are involved with *process.* The act of creating a healthy relationship requires a readiness that evolves through both time and experience. When we affirm "I am now creating a healthy relationship," we are helping to initiate that readiness. The affirmation is a commitment of intention . . . and commitment is a very powerful force. Our subconscious mind receives the message and begins its work.

Keep in mind that even when our conscious mind is not focusing on our intention, our subconscious mind is. Remember those times when a name slipped your mind. You wracked your brain trying to remember the name, but it eluded you. You finally gave up trying. And suddenly, out of nowhere, the name popped into your head. Obviously a part of your subconscious was still working on the "command" even though your conscious mind had stopped.

The beauty of affirmations is that it is not necessary for us to believe the words we are saying for them to work. Our subconscious mind seems to believe the words we speak, whether our conscious mind believes it or not! When we fill ourselves with positive self-talk we see beneficial effects on our health, our attitude, our performance, and more.

Positive affirmations also act like radio signals which send out messages to the outside world—and somehow these signals are received, understood, and responded to. Note all the meaningful coincidences that will begin to happen in your life. For example—did you ever commit to something in you life, such as finding a better job, and, suddenly, you bumped into just the right person who gave you the perfect lead for the job you were looking for? Carl Jung called this kind of meaningful coincidence "synchronicity."

When and how does one use affirmations? The beauty of affirmations is that they can be incorporated easily into our daily living and require no extra time. For example, as we shower, drive, or dress, we can be filling our subconscious mind with empowering and loving thoughts. The key to affirmations is *repetition, repetition, and repetition.* Repeat each affirmation at least ten times to create a positive effect.

I've included many affirmations in this book. Pick the ones that "speak" to you. Create index cards for each one so that you can use them as reminders throughout the day. As you awaken, repeat positive affirmations to yourself instead of the gloom and doom messages from your negative Chatterbox. Instead of saying, "Oh, I don't want to go to work today. It's so boring!" repeat to yourself over and over again, "I am creating a beautiful day." "I am drawing to me all good things." "I am bringing light wherever I go." And so on. One of my diligent students created an affirmation Rolodex which she uses while driving. In this way, her mind is always filled with wonderful thoughts instead of upset as she fights traffic and other hassles in life.

Whenever I am facing a particularly trying time, I create a thirty-minute audiotape of my voice repeating positive affirmations over and over again. I play the tape as I am going to sleep and as I am awakening. This method quiets my Chatterbox to a whisper and allows my Higher Self to be in control.

After you become proficient, you can create your own affirmations that relate specifically to your needs. Keep in mind that AFFIRMATIONS ARE ALWAYS STATED IN THE *PRESENT.* For example . . .

I am now creating a healthy relationship . . .
not
I am going to create a healthy relationship.

Also, affirmations should always be stated in the *positive* instead of the negative.

I am drawing supportive men into my life . . .
not
I am no longer drawing hurtful men into my life.

Affirmations can be part of a larger program of positive thinking. For a look at a beginner's intensive into positive thinking, read Chapter 5 in *Feel the Fear and Do It Anyway.* Also, you can find many books in your bookstore that focus on the use of affirmations and positive self-talk. In the meantime, the constant repetition of the affirmations I've provided will give you a good start.

Quotes to Remember from
Opening Our Hearts to Men

The whole of the human species is crying out for love. If we all take the time to look into our hearts, we will ultimately feel complete and connected . . . within ourselves and as part of the human family.

Getting out into the world can bring silent screams of terror. But we won't find what we want by retreating. In going back, we will only find the silent screams of helplessness.

As long as "they did it to us" remains part of our thinking, we won't find the identity and joy and satisfaction in life that we all are seeking.

To move ahead requires that we not only let go of our own anger, but that we distance ourselves from others who are angry, accusatory, and who have made themselves victims of their own beliefs.

We can't blame men for walking all over us. We can only notice that we are not moving out of the way.

When we take responsibility for moving out of the way of those who try to hurt us, we can begin to open our hearts and see the pain that lies within their souls. We can begin to understand that no matter how heinous the "crime" that was perpetrated, it is the act of a very frightened child who is fighting for its survival in the only way it knows how.

———

We have to stop playing the role of "poor us" and create a new model for ourselves—that of loving, creative, powerful, and abundant adults.

———

What many of us find attractive in our men is inconsistent with what we say we want our men to be, and, as a result, inconsistent with what we say we want ourselves to be!

———

I believe that we women are capable of making profound transformations in our thinking about men and about ourselves, and in so doing make a profound contribution to this world.

———

The sooner *we* make the inner shift, the sooner will the men. Once our tastes change, their behavior will shift to accommodate our tastes.

———

We can't be angry at men for not having accepted equality between the sexes, because we haven't accepted it ourselves!

———

I don't think we need to lower our standards; rather, we need to expand our hearts to see the beauty in another person. Perhaps we should call it raising our standards!

———

As we open our hearts to men, we begin to discover our own inner beauty, inner strength, and inner light.

———

Clearly, when we are judgmental of either ourselves or our men, we lose our joy and lightness—qualities that come only from seeing with loving eyes, not hostile ones.

———

Stop trying to figure out why someone else acts the way he does. The important question is: "Why do we react the way we do?"

———

Do you know how good you make a man feel when you let him know he makes a difference in your life? And do you know how good you will feel when you see his face come alive with joy in being reminded that he does, indeed, make a difference?

———

Intimacy is the feeling we get when we mutually open our minds and hearts in total acceptance of each other to truly hear what the other is saying and feel what the other is feeling. . . . It is the sense of human connection at the level of the soul.

———

Our disapproval of someone else often signifies that we are out of touch with our own inherent beauty and, as a result, are not feeling good enough about ourselves.

———

Security and intimacy go hand in hand.

———

Until we, as a unified body, create the critical mass that prefers warm, soft, delicious, and open men who are comfortable revealing all of who they are, men will continue to be "manly" and closed. They would be crazy not to be!

When we stop judging, men will begin to trust that we are on their side. When they have that trust, they can begin to open up.

The only thing we can safely trust is our ability to handle whatever anyone says or does to us.

If we perceive our mates as human beings who won't always follow our script, we can keep an open heart. If we have fairy tale expectations, our hearts can be easily broken and it is hard to "fix" them again.

Our insecurity is, I believe, only our primitive fear of truly leaving our childhood behind and being on our own. We all want the security of being attached to someone else who will save us. But when we cut the cord and see ourselves standing on our own, we get in touch with our own power.

It is at the level of the Higher Self that we are able to keep our hearts open to the struggles and joys that we all share by virtue of the fact that we are all human beings. This is the place where it is impossible to remain numb to the beauty inherent in our own or another being. We must learn, therefore, how to transcend the petty ego and jump up into a higher plane if we want to experience loving relationships.

There is only one time when it is absolutely appropriate for you to have the last word, and that is when the last "word" happens to be, "I love you"!

Being a woman carries with it many inequities and being a man carries with it many inequities. They are just different inequities. It's time we got off the position that men have it easy. They don't!

―――――

When our neediness forms the basis of a relationship, most men know there is no way they can ever please us. They are smart to run the other way.

―――――

Pointing a finger is a powerless act—the only real power lies in taking control of our reaction to whatever life hands us.

―――――

It kills our sense of self-worth to hurt other people.

―――――

I believe that when we "kill" our men with heartless attitudes and behavior, we also kill a part of ourselves. Psychological numbing is death to our soul. By learning to respect and honor ourselves as we open our hearts to others, we form the basis of a new kind of revolution, the kind of revolution that could abolish war forever. *I believe women have that kind of power.*

―――――

We women are capable of generating a whole new kind of energy in this world—one that can tear down walls between "enemies" instead of building them. Once we understand how important we really are, we won't take our actions in the world so lightly. We will realize that equality is nothing without responsibility.

―――――

To "own our magnificence" is to know in our minds, to feel in our hearts, and to reflect into this world our inner beauty, inner strength, and inner light.

―――――

To come from a place of self-love is to act in a way that has integrity, compassion, caring, respect, kindness, and appreciation of all humankind . . . and that includes one's self.

There is no doubt that to own your magnificence is constantly to affirm that you are a beautiful being and that your life matters . . . and to live accordingly.

When we don't give ourselves credit for what is good about who we are, we set ourselves up for a feeling of inner emptiness that no man, however he may try, can fill up.

There is plenty of time. And despite what my Chatterbox (or anyone else) is telling me, it is all unfolding perfectly.

Having it all really means accepting our choices and having no regrets about the road we didn't travel.

It is only through creating a Higher Life Purpose that we earn peace. It is our gateway to the higher self. It is the key to finding our own magnificence.

Liberation is really about letting the light shine through. It has nothing to do with men, money, power, or anything else that is external. It is purely about the light . . . purely about the light . . .

Understand that everything you do contributes to the pot of energy that defines the world. Always ask yourself, "Am

I contributing loving energy or unloving energy?" I believe every one of us wants to be a source of strength and love.

———

The way we create a loving relationship is to cut away everything in our actions and feelings that doesn't look like a loving relationship!

———

A higher love is part of a grander plan of loving. The more we succeed as a "lover" in the world outside our relationship, the more we will succeed as a "lover" inside our relationship. The more we succeed in putting love and harmony into our outer world, the more we will succeed in putting love and harmony into our inner world. Our life has to be about creating a context for love which touches everything and everyone that comes into our sphere of being . . . and that, of course, includes men.

———

A higher love focuses on the larger picture, not the everyday specifics. It notices that this is a loving and caring man. It does not focus on the fact that he forgot to take out the garbage.

———

As long as we are showering love into the relationship and into the world, we will never be bored. There's too much to do!

———

In order to keep love alive, we must consciously intend to shower it with all the magnificence we can muster.

———

A higher love says stop playing games and losing your soul just so you can keep someone in your life.

———

When we cling to another, we can't become our own person; we become their person. We fall into disharmony with our own inherent need to grow.

Commitment means that we will participate 100 percent full-out in making our relationships the best they could possibly be for however long they may last, whether it is a week, a year, or a lifetime.

Remember, that if on the last day of our lives we can answer yes to the question, "Did you warm the world with your love?" we can be at peace with the knowledge that our lives had meaning . . . and that the world is better off for our having been a part of it.

I foresee a day in the not-too-distant future when the collective opening of our hearts will occur. It will be as though the floodgates of dawn have opened wide apart, showering the world with the blood-red warmth and glow of the sun.

En masse we unleased our anger.
En masse let us now unleash our love.

Notes

Chapter 1

1. Betty Friedan, *The Feminine Mystique* (New York: Dell Publishing, 1963), 7.
2. To learn more about the effects of mental attitude on health, read *Love, Medicine and Miracles* by Bernie Siegel (New York: Harper & Row, 1986) and *You Can Heal Your Body* by Louise Hay (Santa Monica, Calif.: Hay House, 1984). Also listen to Carl Simonton's audiotape, *Live from the Inside Edge* (The Inside Edge, P.O. Box 692, Pacific Palisades, Calif. 90272).
3. Sam Keen, *The Passionate Life: Stages of Loving* (New York: Harper & Row, 1983), 112.
4. Sam Keen, "Facing the Enemy Within," *New Age Journal* (November/December 1987), 43.

Chapter 2

1. Merle Shain, *Hearts That We Broke Long Ago* (New York: Bantam, 1983), 37.
2. For an in-depth look at transactional analysis, read *Games People Play* by Eric Berne (New York: Grove Press, 1964) and *I'm OK—You're OK* by Thomas A. Harris, M.D. (New York: Harper & Row, 1967). For a look at how transactional analysis applies specifically to anger and depression, read *Cry Anger* by Jack Birnbaum, M.D. (New York: Paperjacks, Ltd., 1973).
3. Susan Jeffers, *Feel the Fear and Do It Anyway* (New York: Fawcett Columbine, 1988).

4. Zig Ziglar, *Top Performance: How to Develop Excellence in Yourself and Others* (New York: Berkley Books, 1987), 22.

Chapter 3

1. Robert Fuller, "Chasing Our Shadow: Breaking the Cycle of the Arms Race Will Require a Psychotectonic Shift: An Interview by David Hoffman," *New Age Journal* (January/February 1988), 32.
2. Tessa Albert Warschaw, *Rich Is Better* (New York: Doubleday, 1985), xxi.
3. Another book that will help improve your relationship with money is: *Moneylove* by Jerry Gillies (New York: Warner Books, 1978).
4. Harold Kushner, *When All You've Ever Wanted Isn't Enough* (New York: Summit Books, 1986), 127.

Chapter 4

1. For information regarding a poster of A THANK YOU LETTER TO MEN, write to: Hay House, Dept. SJ, P.O. Box 6204, Carson, CA 90749-6204, (800)654-5126.

Chapter 5

1. For an in-depth discussion of the Chatterbox and Higher Self, read: *Feel the Fear and Do It Anyway* by Susan Jeffers (New York: Fawcett Columbine, 1988).
2. Toni Grant, *Being a Woman* (New York: Random House, 1988), 21.
3. Hal Stone and Sidra Winkelman, *Embracing Our Selves* (DeVorss and Co., Box 550, Marina Del Rey, Calif. 90294).
4. "The Nuclear Lagoon," *Global Report,* British Broadcasting Corporation, 1983.
5. Ram Dass, *Who Are You* (The Soundworks, Inc., 911 N. Fillmore St., Arlington, Va. 22201). [Audiotape]
6. David Hoffman, "Chasing Our Shadow: An Interview With Robert Fuller," *New Age Journal* (January/February 1988), 75.
7. Ibid., 75.

Chapter 6

1. Bob Mandel, *Two Hearts Are Better Than One* (Celestial Arts, Box 7327, Berkeley, Calif. 94707).
2. Lillian Rubin, *Intimate Strangers* (New York: Harper & Row, 1983).
3. Michael McGill, Ph.D., *The McGill Report On Male Intimacy* (New York:

Notes

Harper and Row, 1985). Steven Naifeh and Gregory White Smith, *Why Can't Men Open Up?* (New York: Warner Books, 1984).

Chapter 7

1. Bobbie Probstein, *Return to Center: The Flowering of Self-Trust* (DeVorss and Co., Box 550, Marina Del Rey, Calif. 90294).
2. Ibid., 198.
3. Ibid., 241.

Chapter 8

1. Warren Farrell, *Why Men Are the Way They Are* (New York: McGraw-Hill, 1986).
   Herb Goldberg, *The Hazards of Being Male* (New York: New American Library, 1976).
   Anthony Astrachan, *How Men Feel* (New York: Doubleday, 1986).
   Ken Druck, *Secrets Men Keep* (New York: Doubleday, 1985).
   Edward Klein and Don Erickson, eds., *About Men* (New York: Poseidon Press, 1987).
2. Goldberg, 3.
3. Sam Keen, *The Passionate Life: Stages of Loving* (New York: Harper & Row, 1983), 114.
4. Farrell, xvi.
5. Farrell, 105.
6. Astrachan, 15.
7. Noel Perrin, "The Androgynous Man," in Klein and Erickson, 245.
8. For information about *Single Dads,* write to Castelton Publishing Co., 6565 S. Dayton, Suite 2000, Englewood, Colo. 80111.
9. Astrachan, 200.
10. Michael Blumenthal, "No Big Deal," in Klein and Erickson, 136.
11. Merle Shain, *Hearts That We Broke Long Ago* (New York: Bantam, 1983), 82.

Chapter 9

1. Sam Keen, *The Passionate Life: Stages of Loving* (New York: Harper & Row, 1983), 30.
2. Alan Cohen, *Rising in Love: The Journey into Light* (South Kortright, N.Y.: Eden, 1983), 33.
3. *The Random House Dictionary of the English Language,* 2nd ed., unabridged (New York: Random House, 1987).

4. Colette Dowling, *The Cinderella Complex* (New York: Summit Books, 1981), 31.
5. Merle Shaine, *Hearts We Broke a Long Time Ago* (New York: Bantam, 1983), 72.
6. A wonderful audiotape on this subject is *Celebrating Your Relationships* (Warner Erhard Audiotapes, 765 California St., San Francisco, Calif. 94108).
7. John Powell, *Unconditional Love* (Niles, Ill.: Argus Communications, 1978), 57.
8. Harold Kushner, *When All You've Ever Wanted Isn't Enough* (New York: Summit Books, 1986), 23.
9. Marianne Williamson is a spokesperson for the Course in Miracles, a study program often described as "spiritual psychotherapy." While the course talks about God and the teachings of Christ, those who are not "believers" should not be put off. People of all religious persuasions are students of the course. One can substitute the term "Higher Self" or "Inner God" or whatever is acceptable and receive the full impact of the message. Send for information about Williamson's entertaining and highly inspirational tapes to: Miracle Projects, 1550 N. Hayworth Ave., Suite 1, Los Angeles, Calif. 90046.

Chapter 10

1. S. Kriyananda, *How to Spiritualize Your Marriage* (Ananda Publications, 14618 Tyler Foote Rd., Nevada City, Calif. 95959), 18.
2. J. G. Bennett, *Transformation* (Claymont Communications, Claymont Court, Box 296, Charles Town, W. Va., 25414), 28.
3. Stewart Emery, *Conscious Love,* New Dimensions Series (The Soundworks, Inc., 1912 N. Lincoln St., Arlington, Va. 22207). [Audiotape]
4. Marianne Williamson, *A Course in Miracles* (Miracle Projects, 1550 N. Hayworth Ave., Suite 1, Los Angeles, Calif. 90046). [Audiotape]
5. Werner Erhard, *Relationships: Making Them Work* (Werner Erhard Audiotapes, 765 California St., San Francisco, Calif. 94108). [Audiotape]
6. Harold Kushner, *When All You've Ever Wanted Isn't Enough* (New York: Summit Books, 1986), 82.

Books
and Audiotapes

Assagioli, Roberto. *Psychosynthesis.* New York: Penguin, 1976.

Astrachan, Anthony. *How Men Feel.* New York: Doubleday, 1986.

Bennett, J.G. *Transformation.* Charles Town, W. Va.: Claymont Communications, 1978. (Claymont Court, P.O. Box 926, Charles Town, W. Va. 25414.)

Berne, Eric. *Games People Play.* New York: Grove Press, 1964.

Birnbaum, Jack. *Cry Anger.* New York and Toronto: Paperjacks, Ltd., 1973.

Bloodworth, Venice. *Key to Yourself.* Marina del Rey, Calif.: DeVorss & Company. (Box 550, Marina del Rey, Calif. 90294.)

Cohen, Alan. *Rising in Love: The Journey Into Light.* South Kortright, N. Y.: Eden Company, 1983. (South Kortright, N. Y. 13842.)

Colgrove, Melba; Bloomfield, Harold; and McWilliams, Peter. *How to Survive the Loss of a Love.* New York: Bantam Books, 1976.

De Angelis, Barbara. *How to Make Love All the Time.* New York: Rawson Associates, 1987.

Dowling, Colette. *The Cinderella Complex.* New York: Summit Books, 1981.

Druck, Ken. *Secrets Men Keep.* New York: Doubleday, 1985.

Emery, Stewart, with Neal Rogin. *Actualizations: You Don't Have to Rehearse to Be Yourself.* New York: Dolphin/Doubleday, 1977.

Emery, Stewart. *Conscious Love.* New Dimensions Series. Arlington, Va.: The Soundworks Inc. (1912 N. Lincoln St., Arlington, Va. 22207.) (Audiotape)

Erhard, Werner. *Relationships: Making Them Work.* San Francisco, Calif.: Werner Erhard Audiotapes. (765 California Street, San Francisco, Calif. 94108.) (Audiotape)

Fankhauser, Jerry. *The Power of Affirmations.* Farmingdale, N.Y.: Coleman-Graphics. (99 Milbar Blvd., Farmingdale, N.Y. 11735.) (Audiotape)

Farrell, Warren. *Why Men Are the Way They Are.* New York: McGraw Hill, 1986.

Friedan, Betty. *The Feminine Mystique.* New York: Dell Publishing, 1963.

Gillies, Jerry. *Moneylove.* New York: Warner Books, 1978.

Goldberg, Herb. *The Hazards of Being Male.* New York: New American Library, 1976.

Grant, Toni. *Being a Woman.* New York: Random House, 1988.

Harris, Thomas A. *I'm OK—You're OK.* New York: Harper & Row, 1967.

Hay, Louise, L. *You Can Heal Your Life.* Santa Monica, Calif.: Hay House, 1984.

Jeffers, Susan. *The Art of Fearbusting.* Hay House: P.O. Box 6204, Dept. SJ, Carson, CA 90749-6204, (800)654-5126, 1986. (Audiotape)

————. *Dare to Connect: Reaching Out in Romance, Friendship, and the Workplace.* New York: Fawcett Columbine, 1992.

————. *Dare to Connect: Reaching Out in Romance, Friendship, and the Workplace.* Hay House: P.O. Box 6204, Dept. SJ, Carson, CA 90749-6204, (800) 654-5126, 1992. (Audiotape)

————. *A Fearbusting Workshop.* Hay House: P.O. Box 6204, Dept. SJ, Carson, CA 90749-6204, (800)654-5126, 1987. (Audiotape)

————. *The Fear-less Series: Inner Talk for Peace of Mind, Inner Talk for a Confident Day, Inner Talk for a Love That Works.* Hay House: P.O. Box 6204, Dept. SJ, Carson, CA 90749-6204, (800)654-5126, 1990. (Affirmation Audiotape)

————. *Feel the Fear and Do It Anyway.* New York: Fawcett Columbine, 1987.

————. *Feel the Fear and Do It Anyway.* Nightingale Conant Audio: 7300 North Lehigh Avenue, Chicago, IL 60648, (800) 572-2770, 1988. (Audiotape)

————. *Flirting From the Heart.* Hay House: P.O. Box 6204, Dept. SJ, Carson, CA 90749-6204, (800)654-5126, 1987. (Audiotape)

————. *Opening Our Hearts to Each Other.* Hay House: P.O. Box 6204, Dept. SJ, Carson, CA 90749-6204, (800)654-5126, 1989. (Audiotape)

Kanin, Garson. *It Takes a Long Time to Become Young.* New York: Doubleday, 1978.

Keen, Sam. *The Passionate Life: Stages of Loving.* New York: Harper & Row, 1983.

Keyes, Ken. *A Conscious Person's Guide to Relationships.* Marina del Rey, Calif.: Living Love Publications, 1979. (Distributed by DeVorss & Company. P.O. Box 550, Marina del Rey, Calif. 90291.)

Klein, Edward, and Erickson, Don (Editors). *About Men.* New York: Poseidon Press, 1987.

Kriyananda, S. *How to Spiritualize Your Marriage.* Nevada City, Calif.: Ananda Publications, 1982. (14618 Tyler Foote Road, Nevada City, Calif. 95959.)

Kushner, Harold. *When All You've Ever Wanted Isn't Enough.* New York: Summit Books, 1986.

Mandel, Bob. *Two Hearts Are Better Than One.* Berkeley, Calif.: Celestial Arts, 1986 (P.O. 7327, Berkeley, Calif. 94707.)

McGill, Michael. *The McGill Report on Male Intimacy.* New York: Harper & Row, 1985.

Murphy, Joseph. *The Power of Your Subconscious Mind.* New York: Bantam Books, 1963.

Naifeh, Steven, and White Smith, Gregory. *Why Can't Men Open Up?* New York: Warner Books, 1984.

Paul, Jordan, and Paul, Margaret. *From Conflict to Caring.* Minneapolis, Minn.: Compcare Publishers, 1988. (2415 Annapolis Lane, Minneapolis, Minn. 55441.)

Powell, John. *Unconditional Love.* Niles, Ill.: Argus Communication, 1978.

Probstein, Bobbie. *Return to Center: The Flowering of Self-Trust.* Marina del Rey, Calif.: DeVorss & Co., 1985. (P.O. Box 550, Marina del Rey, Calif. 90294.)

Ram Dass. *Who Are You.* Arlington, Va.: The Soundworks, Inc. (911 North Fillmore Street, Arlington, Va. 22201.) (Audiotape)

Rubin, Lillian. *Intimate Strangers.* New York: Harper & Row, 1983.

Shain, Merle. *Hearts We Broke Long Ago.* New York: Bantam, 1983.

Siegal, Bernie. *Love, Medicine and Miracles.* New York: Harper & Row, 1983.

Simonton, Carl. *Live From the Inside Edge.* Pacific Palisades, Calif.: Inside Edge. (P.O. Box 692, Pacific Palisades, Calif. 90272.) (Audiotape) Write to The Inside Edge for their list of talks by leading speakers on personal growth.

Stone, Hal, and Winkelman, Sidra. *Embracing Our Selves.* Marina del Rey, Calif.: DeVorss & Company, 1985. (P.O. Box 550, Marina del Rey, Calif. 90294.)

Warschaw, Tessa, Albert. *Rich is Better.* New York: Doubleday, 1985.

Wilde, Stuart. *Affirmations.* Taos, N.Mex.: White Dove International, Inc., 1987. (P.O. Box 1000, Taos, N.Mex. 87571.)

Williamson, Marianne. *The Choice to Love.* Los Angeles, Calif.: Miracle Projects. (1550 N. Hayworth, Suite #1, Los Angeles, Calif. 90046.) (Audiotape)

Ziglar, Zig. *Top Performance: How to Develop Excellence in Yourself and Others.* New York: Berkley Books, 1987.

About the Author

Susan Jeffers, PhD. received a doctorate in psychology from Columbia University. She is a noted public speaker, workshop leader, and media personality. She has created numerous audiotapes and other instructional materials on the subjects of fear and relationships and is the author of *Feel the Fear and Do It Anyway* and *Dare to Connect: Reaching out in Romance, Friendship, and the Workplace* (1992). Dr. Jeffers lives with her husband in New Mexico.